THE
THEOCONS

THE
THEOCONS

Secular America Under Siege

DAMON LINKER

DOUBLEDAY

New York   London   Toronto   Sydney   Auckland

PUBLISHED BY DOUBLEDAY

Published in the United States by Doubleday, an imprint of The Doubleday Broadway
Publishing Group, a division of Random House, Inc., New York.
www.doubleday.com

Library of Congress Cataloging-in-Publication Data
Linker, Damon, 1969–
The theocons : secular America under siege / by Damon Linker.— 1st ed.
p. cm.
Includes bibliographical references and index.
1. Religious right—United States. 2. United States—Religion. 3. Religion and politics—
United States. 4. Church and state—United States. 5. Presidents—United States—Religion.
6. Bush, George W. (George Walker), 1946– —Religion. I. Title.
BR526.L494 2006
320.5'50973—dc22
2006012398

ISBN-13: 978-0-385-51647-1
ISBN-10: 0-385-51647-9

PRINTED IN THE UNITED STATES OF AMERICA

1   3   5   7   9   10   8   6   4   2

First Edition

FOR BETH

Ideologists are "terrible simplifiers."

Ideology makes it unnecessary for people to confront individual issues on their individual merits. One simply turns to the ideological vending machine, and out comes the prepared formulae. When these beliefs are suffused by apocalyptic fervor, ideas become weapons, and with dreadful results.

—DANIEL BELL

The ordinary resources of empirical observation and ordinary human knowledge give us no warrant for supposing that all good things are reconcilable with each other.

—ISAIAH BERLIN

An unbridled passion for the total elimination of this or that evil can be as dangerous as any of the delusions of our time.

—RICHARD HOFSTADTER

Complexity is the destiny of thoughtful individuals,
from which they will never be rescued.

—LEON WIESELTIER

Ten thousand difficulties do not make one doubt.

—JOHN HENRY NEWMAN

CONTENTS

PREFACE   XI

INTRODUCTION
The End of Secular Politics   1

1

THE ORIGINS OF AN IDEOLOGY   15

2

THE PATH TO POWER   53

3

FROM DESPAIR TO REDEMPTION   87

4

THEOCONS AT WAR   117

5

THEOCON NATION   147

6

AMERICA'S THEOCONSERVATIVE FUTURE   176

7

AGAINST THE THEOCONS   208

ACKNOWLEDGMENTS   228

NOTES   231

INDEX   261

PREFACE

O N T H E E V E N I N G of October 22, 1962, President John F. Kennedy addressed the American people about a grave danger confronting the United States. Aerial surveillance of Cuba revealed that the Soviet Union had begun to construct a series of offensive nuclear missile sites on the island—sites from which the Soviets would be capable for the first time of striking any city in the southeastern United States, including Washington, D.C. In response to the Soviet threat, the president committed the country to an extraordinarily risky policy of imposing a naval blockade, forcibly searching all vessels bound for Cuba, and turning back any and all ships found to contain cargoes of offensive weapons. Having just set the country on a path that could easily lead to worldwide nuclear conflagration, Kennedy concluded his address to the nation with these words: "Thank you and good night."

Thirty-nine years later, addressing the country at another moment of national crisis, President George W. Bush struck a very different note. Speaking from Washington's National Cathedral on

September 14, 2001, three days after the massive terrorist attacks of September 11, the president assured the nation that America's duty was clear—not only to "answer these attacks," but also to "rid the world of evil." Bush then explicitly asked "Almighty God" to "watch over our nation" and "grant us patience and resolve in all that is to come." Having committed the country to a breathtakingly bold new policy and having appealed to God for assistance in its implementation, Bush concluded his address by invoking St. Paul's Letter to the Romans (8:38–39): "As we have been assured, neither death nor life, nor angels nor principalities nor powers, nor things present nor things to come, nor height nor depth, can separate us from God's love. May he bless the souls of the departed. May he comfort our own. And may he always guide our country. God bless America."

Something has happened to the United States during the past four decades. In 1962 a president informing the American people about a potentially catastrophic threat to the country and the world felt no need to invoke the blessings of the divine—and no one considered it an oversight because no one expected otherwise.[1] By 2001 expectations had changed so dramatically that it was hardly noticed when a different president, responding to another national crisis, led the country in prayer from the altar of a cathedral. Indeed, it would have been far more noteworthy had Bush failed to invoke God in his address, breaking from the tradition started by Ronald Reagan of politicians concluding their major speeches with "God bless America." Bush's decision to paraphrase the New Testament on God's boundless love certainly went several steps beyond previous expressions of presidential piety, but it merely built on and solidified a trend that had been under way for quite some time.

This is a book about a vitally important (and unjustly neglected) aspect of this transformation. It tells the story of how a small group of "theoconservative" intellectuals has decisively contributed to the unprecedented rise of public religiosity in our time. As the story begins in the mid-1960s, the men who would become the "theocons" march for civil rights and against Vietnam—and ponder the morality of advocating the violent overthrow of the American government in the name of divine justice. Searching for a new ideological orientation during the tumult and uncertainty of the 1970s, they end up rallying to the side of Ronald Reagan during the 1980s and propose to inject conservative Christianity—and conservative Catholicism, in particular—into the nation's politics. Then, facing various political and cultural setbacks during the 1990s, they recapitulate their youthful radicalism on the far right, stopping just short of advocating a religious revolution against the godless American "regime." With the election of 2000, the theocons rise to the peak of political power and influence in Washington, where their ideas inspire the most controversial and divisive policies of the Bush administration. The story ends with an examination of the theocons' deeply troubling vision of the nation's future—a future in which the country is thoroughly permeated by orthodox Christian piety, and secular politics are driven out in favor of an explicitly theological approach to ordering the nation's public life.

The history that follows is based largely on the published writings of the members of this enormously influential and understudied movement—a movement to which I once belonged and from which I now strongly dissent. Later chapters also include some anecdotal material, which is based on my experience of working closely with the theocons for just over three and a half years, from May 2001 through February 2005. Unless stated otherwise in a footnote, I am the source for this material.

I have written this book to alert Americans—and especially those who cherish our nation's tradition of secular politics—to the threat that the theocons pose to the country. Until now, their aims and influence have been largely ignored by the mainstream media and even by scholars of recent political and religious history. For the past three decades the theocons have devoted their considerable polemical and analytical talents to analyzing and assaulting every conceivable aspect of secular liberalism, but the attention hasn't been returned. It is long overdue. Before political secularists can hope to triumph at the voting booth, they will have to begin to defend themselves on the battlefield of ideas. And before they can do that, they must familiarize themselves with the men who have placed them in the dock and charged them with treason against the American experiment in constitutional democracy. I will consider this book a success if it manages to contribute in some small way to preparing would-be champions of secular politics to defend themselves against their self-declared enemies.

THE
THEOCONS

INTRODUCTION

The End of Secular Politics

GEORGE W. BUSH has gone out of his way to blur the line between religion and politics in America—this is acknowledged by his strongest supporters no less than by his most strident critics. What is much less widely recognized is how extensive these efforts have been. The president has nominated judges who advocate a greater role for religion in the public life of the nation. He has created a network of offices throughout the Washington bureaucracy whose task is to direct billions of dollars in annual grants to churches, synagogues, and mosques. He has acted to curtail abortion rights at home and abroad. He has endorsed a constitutional amendment banning same-sex marriage. He has thrown his support behind "abstinence-only" sex education in public schools. He has empowered the Federal Communications Commission to levy massive fines against television and radio stations that broadcast "indecent" material. He has strictly limited government funding for embryonic stem-cell research. He encouraged congressional Republicans to intervene in the "right to die" case of Terri Schiavo. And he routinely describes the United

States as a nation on a messianic mission to spread democracy and "end tyranny in our world."

This extraordinary list of policies and statements represents a concerted, coordinated effort by the executive branch of government to advance a religious agenda—and even to move the political culture of the nation in an explicitly religious direction. The president himself has admitted as much. In an on-the-record conversation at the White House with a group of religious editors and writers in May 2004, Bush declared that "the job of a president is to help cultures change"—and that the government can bring about such a cultural transformation by "standing with those who have heard a call to love a neighbor." The direct funding of religious organizations, for example, "recognizes that there is an army of compassion that needs to be nurtured, rallied, called forth, and funded" by the state. In undertaking such explicitly religious projects, the government plays an important, even essential role in "changing society one soul at a time."[1]

Though his supporters emphatically deny it, Bush's extensive advocacy of religion is unprecedented in American history. It is so exceptional, in fact, that as his second term enters its final years most political analysts remain disoriented, unsure what to make of the president's push to increase the power and presence of religion in the United States. By far the most common explanation points to evangelical Protestants and their ascendancy as a potent force in American politics since the early 1980s. According to one version of the story, the president and his political strategist Karl Rove have deliberately (and cynically) cultivated the evangelical vote by telling conservative Protestant voters what they want to hear. Bush's decision to champion several items on the social conservative agenda, like his ample use of religious rhetoric in his speeches, is thus merely an example of political expediency. A second version of the evangelical story focuses on the depth of the president's own piety. For those who prefer this account (including the president himself), Bush's religious policies and rhetoric should be seen as an outgrowth of his "born-again" experience in the 1980s. Simply put, Bush is himself an evangelical Protestant working to foist his idiosyncratic faith on the nation.

That evangelicals have played an important role in the rise of theological politics in the United States is undeniable. Yet their influence has been far less decisive than the mainstream media would have us believe. As I argue in the pages that follow, the overtly religious policies and rhetoric of the Bush administration have been inspired by an ideology derived from Roman Catholicism. With their deep historical roots and universalistic aims, Catholic political and cultural ideas provide George W. Bush and like-minded politicians in the Republican Party with a nondenominational language and morality that appeals to a wide array of Americans, transcending any one demographic group. This language and morality has gone a long way toward unifying the conservative movement, and many on the right clearly believe it has the potential to permeate American political culture to such an extent that the separation of church and state as we have known it will cease to exist.

Conservative writer Joseph Bottum has sent out the clearest warning, asserting that those who fear the rise of public religiosity are "right to be afraid." Non-Catholic ways of talking and thinking about morality—be they secular liberalism, nonreligious strains of conservatism, or "emotive evangelicalism"—are on the verge of losing "the battle to set the nation's rhetoric." According to Bottum, advocates of these outmoded ways of thinking and speaking about American politics "are welcome to come along for the ride," but from now on "the nation will be moving to the beat of a different political philosophy." The president of the United States (as well as the bulk of his party) intends to overthrow secular assumptions about how to order the political life of the nation and to replace them with an outlook derived from none other than "Christ the philosopher."[2]

For readers accustomed to mainstream journalistic accounts of American politics, these assertions may seem bold—even implausible.

Is it really conceivable that in pursuing its spiritual agenda the Bush administration has been motivated by, and has actively sought to promulgate, a comprehensive religious ideology? The argument of this book is that, however fantastic it might sound, this is precisely what has been happening in the United States during the past several years—and that responsible American citizens owe it to themselves and their country to become acquainted with the origins and aims of this enormously influential but little-understood ideology, which I call *theoconservatism*.[3]

Theoconservatism teaches that a secular society is both undesirable and unsustainable; that for most of its history the United States has been a thoroughly Christian nation founded on absolute moral principles that make no sense outside of a religious context; that the liberal and secular drift of American culture since the 1960s is the result of an organized effort by liberal and secular elites in the nation's education and media establishments to impose their corrupt views on the nation through antidemocratic means (especially through the courts); that the practical consequences of secularization are a sex-saturated popular culture, the collapse of crucially important social institutions (such as traditional marriage), a general separation of law from religiously based moral principles, and the rise of a "culture of death" in which abortion and euthanasia are widely permitted and practiced; that the solution to secularization is to bring modern America (back) into line with the moral strictures of biblical religion; and that this reversion can be accomplished by allowing the country's Christian essence to reassert itself democratically—primarily by citizens voting for conservative Christian politicians who advance religion in public life through public policy, court appointments, and constitutional amendments, but also by proposing popular referenda (such as the anti-gay-marriage initiatives that passed overwhelmingly in twelve states during the 2004 election cycle) which frustrate the tyrannical ambitions of secularists.

This is the revolutionary religious ideology that is transforming the political and cultural landscape of our time. When Karl Rove speaks (as he often does) about fashioning a GOP governing majority that will last for over a generation, he means that he believes it possible to use theoconservative ideas to unite a broad and stable electoral coalition. Evangelicals will be an important part (perhaps even the core) of this coalition, but they will not be its only members. A large portion of Catholics (52 percent of whom cast ballots for Bush in his campaign against the Catholic John Kerry) will join it, as will significant numbers of suburban and so-called "exurban" voters, many of whom are concerned about moral trends in the country during the past several decades. If Rove is right—if this coalition consistently unites behind candidates who champion theoconservative ideology—then the explicitly religious stance of George W. Bush's presidency will come to be seen not as an electoral and historical aberration but rather as the first stage in a cultural counterrevolution whose ultimate goal is nothing less than the end of secular politics in America.

This is a book about theoconservative ideology—what it thinks is wrong with the United States, what it believes can be done to change the country's course, how it came to exercise so much influence in Washington, and how responsible citizens should respond to its potent challenge to the secular political order. But ideologies don't just appear out of thin air. They have authors and promoters, and they have histories. Before there was theoconservatism, there were theoconservatives (or "theocons")—a tightly knit group of ambitious and deeply conservative writers who set out over thirty years ago to devise a comprehensive political program that would reverse the secularizing direction of the country since the 1960s. *The Theocons* tells their story, tracing the development of their ideas and charting their rise to positions of power and influence in the conservative intellectual world. Finally, as a study of theoconservatism's political ascent, *The*

Theocons necessarily provides a broad overview of recent American political and cultural history. No matter how critical we might be of the theocons and their influence—and this book will be quite critical—we must recognize that their history is, in some sense, our history. What was it about late twentieth-century America that inspired a group of intellectuals to fashion a right-wing political-religious ideology? And what is it about early twenty-first-century America that is leading large (and perhaps growing) numbers of its citizens to find that ideology persuasive? No serious study of theo-conservatism can ignore these important and difficult questions.

Although the theocons exercise considerable influence on American politics in our time, they are not household names, even among the politically informed. Some of this obscurity can be explained by the general religious illiteracy of the mainstream media. Then there is the fact that the theocons themselves believe it politically efficacious to keep a low public profile from which they can influence politics and policy quietly, behind the scenes. When they are mentioned at all, they are usually described as "Catholic neocons," implying that they are merely the religious faction of the much more widely known neoconservative movement.[4] This is a mistake. Despite a number of biographical and ideological affinities between the neocons and theocons, the differences between them are real and important.

Most neoconservatives, for example, are secular and Jewish. All theocons, by contrast, are deeply religious, and most are Catholic. In the late 1960s, the men who went on to become the first neocons were moderate liberals who opposed the revolutionary ambitions of the counterculture. The proto-theocons, on the other hand, were leftist revolutionaries who proposed (as in the title of one of their books) "a theology for radical politics." While the neocons moved to the center-right during the 1970s, giving a modest "two cheers" for the market economy, the theocons went much further, praising the sanctity of the entrepreneurial spirit and suggesting that by starting a business and creating jobs the capitalist does God's work in the world. Whereas the neocons view the American founding in secular terms, the theocons claim that the country is founded on principles of natural law ultimately derived from medieval Christendom. Neocons and theocons both advocate a foreign policy geared toward the promotion of democracy around the world using military force, but the theocons defend it by speaking of America as a "sacred enterprise" with a providential mission to enforce divinely sanctioned order in the world. While the neocons treat religion as a useful means to achieving their political goals, the theocons believe that Christianity is the indispensable bedrock of American democracy. Neoconservatism and theoconservatism are thus distinct ideologies—and despite the extraordinary amount of attention focused on the first during the past few years, it is the second that is coming to exercise the greater influence on conservative politics in contemporary America.

The founder of the theocon movement, as well as the man who has long served as its de facto leader and inspiration, is Richard John Neuhaus (a long-time Lutheran minister who converted to Catholicism in 1990 and became a priest the following year). While others have contributed in important ways to fashioning theoconservative ideology, Neuhaus's intellectual impact has been essential—just as his political savvy has maximized the ideology's influence. A handsome, charismatic man who delights in public attention, Neuhaus began his life of political engagement by marching alongside Martin Luther King Jr. in the civil rights and anti–Vietnam War movements of the 1960s. By 1984 he was vying for intellectual leadership of the religious right, arguing that religion was being systematically excluded from public debate and advocating a robust effort to reverse the trend. In subsequent years Neuhaus has worked to forge a potent political and religious alliance between conservative Catholics and evangelical Protestants. He served as a close advisor to George W. Bush in his 2000 presidential campaign and continues to meet with him to discuss cultural and religious issues. Neuhaus also exercises influence through his magazine *First Things*, which is read in the Bush White

House, and especially through his ten-thousand-to-fifteen-thousand-word column in the journal, which serves as monthly marching orders for the theoconservative movement.

Along with Neuhaus, the two most important theocons are Michael Novak and George Weigel, both of them staunch Catholics. Like Neuhaus, Novak was a prominent radical in the 1960s who moved sharply rightward during the 1970s. In his most important book, *The Spirit of Democratic Capitalism* (1982), Novak enumerated several ties between entrepreneurialism and Catholicism. Over the past two decades, Novak has devoted his considerable talent and energy to making moral and religious arguments against the income tax, to demonstrating the Christian character of the American founding, and to providing theological justification for President Bush's project of democratizing the Middle East.

George Weigel's influence on the development of theoconservatism has been somewhat different. Best known in the literary world as the author of a thousand-page biography of Pope John Paul II, *Witness to Hope*, Weigel has contributed to theocon ideas in the areas of American political thought and international relations. Emphasizing the root compatibility between Catholicism and American democracy, Weigel argues both that American principles derive from medieval Catholic sources and that the country's political institutions require a religious foundation in order to maintain their vitality. In foreign policy, Weigel has worked to recover what he calls the "just war tradition of Catholic reasoning," which he has used to justify Ronald Reagan's revival of the arms race with the Soviet Union, the 1991 Gulf War, the war on terror, and the ongoing war in Iraq. While in the past few years the neoconservatives have revived and sought to legitimize the myth of American exceptionalism, Weigel has significantly augmented these efforts by bringing theological and providential ideas to bear on discussions of America's role in the world.

In addition to the Neuhaus-Novak-Weigel core, theoconservative ideology has been influenced—and its political goals decisively advanced—by the work of two scholars: Robert P. George and Hadley Arkes. George is the holder of Woodrow Wilson's John P. McCormick Chair in Government at Princeton University, director of the influential and well-funded James Madison Program in American Institutions at Princeton, and a member of the President's Council on Bioethics; he is also the coauthor (with the University of Notre Dame's Gerard V. Bradley) of the Federal Marriage Amendment that President Bush endorsed in 2004. Boyish and always smartly dressed, George frequently surprises his opponents with the passionate ferocity of his right-wing rationalism, which inevitably ends up justifying his own conservative Catholicism. George is unshakably convinced that, beginning with a short list of (supposedly) universally accepted premises, rational argument can establish with absolute clarity and persuasiveness that abortion, euthanasia, embryonic stem-cell research, and same-sex marriage (and perhaps even contraception and masturbation) should be outlawed in any decent society, Christian or non-Christian.

Arkes (who is Jewish and one of a handful of non-Catholics in the theocon inner circle) is a student of Harry Jaffa, himself the most politically engaged and stridently right-wing student of the controversial conservative philosopher Leo Strauss. In a series of books and articles, Arkes has argued that the principle of natural rights enunciated in the Declaration of Independence forms the basis for a distinctly American form of natural law reasoning. On its basis, and without making a single reference to Catholic theology, one can supposedly establish beyond a shadow of a doubt that abortion is always an absolute evil that must be banned in all cases. It is this conviction that led him to author and then lobby Congress to pass the Born-Alive Infants Protection Act, which President Bush signed into law in 2002. Like the other theocons, Arkes believes that same-sex marriage, euthanasia, cloning, and embryonic stem-cell research are fundamentally incompatible with American legal and political principles—and that America's moral vision has been obstructed by a liberal-secularist conspiracy that seeks to corrupt the nation through the courts, the media, and the universities.

Surrounding these five central figures are several sympathetic writers, scholars, and public officials whose work has contributed in varying degrees to advancing theoconservative ideology in theory and practice. These include: Supreme Court justices Antonin Scalia and Clarence Thomas, both of whom have sought to develop a jurisprudence that permits and encourages a substantial role for religion in American public life; Leon Kass, former chairman of the President's Council on Bioethics and advocate of a profoundly conservative approach to moral reasoning derived from Aristotle and the Hebrew Bible; Harvard Law School's Mary Ann Glendon, who chairs the Pontifical Academy for the Social Sciences in Rome and has written in favor of a constitutional amendment banning same-sex marriage; Gilbert Meilaender, a member of the President's Council on Bioethics and staunch defender of traditionalism in society and the family; Rabbi David Novak of the University of Toronto, who has lent crucial support to theocon efforts at building an alliance between theologically orthodox Christians and Jews; and Judge Robert Bork, who since his rejection by the Senate in 1987 for a spot on the Supreme Court has drifted into the theocon orbit, writing a series of blistering attacks on the "tyrannical" influence of liberal secularism on American democracy.

As with so much else in our ideologically charged politics, the story of how this group of writers and intellectuals came to transform the political landscape of the nation begins in the 1960s. In chapter 1 we meet Neuhaus and Novak, religiously inspired radicals whose fervent faith inspired them to protest in favor the civil rights movement and against the Vietnam War—and even to contemplate the violent overthrow of the United States government. Stopping just short of revolution, the two men underwent independent ideological transformations during the 1970s, eventually coming to believe that the nation was plagued by a grave spiritual crisis. Both authors sought a solution to this crisis in the creation and dissemination of a comprehensive religious ideology that they hoped would unify and exalt the nation. Novak's version of the ideology effectively spiritualized the "Reagan revolution" of the early 1980s by portraying America's political, cultural, and economic system of "democratic capitalism" as the political system that best reflects God's intentions in the world.

Neuhaus's approach was somewhat different—and, in the end, much more influential. Largely absorbing Novak's proposals but going far beyond them, Neuhaus suggested that America's spiritual woes could be cured by a populist insurrection against the secularism of the nation's cultural elite. Jerry Falwell's Moral Majority was an early attempt at just such an insurrection, but it had failed to galvanize the nation. In the book that would become the manifesto of the theoconservative movement (*The Naked Public Square: Religion and Democracy in America* [1984]), Neuhaus made his first attempts to devise a potent ideological program that would enable these newly politicized evangelical Protestants to contend much more effectively for political and cultural power in the United States.

With the fundamentals of theoconservative ideology in place, Neuhaus turned his attention to maximizing its influence. Chapter 2 charts theoconservatism's path to power from the mid-1980s through the mid-1990s—a period of strategizing and institution-building, deal-making and diplomacy. On one front, the theocons persuaded their ideological cousins, the neocons, to help them establish their own network of magazines, think tanks, and institutes that would give them influence in Washington and around the country. On a second front, Neuhaus and Weigel refashioned theocon ideology in Roman Catholic terms and allied the movement with powerful conservative forces within the Catholic Church (including Pope John Paul II and Joseph Cardinal Ratzinger, now Pope Benedict XVI). Finally, the theocons forged an enormously important alliance between leading orthodox Catholics and conservative evangelical Protestants. In their joint statement of 1994, "Evangelicals and Catholics Together," the two groups announced that from then on they would work together toward the common goal of eradicating secularism and augmenting the presence of Catholic-Christian piety in American public life.

Despite these accomplishments, the mid-1990s were a time of profound disappointment for the theocons. A series of court rulings on abortion, euthanasia, and gay rights convinced them that a cadre of secular liberal elites continued to usurp the right of the American people to govern themselves on the most morally pressing issues of the day. Theocon ideology predicted that such provocations would spark a widespread populist revolt in the country. Yet aside from the fleeting "Gingrich revolution" in 1994, there was no such rebellion. Chapter 3 tells the story of how this disjunct between theoconservative ideas and American reality provoked the theocons into reverting to radicalism—but this time from the far right. In the notorious "End of Democracy?" symposium in Neuhaus's magazine *First Things*, the theocons declared that the proper response to the "judicial usurpation of democracy" by godless and immoral judges ranged "from noncompliance to resistance to civil disobedience to morally justified revolution."[5]

By the end of the decade, theocon radicalism had been transmuted into passionate support for George W. Bush's presidential campaign. With Bush's 2000 victory, theocon ideas rose for the first time to the pinnacle of political power in the United States. Yet for all of the high hopes that accompanied Bush's victory, events soon conspired to give the theocon cause even more momentum. Chapter 4 explores the effect of September 11 on the theoconservative agenda and examines how the theocons adapted their theological ideas about America's role in the world to the post–September 11 context. From the very beginning, the theocons described the war on terror as a just and unambiguously good war—and insisted that it was a religious war being fought in the name of Christian civilization against its mortal enemies. Once the Bush administration turned its attention to an impending war in Saddam Hussein's Iraq, the theocons began to make even bolder claims, asserting that the United States had the moral duty to act as the world's enforcer of justice—punishing those who would flout American authority—regardless of whether the other nations of the world recognized the legitimacy of the policy. This holy war for universal justice would likely include military altercations with several nations in the Muslim Middle East, but it also necessitated the advent of a "cold" war with Europe—a continent seemingly unwilling to defend the Christian essence of Western civilization against the challenge of militant Islam.

Chapters 5 and 6 turn back to domestic affairs, where the theocon influence under President Bush has been most profound. In chapter 5, the theocons push their agenda on several fronts during Bush's first term in office. They promote legislation designed to curtail abortion rights. They act as a brake on biotechnological innovation and development. They author a constitutional amendment to ban same-sex marriage and persuade the president to endorse it. And they convince the U.S. Conference of Catholic Bishops to intervene in the 2004 election on behalf of the Republican Party. Chapter 6 looks to the future. The theocon-inspired federal intervention in the Terri Schiavo case, the drive to substitute "intelligent design" for biological science in the nation's public schools, the push to revive the patriarchal family, the defense of absolute authority in the church, and the revival of premodern interreligious tensions—in these recent trends and developments we gain glimpses of a possible, and ominous, American future, one in which the theocons have fully succeeded in realizing their goals for the nation.

The theocons do not aim to transform the country into a Christian version of Afghanistan under the Taliban—a goal that could only be achieved by pursuing the wholesale destruction of American liberal democracy and the establishment of theocratic totalitarianism in its place. Yet they do propose to sanctify and spiritualize the nation's public life, while also eliding fundamental distinctions between church and state, the sacred and the secular. Such efforts, if successful, would

not be fatal to the nation, but they would cripple it, effectively transforming the country into what would be recognized around the world
as a Catholic-Christian republic. I hope that prospect is disquieting
enough to inspire thoughtful American citizens to educate themselves
about the theocons, their ideology, and the very real threat that they
pose to the United States.

1

THE ORIGINS OF AN IDEOLOGY

R ED STATE AND blue state, conservative and liberal, pro-Bush and anti-Bush, prolife and prochoice, religious and secular— the culture war that divides America is about many things, but it is in large part about the legacy of the 1960s. Most "blue" Americans feel at peace with the cultural revolution that began roughly four decades ago, believing that for all of its excesses the decade of the 1960s made the country freer and more just than it once was. Others, however, are more troubled. Some of these "red" Americans feel deeply ambivalent about the profound cultural changes wrought by the 1960s, while still others take a more strident view, convinced that the decade inaugu-rated a period of moral decadence that continues to this day, dimin-ishing the nation, coarsening its culture, corrupting its children. Theoconservative ideology has played a crucial role in legitimizing this last view—the outlook of those who take it as axiomatic that (in the words of founding theocon Richard John Neuhaus) the 1960s were "a slum of a decade."[1]

But this highly tendentious account of the 1960s obscures the historical record, which shows that the theocons themselves were once enthusiastic participants in the very activities they now passionately decry. During the 1960s, Neuhaus was moved by his religious faith to join the civil rights and anti–Vietnam War movements, flanking Martin Luther King Jr. in protest marches, clashing with Mayor Daley's police force on the streets of Chicago at the 1968 Democratic National Convention. Although a well-known advocate of free-market capitalism and cultural conservatism today, theocon Michael Novak, too, was a member of the far left during the 1960s, advocating a religiously inspired revolution in consciousness that would lead the country toward greater freedom in all areas of life, including sexuality. For both men, participating in leftist political agitation was a means of bringing the country into greater conformity with its own principles of justice and freedom, which they understood in explicitly religious terms.

After the 1960s, these figures of the far left would migrate right, sometimes gradually, sometimes in sudden lurches. This chapter tells the story of how, between the mid-1960s and the publication of Neuhaus's seminal *The Naked Public Square* in 1984, these two radicals became the authors of the ideology that currently dominates the Republican Party and, increasingly, the nation as a whole. The story is, in many of its details, one of dramatic change—from sweeping criticism of the United States and its policies to a defense of the country in theological terms, from a passion for political violence to an enthusiastic justification of capitalism, from support for the sexual revolution to intense hostility to its cultural effects. Through all these changes, however, Neuhaus and Novak would remain political radicals, patriots to an America they believed to be deeply and pervasively religious, and agitators who delighted in challenging political authority in the name of their faith. In the 1960s, their religious ideals inspired them to fight for greater justice and freedom in the United States. Two decades later, those same ideals convinced them that above all else the country needed to combat the spread of secularism and push for the expansion of public religiosity. Both positions derived from the same theological sources.

QUESTIONING AUTHORITY

Richard John Neuhaus always had a troubled relationship to authority. Born on May 14, 1936, in the agrarian community of Pembroke, Ontario, Richard was the sixth son of a conservative Lutheran pastor, Clemens Neuhaus (there were eight children in all). Nicknamed "The Pope" by his seminary classmates, Clemens was a stern authority figure—one whom, according to Richard, "you did not directly cross . . . without direct repercussions."[2] Pastor Neuhaus's decision to send his son to a Lutheran high school in Nebraska, several hundred miles away from the family, may have been one such repercussion. Continuing his pattern of youthful defiance, Richard managed to get himself expelled from the school by the age of sixteen. Over the next few months, the teenage Neuhaus became a naturalized American citizen and relocated to Cisco, Texas, where he ran a gas station and grocery store, becoming the youngest member of the local chamber of commerce.[3] Eventually resolving to follow in the footsteps of his father by becoming a Lutheran minister, he somehow managed to get around his lack of a secondary school diploma to gain admittance to and graduate from Concordia College in Austin, Texas. He completed his pastoral training at Concordia Theological Seminary in St. Louis; ordination followed in 1960.

From the beginning of his ministry, Neuhaus proved himself to be a highly unusual Lutheran. As the leader of the sixteenth-century Protestant Reformation, Martin Luther had taught that an unbridgeable, infinite chasm exists between human law, which is inevitably flawed, and the gospel's message of perfect, unconditional love. This teaching, which is often called the "two kingdoms" theory, has been criticized for producing complacent citizens who react to political injustice with indifference, in the belief that it would be an act of pride-

ful impiety to expect better from human institutions. At its best, the
Lutheran emphasis on human imperfection can encourage political
wisdom and humility, as it did, for example, in the case of theologian
Reinhold Niebuhr, whose writings and political activity in the middle decades of the twentieth century were models of moderation and
responsibility.

Although he clearly admired Niebuhr and at times even liked to
think of himself as his successor, the young Reverend Neuhaus very
quickly showed himself to be a theological and political radical who
planned to treat his preaching as an occasion for political protest—
for narrowing and even eliminating the gap between Luther's two
kingdoms. Drawing on more volatile, eschatological strands in the
Christian tradition and feeding off of his own irrepressible rebellious-
ness, Neuhaus made a habit of disobeying temporal political authorities in the name of upholding and enforcing a higher, divine
authority whose wishes he (along with a few like-minded allies) had
somehow managed to discern. It was an explosive mixture—one in
which the very longing to obey encouraged acts of disobedience.

Neuhaus fell into this radical pattern very soon after his ordination. After a short stint as a pastor in the small town of Massena, New
York, Neuhaus requested and received a difficult inner-city assign-
ment—to take over St. John the Evangelist, a parish straddling the
neighborhoods of Bedford-Stuyvesant and Williamsburg in Brooklyn, New York. The German immigrants who worshipped at St. John's
had long ago begun their flight from the area, and very few of the recent arrivals (most of them black and desperately poor) were Lutherans. When Neuhaus arrived in April 1961, there were two dozen
regular parishioners, and the church was on the verge of being shut
down for good. Over the next few years, the charismatic and articulate minister revived the church by turning it into a vibrant center for
political agitation—in favor of civil rights, and against the Vietnam
War.[4]

At first Neuhaus's political activity focused on local issues in New

York City, but before long he began to take on the authority of the federal government, at home and abroad. Like many activists of the time, he portrayed his protest as an effort to bring the country into greater conformity with its own democratic ideals—though Neuhaus invariably viewed those ideals through the lens of his piety, as expressions of a moral vision ultimately traceable to God. In the fall of 1965, after President Lyndon Johnson insinuated that all opposition to American military policy in Vietnam bordered on treason, Neuhaus signed a declaration with Rabbi Abraham Joshua Heschel and Father Daniel Berrigan defending their God-given and patriotic right to engage in prophetic protest. Within weeks the three men founded Clergy Concerned About Vietnam (eventually renamed Clergy and Laity Concerned About Vietnam, or CALCAV), the most important religiously based antiwar organization of the time.[5] The following summer, Neuhaus led an Independence Day fast in order to draw attention to the injustice of American actions in Vietnam.[6] Soon he began to act as the New York liaison for the Reverend Martin Luther King Jr. in his attempt to bring the civil rights movement, which had begun and flourished in the rural South as a religiously inspired crusade for justice, to the slums of the urban North.[7] But perhaps nothing captures Neuhaus's distinctive combination of religious faith, hostility to political authority, and patriotic reverence for the ideals of his adopted homeland more than his decision to lead his parish in a protest at which young people were invited to turn in their draft cards at the altar—provided they did so while singing "America the Beautiful."[8]

As the decade progressed and the protest movement began to question authority more radically, Neuhaus's own rhetoric and actions grew increasingly extreme. Challenging St. Paul's injunction in his Letter to the Romans to obey lawful political authorities, Neuhaus spoke of the need to build a "vital and virile subculture" that would "knock out some of the mythology of Romans 13, . . . [and] this whole notion that they [the powers that be] know more than we do."[9]

He even went so far as to insinuate in his sermons that the Vietnam War might very well be divine punishment for the collective sins of the United States, describing the Vietnamese people as "God's instruments for bringing the American empire to its knees."[10] By the time of the 1968 Democratic National Convention in Chicago—just weeks after the assassinations of Robert Kennedy and Reverend King— Neuhaus, like so many others in the movement, was primed for direct confrontation with the authorities. That week he would be arrested by Mayor Richard Daley's police in a march down Michigan Avenue.[11] Over the coming months, he would be arrested many more times in cities around the country.

It was in the midst of this radical political activity that Neuhaus began to reflect on whether he should advocate an armed insurrection to overthrow the government of the United States. He and his somewhat less radical friend, sociologist Peter Berger, decided that they would each write an extended essay on the topic and publish them both as a single book, titled *Movement and Revolution* (1970). In his contribution, Berger discussed why, despite the manifest injustices that marked race relations and the war in Vietnam, the United States was neither ripe for revolution nor likely to become so anytime soon. Neuhaus, by contrast, was much more willing to entertain the prospect of revolutionary violence. Although he agreed with Berger that the country was not quite ready for a coup d'etat, he differed from his friend in being "more willing to consider the revolutionary alternative."[12] Above all, Neuhaus was interested in examining "the problems and possibilities, the rights and the wrongs, of making revolution."[13] While he shared the revolutionary longings and goals of his fellow radicals, he also worried that they had failed to confront the bloody reality of revolution and the moral dilemmas its leaders would inevitably face. In his contribution to the book, "The Thorough Revolutionary," Neuhaus set out to clarify the stakes—to act as a moral tutor to the American left.

The first step in the tutorial involved an examination of why so

many members of the movement had concluded that the time for revolution had already arrived. Building on C. Wright Mills's radical
concept of a "power elite" that rules American society without democratic accountability, Neuhaus proposed that the country was controlled not by an impersonal "system," as many other radicals claimed,
but by a "regime." This regime was not "coextensive with the society"
but was rather "the *actual* power-wielding group in the society, including not only—not even primarily—those who are publicly recognized because they hold office through electoral politics, but also, for
example, the leadership of the military-industrial complex." This elite
regime had acted so unjustly in recent years that many had understandably concluded that it needed to be overthrown by force in the
name of "the people," which was the nation's only legitimate "source
of public authority."[14]

Neuhaus clearly sympathized with and even endorsed much of
this argument, viewing the prospect of a populist revolution in the
United States with considerable enthusiasm. Yet his ultimate aim was
not to encourage an immediate political uprising but instead to urge
his peers on the left to undertake their radical actions in the light of
the Christian "just war" tradition of moral reasoning. Above all, he
wanted them to understand that revolution is a bloody business. Disgusted that too many of his fellow leftists treated armed rebellion as
if it were a "politicized Woodstock Festival" and no more profound
than smoking "pot in Grant Park and skinny-dipping at public
beaches," he sought to remind them that the overthrow of political
authority begins with "propaganda, disruption, subversion," and that
it employs "guerrilla warfare" and "acts of terror," including campaigns
"to kill, kidnap, or otherwise intimidate any persons or institutions"
that would seek to undermine the revolution by bribing the people
with reformist half-measures. This is the reality of revolution—and
those who flinched from it (including Che Guevara, whose failure to
topple the Bolivian government Neuhaus traced to his "unwillingness

to use terrorism")[15] showed that they lacked the "manhood" to determine whether or not decisive action is necessary, and what that action
should be.[16]

Having faced the ugly reality of revolution and reflected on its
likely moral costs, Neuhaus reluctantly concluded that the time for
coordinated political violence had not yet arrived—though he made
a point of reaffirming "the right to armed revolution" and asserted
that the possibility of successful reform rendering such revolution unnecessary was "improbable."[17] In the end, he sided with Bobby Seale
of the Black Panther Party in considering fifty to a hundred years a realistic time frame for a morally justified revolution in the United
States.[18] Over the next several months, Neuhaus would undertake a
failed campaign for Congress on a far-left platform and continue his
agitation on the streets and from the pulpit as he awaited the coming
conflagration.

THE CATHOLIC IMAGINATION AND
RADICAL POLITICS

While Neuhaus walked a tightrope between political revolution and
responsibility in the slums of Brooklyn, his fellow leftist Michael Novak embraced a form of cultural radicalism that aimed above all at a
"revolution in consciousness."[19] It was a difference with roots in Novak's fervent, if idiosyncratic, Catholic faith. Born on September 9,
1933, to a deeply Catholic Slovak-American family in rural Johns-
town, Pennsylvania, Novak spent several years of his youth in seminary with the intention of becoming a priest. Although he eventually
concluded that his vocation was as a layman, his writing and study
would continue to focus on Catholicism. By the fall of 1963, he had
landed a contract with *Time* magazine to write reports on the Second
Vatican Council. Those reports would become Novak's first book of
nonfiction, *The Open Church* (1964).[20] This book, as well as its 1965
successor (*Belief and Unbelief*), shows Novak to have been an enthu-

siastic advocate of the *aggiornamento*, or "updating," of the Catholic Church in Vatican II. He was, in other words, a member of the Catholic left who enthusiastically embraced the council's call to foster a vibrant synthesis between modernity and the church.

If Neuhaus's impatient desire to bridge the infinite gulf separating the divine and human kingdoms marked him as a radical dissenter from the Lutheran mainstream, Novak's emphasis on the ideal of synthesis grew out of distinctly Catholic hopes and concerns. Because the identity of the Catholic Church is wrapped up with its status as a (small-c) catholic institution, many of its greatest theologians have sought to portray the church as a dynamic unity containing a multitude of interdependent parts, each of which perfectly balances and complements the others. In reality, of course, these parts inevitably have to submit their independence to the ecclesiastical authority of Rome, producing a synthesis far less egalitarian and more rigidly hierarchical than the image of dynamic unity would imply. Yet the image has remained a vital element of the Catholic imagination over the centuries—and never more so than in the years immediately following Vatican II, when hopes were raised of applying the synthetic ideal not only to the internal life of the church but also to the church's relations with other religions, and even with secular modernity as a whole. For the first time in its history, Catholics were presented with the possibility of a truly catholic synthesis.

Even in an era dominated by the lust for synthesis, Novak's early attempt to fashion a thoroughly synthetic political theology was breathtaking in its extremism, even threatening to blur the categorical distinctions that make coherent thinking possible. In *A Theology for Radical Politics* (1969), Novak endorsed the radically democratic (and borderline heretical) outlook of French Catholic novelist George Bernanos, who famously asserted that "grace is everywhere," and went on to proclaim that "by the fact that anything is, it is already good, already gracious, already redeemed."[21] Recognizing that such absolute affirmation appeared to deny original sin, the need for salvation, the

sacraments that make salvation possible, and thus a role for the institutional Catholic Church, Novak endorsed a "religionless Christianity" and a "secular sanctity."[22] It was simply an error, he claimed, "to set
world over against church, secular thought over against Christian theology, man over against God." The entire Christian tradition, in fact,
was "too narrow and parochial." In its place, modern men and women
needed to substitute an awareness that "the Holy Spirit blows where he
wills" and that "Christ is alive everywhere in human history."[23] In Novak's radical theology, institutional Catholicism would be fulfilled by
willing itself out of existence, and Christianity's urge to sanctify the
world would be consummated in the triumph of secularism.

When it came to the political implications of these paradoxical,
even unintelligibly contradictory, positions, Novak made it clear that
he believed they implied the need for revolution to overthrow established political institutions as well as settled ways of thinking. At a
practical level, this led Novak to travel in many of the same radical
circles as Neuhaus. (Both men, for example, participated in a tense
meeting between CALCAV and Secretary of Defense Robert McNa-
mara in February 1967.)[24] But whereas Neuhaus was motivated primarily by righteous indignation against the actions of the "powers
that be," Novak focused more intensely on cultural concerns, insisting that the United States as a whole was failing to live up to its full
spiritual potential. In Novak's view, the problem with modern America was not so much its injustice as its "appalling mediocrity" and the
"irrationality of [its] merely technical progress."[25] Looking at the
country, Novak saw only "the vacant eyes watching television and
drinking beer; the tired eyes of men on the commuter train; the effi-
cient eyes of the professor and the manager; the sincere eyes of the
television politician." Overwhelmed with "anguish" at the spectacle,
Novak lamented that "the suffering and sacrifices of past generations"
had culminated in "a grown man with a can of beer" finding his fulfillment "in a televised game, watched by thirty million others," and
foolishly believing his country to be "free, brave, and just."[26]

According to Novak, these moral and aesthetic defects implied that the American Revolution of 1776 had been left "unfinished," since it had merely increased "the quotient of human freedom realized by each of us" without specifying what that freedom should be used for.[27] By contrast, the coming revolution—which was primarily a "religious task" involving "education as conversion"—would bring "the Protestant, rationalistic, pragmatic, and scholastic era" to an end and signal the advent of "a new age in the history of religion."[28] Once this new age had begun, individual and collective rights and duties would mesh perfectly in every sphere of life. Socialism would thus be freely established in economics, at the same time that an exponential increase in the "revolutionary consciousness" of ordinary Americans would both unify and ennoble the nation.[29]

Echoing those writers of the New Left whose radical agendas encompassed the whole of life, the former seminarian even prophesied that the coming revolution would lead to dramatic improvements in sexual experience. Unlike our society, which "tolerates violence and murders by the dozen in movies and on evening television but outlaws manifestations of sexual love," the America of the future would recognize that it is more moral to "caress a woman's breasts" than to "strike a man in the face in a barroom brawl" and cleaner to "enter a woman with gentleness" than to "plunge a knife into a man again and again." No longer would Christian society repress "vital and sacred instincts" and conceive of God as "the transcendent, all-seeing Eye who detects every violation of sexual taboos." Instead, postrevolutionary America would throw off "the idol of inhibition, repression, and shame" and begin to treat sex as a spontaneous expression of divine love.[30]

This, at any rate, was Novak's ecstatic vision of a postrevolutionary order. Only when he turned to the question of how this state of social perfection might be realized in the United States did his vision grow darker. The sad fact was that "the good people, the churchgoers, the typical Americans" were not the allies of the radical reform that the country required. They were, on the contrary, its "enemy," and they needed to be treated as such. Thus if, in the end, after being shown "how desperately inadequate our society is," they still failed to recognize the need for revolution, it might become necessary to place "the American majority . . . for a change, in the line of fire."[31] Unlike Neuhaus, then, Novak did not attempt to distinguish between "the people" and their elite oppressors. Indeed, like the most violent revolutionaries of the twentieth century, he combined radically egalitarian ideals with open hostility to large numbers of his fellow citizens.

Ultimately, though, Novak joined Neuhaus in refusing to countenance violence, concluding his essay on revolution by asserting that, although "the question of the employment of arms and open violence" needed to remain open, the moment had "clearly not arrived for armed revolution" in the United States.[32] Having stopped just inches short of advocating insurrection, both men chose not to take the final step. Over the next few years, events in the country and the world would lead them to reevaluate the ideas that had brought them to the brink in the first place.

FAILED REVOLUTION AND ITS AFTERMATH

Dealing with disappointment when an anticipated revolution fails to materialize is a perennial burden for political radicals—one that can be handled in many different ways. Some, like Karl Marx, whose hopes were dashed when the political violence that convulsed Europe in 1848 failed to produce the communist revolution he anticipated, become more convinced than ever of the uprising's eventual inevitability. Others, by contrast, lose their faith in radical politics altogether. Some of the deradicalized seek to insulate themselves from further disillusionment by withdrawing entirely from public life, while still others reinvent themselves as political centrists or pragmatists.

And then there were the responses of Neuhaus and Novak. The failure of the 1960s revolution convinced each of them that he had misunderstood something vitally important about the United States. Yet neither writer gave up his hopes for radical change. The two merely modified their views about what changes needed to be made— and prepared themselves for a longer and potentially more frustrating process of reform. Although both men began their reevaluation as disappointed leftists, by the time it was over they would embrace the Republican Party as the political force in American life most likely to adopt and institute their radical vision. For Neuhaus, the move to the right would come in two stages, from 1972 to 1976 and from 1979 to 1984. Novak's evolution would be more continuous, beginning in 1970 and ending in 1982. When these transformations were complete, the fundamentals of theoconservative ideology would be in place.

Becoming the Christian Marx

Neuhaus pronounced the end of the protest movement quite early—in the spring of 1972, a mere two years after the peak of his revolutionary engagement. In later years he would trace his disillusionment with the left to several factors, including both moral revulsion at the Supreme Court's *Roe v. Wade* (1973) decision legalizing abortion and disgust at the excesses of the counterculture.[33] But this is revisionist history. Not only did his announcement of the movement's demise predate the *Roe* decision by nearly a year; his statements from the time about abortion and the counterculture show that his reaction to both was, at first, quite muted. While he had come out in opposition to the relaxation of restrictions on abortion as early as 1967, there is no evidence from the months and years following *Roe* that Neuhaus considered abortion to be the most pressing issue facing the country—let alone that he believed, as he later would, that the decision had been the gravest act of judicial injustice in the United States since *Dred Scott v. Sanford* (1857) denied the citizenship and humanity of black Americans.[34]

As for the counterculture, Neuhaus's original views were similarly restrained. Although he never showed anything but contempt for those members of the movement who put the quest for, in his words, "the perfect orgasm" ahead of the pursuit of justice, he did embrace other "progressive" causes, signing a petition in November 1966 that called on the Catholic Church to liberalize its position on birth control, and later advocating the widespread use of contraception as a way to decrease the number of abortions in the country.[35] He even went so far as to denounce those who equated "morality with correct sexual behavior, attributing to God an inordinate, if not exclusive, concern for mankind from the waist down." "Christian ethical preoccupation with sex," he believed at the time, "has had an inestimably deleterious effect on the credibility of the Church's witness in the world."[36] Even as late as 1978, he would acknowledge the justice behind the feminist and the gay rights movements.[37] Neuhaus's shift to the right on cultural and moral matters thus came much later—after his broader theological and ideological reorientation had already taken place.

Somewhat more significant in explaining Neuhaus's political evolution was the deescalation of the Vietnam War, as well as the behavior of his fellow radicals after the fall of Saigon. On the one hand, the process of Vietnamization (the gradual transfer of military responsibilities from American to South Vietnamese troops during the early 1970s) convinced him that the left had won the argument about the injustice of the conflict, which effectively eliminated one of the movement's central issues.[38] On the other hand, he was appalled by the reaction of his comrades-in-arms when he asked them to sign a petition in 1975 condemning the Communist government in Hanoi for its human rights record and disgraceful treatment of political prisoners, which precipitated a major refugee crisis as thousands fled the country on primitive bamboo boats. Only half of the 104 leftists Neuhaus approached would sign on to the protest. In his telling of the story, the rest were unwilling to take a public stand that could be interpreted as a concession to anti-Communist claims about the evils of Marxist government. This, he believed, was an example of anti-American animus and vindictiveness trumping moral principle, and he would have none of it.[39]

Yet, however much the morally ambiguous conclusion to the Vietnam War contributed to Neuhaus's disaffection with the left, the fact is that the beginnings of his ideological shift began much earlier, with his 1972 obituary for the protest movement.[40] Writing more than three years after Richard Nixon had been voted into the White House, and perhaps sensing the president's momentum going into his upcoming bid for reelection against the movement's preferred candidate (George McGovern), Neuhaus's mood was dark, shot through with disappointment. The radicalism of the 1960s, he now claimed, had been "fruitless." Because the movement "lacked the confidence of the majority of the people," its revolutionary goals could never have been achieved.[41] A morally justified revolution requires widespread popular support—it must be a populist revolution. And to that the 1960s left never even came close. And now that the "unrelieved indignation" that coursed through the country during the 1960s had begun to fade, its prospects were more remote than ever. Hence those who wished to continue pushing for dramatic changes in the nation needed, above all, to be patient. "The leaders we can count on for the '70s know the loneliness of the long-distance radical, and have overcome their fear of it." As for himself, Neuhaus confessed that his "own search for radical definition has progressively become *Christian* radicalism."[42]

The emphatically Christian form of radicalism to which Neuhaus referred in his 1972 essay would take shape over the next several years, as he slowly came to terms with his disappointment at the failure of the leftist revolution, as well as with a series of more recent and equally disturbing developments in the country. Military and moral defeat in Vietnam, a criminal conspiracy in the White House leading to a presidential resignation, lingering racial unrest in the nation's cities,

a crippling gasoline shortage and subsequent economic stagnation—
Neuhaus was hardly alone in concluding that the United States had
entered a period of profound uncertainty, even paralysis. Indeed, by
the mid-1970s it had become the conventional wisdom among the
nation's leading writers and intellectuals, many of whom wrote books
and articles intended to diagnose and prescribe a cure for the country's ills. Neuhaus's contributions to this literature were unique in two
respects. First, they were unusually ambitious, seeking to explain not
only why the nation currently suffered from such a lack of confidence
and sense of purpose but also why during the previous decade the
country's leaders had perpetuated grave injustice (in race relations and
foreign policy), as well as why the American people failed to rise up
against this injustice once the movement had brought it to their attention.[43] Neuhaus's writings in this period were also unique in that
they traced these manifold and long-standing problems to a single
source—a national "crisis of meaning," by which he meant a crisis of
religion.[44]

This crisis, Neuhaus claimed, had its roots in a spiritual conflict
between a narrow band of elites and the vast majority of the American people. Building on and radicalizing his earlier portrait of a country ruled by a hostile and unjust "regime," Neuhaus now portrayed a
nation governed by a class of decadent intellectuals who espoused a
form of "secularized liberalism that has been cut off from its religious
roots and robbed of its power to provide meaning." Meanwhile, the
vast majority of Americans made their way in the world using concepts, ideas, and principles derived from "explicit religion," which for
all practical purposes meant "some form of Christianity or Judaism."
Yet this religious majority had been excluded from "participating with
religious seriousness in the political process" by the "religiously
'emancipated,'" who held a "virtual monopoly" on "respectable public discourse." As a result, "millions of Americans" felt understandably
"alienated" from the public life of the nation.[45] It was this alienation

that by the mid-1970s had dulled the nation's moral senses and sapped its spiritual strength.

Neuhaus maintained that overcoming this alienation was a matter of extreme urgency. Failure to respond to it effectively could lead to a far deeper national malaise, even to a loss of the "moral cohesion without which a nation eventually collapses."[46] As he put it, in characteristically prophetic and apocalyptic terms, "Unless there is a new and widely convincing assertion of the religious meaning of liberal democracy, it will not survive the next century."[47] And because of America's unprecedented influence on the world as a whole, such a wholesale spiritual implosion in the United States could initiate a worldwide "new dark age."[48] Neuhaus even suggested that the stakes were so high and the challenges so great that the country required the aid of someone with extraordinary theoretical and practical vision—indeed, someone with the vision of a "Christian Marx." Not that Neuhaus endorsed communism or any other aspect of Marxist ideology. He simply meant to highlight Marx's remarkable ability to fashion a comprehensive system of thought that inspired millions, providing them with final, authoritative answers to every human question. Only a man of such enormous gifts would be capable of giving the United States what it so manifestly craved and required—namely, an ideological "alternative both to Marxism and secularized liberalism" that would grant the nation "a definition of reality, an ideology, based on Jewish-Christian religion, that [was] as creative, comprehensive, and compelling as was Marx's definition of reality."[49]

Neuhaus's writings from the mid-1970s were his first attempts to step into this exalted role—to become America's Christian Marx, to author a comprehensive religious ideology that would enable the United States to break out of its spiritual crisis. At the most basic level, this ideology would have to be more radically and consistently populist than the one that had prevailed during the 1960s. Unlike the progressive elites of the previous decade, who issued revolutionary

declarations from on high and expected the American majority to follow along, the intellectuals of the present and future needed to take
precisely the opposite approach—to tease out, clarify, and amplify
what the majority already believed. Against such authors as Richard
Hofstadter and Daniel Bell, who criticized the politically volatile
"paranoia" associated with populist politics in America, Neuhaus
pointed out that "paranoiacs can be persecuted too." Indeed, "there is
a kind of persecution felt by many ordinary Americans in the thinly
veiled disdain with which they are viewed by many intellectuals."[50]
The genuinely populist intellectuals that America needed would have
to overcome the pernicious effects of such persecution and disdain by
empowering the people both politically and intellectually.

Neuhaus claimed that his proposed fusion of extreme populism
and theological ideas would lead to a "radical rethinking of the role of
religion in the public realm."[51] The point of such rethinking was not
to engage in a nationwide "return to religion," but rather to become
"more honest and articulate about the religious dynamics that do in
fact shape our public life" without our being fully aware of it.[52] Drawing on the work of theologian Paul Tillich, Neuhaus asserted that,
whether or not it is publicly acknowledged, in all times and places
politics is ultimately a function of culture, and culture is ultimately a
function of religion.[53] The fate of democracy in America was thus in-
separable from the fate of public religiosity in America. Over the past
several generations, fashionable secularist theories had not so much
eradicated as concealed this truth from us. Yet unlike the corrupt and
corrupting secularist intellectuals who had come to set the terms of
public debate in the country, ordinary Americans continued at a basic, intuitive level to understand the crucial role of religion in healthy
and vibrant politics—and to sense that the "American experiment"
requires a "transcendent point of reference to which we are corpo-
rately accountable."[54] It was the duty of intellectuals to learn this lesson from the people and begin constructing arguments to justify their
wisdom.

Once the new breed of religious intellectuals had succeeded in convincing the American people that it is legitimate to make "religious, specifically biblical, truth claims" in public, they could then take their national tutorial to the next level—by seeking to transform the way Americans think of their country and its role in world history.[55] In place of the notion of a "contract" among equal citizens, which secular intellectuals and academic political theorists had done their best in recent years to spread among the American people, Neuhaus proposed that the American experiment in self-government be reconceived in terms of a communal "covenant" under God. Unlike the signatories to a contract, who view the world through the lens of individual self-interest, the members of a covenantal community think and act in light of a time in which "judgment is rendered, forgiveness bestowed, renewal begun, and the experiment either vindicated or repudiated."[56] Which is to say that talk of a covenant raises questions about the eschaton—the "end times" in which individuals and peoples will be judged by the Lord.[57] In one of the most remarkable passages he would ever write, the native Canadian drew out the political and theological implications of such eschatological thinking by announcing that when he died and stood face-to-face with his creator, he expected to do so "as an American." He also advised his readers to follow his example in seeking "the vindication of myself in my historical particularity, and of the American experiment of which I am a part."[58] God, Neuhaus wished his readers to believe, is watching and judging every act we make as individuals and as a nation—and we ought to order our public life in light of his divine oversight.

Responding to the liberal concern that encouraging communal speculation about God's plans for the nation would inspire religious extremism and heighten sectarian conflict, Neuhaus claimed that it would have a much more salutary effect, curing America's spiritual malaise by generating "a unifying source of meaning."[59] By "renewing our religious understanding of the American experience," the revival of "eschatological urgency" would lead the country to unite with confidence and in common purpose as never before—or at least for the first time since a "relentless secularism in the public realm" began to "eviscerate" American society.[60] Indeed, Neuhaus went so far as to argue that it was in fact the *exclusion* of eschatological speculation from public life that was "unhealthy, unnatural, and possibly lethal to our hopes for a common purpose as a people," and perhaps even "lethal to our hopes for continued life together."[61] Eventually religious Americans would grow weary of subverting their faith to secular pieties and demand an end to the tyranny of public godlessness. Many years before it would become common to speak of a "culture war" in the United States, Neuhaus prophesied the disintegration of America along cultural and religious lines, with secularists and religious believers going their separate ways or, one imagines, even coming to blows.

From Counterculture to Incarnational Capitalism

Michael Novak had somewhat further to go on his journey to the right than Richard Neuhaus. As an advocate of revolution in personal and social matters no less than in politics, Novak had placed himself far outside of the American mainstream at its most leftward fringe. This was perhaps most apparent in the highly aesthetic and elitist character of his radicalism. As we have seen, in 1969 he considered "the good people, the churchgoers, the typical Americans" to be the "enemies" of his radical ideals, and he even entertained the possibility of placing these average citizens "in the line of fire."

It was perhaps predictable, then, that the first step in Novak's ideological evolution involved a populist turn. Oddly enough, this initial shift began on a road trip, during the three months of 1970 when he traveled around the country with Sargent Shriver, working as a speechwriter-for-hire for a series of Democratic congressional candidates. In his travels he "met the American people in the flesh" for the first time and was instantly consumed with shame about what he had written in *A Theology for Radical Politics.*[62] The individuals he came to know struck him as decent and moral—the very model of upstanding citizens. Before long he had concluded that "there was more health in the people than in their literary elites, including me."[63]

Novak would seek redemption for his earlier views in *The Rise of the Unmeltable Ethnics*, the 1972 book in which he reinvented himself as a rabid populist and broke decisively with the cultural radicalism of his 1969 position.[64] *Ethnics* was at once a love letter to immigrants, like his own parents, from southern, central, and eastern Europe, and a strident polemic against America's WASP elite, which Novak blamed for everything from his own boyhood ethnic insecurities to the destructive influence of the New Left (which he now treated with contempt) on American culture and civility. Read in the context of George McGovern's failed 1972 presidential campaign (for which Novak worked), the book can be seen as a warning to the Democratic Party not to identify itself too closely with (in Novak's words) the "educated, wealthy, [and] powerful."[65] The winning electoral coalition for the future would, by contrast, unite inner-city blacks and ethnic whites against their common enemy, which Novak described as the "concentrated power" of the WASP establishment. It is hardly surprising that neither the Democrats nor the Republicans were interested in adopting such a divisive strategy and rhetoric, although Novak did eventually succeed in persuading the Ford administration to open a White House Office of Ethnic Affairs.

But like the political and cultural radicalism that preceded it, Novak's focus on ethnicity would not last. As Novak gained ever-greater appreciation for the everyday virtues of immigrant communities like the one in which he was raised, his views of religion, politics, and economics headed off in new and surprising directions. On the one hand, he developed a greater respect for the conservative Catholic piety of his parents' generation. Although he remained a passionate defender of Vatican II, he began to wonder whether it might be pos-

sible to fashion a less heterodox interpretation of the council's meaning and intent than the one he had endorsed in the mid- and late
1960s. On the other hand, Novak came to admire the work ethic,
economic dynamism, and entrepreneurial spirit he observed among
ordinary Americans. Before long, this admiration blossomed into an
intense infatuation with free-market capitalism. Proudly declaring
himself to be a "closet capitalist," and denouncing the "closet socialists" among his peers, he now publicly "confessed" his long-standing
admiration for the flexibility, creativity, productivity, and resiliency of
the free market.[66] No amount of anticapitalist ideology could conceal
the glorious fact that capitalism had done more than any other economic system in human history to improve living conditions for the
poor, just as it had generated more wealth and technological innovation for the human race as a whole. For the former leftist critic of all
things American, including capitalism, it was clearly a case of love at
second sight.

But Novak also believed that capitalism, despite its remarkable and
unheralded strengths, had a serious problem—much the same problem, in fact, that Neuhaus diagnosed around the same time as a "crisis
of meaning." According to Novak, capitalists "have not been trained to
think—have, indeed, been tutored *not* to think, not to theorize, not to
dream." As a result, the capitalist system is "brute and inarticulate,
mute in the language of the spirit."[67] Whereas socialism provided its
followers with a secular religion to substitute for the traditional religions it forbade them to practice, capitalism inculcated no equivalent
overarching metaphysical justification of itself. It was thus incapable of
matching the humanistic aspirations of socialism—at least in theory. In
practice, it won hands down. But that was insufficient. Democratic
capitalism lacked a "single text setting forth our social vision," and that
was its "most stunning single deficiency."[68] And so, just as Neuhaus set
out to become a Christian Marx who would provide the United States
with a comprehensive religious ideology, Novak resolved to develop a
theological defense of capitalism—of "the system of symbols, values,

ideas, rituals, practices, and institutions that define the attitudes and daily operations of our people, and that give substance and meaning to their political and economic activities."[69]

In his effort to provide capitalism with a theological justification, Novak received unlikely inspiration from the work of sociologist Daniel Bell, in particular from his 1976 book *The Cultural Contradictions of Capitalism.* Bell denied that modern societies could be adequately understood as simple wholes and defended a pluralistic view in which distinct spheres of politics, economics, and culture each operated according to its own norms, types of behavior, and dynamics of change. He then went on to claim that American society was suffering from a contradiction between the spheres of economics and culture, with capitalism creating hedonistic needs, desires, and wants in citizens that subverted the conservative cultural ties of family, community, morality, and religion on which capitalism itself depended for its ongoing survival and strength.

It was a pessimistic, even tragic, thesis—one profoundly at odds with Novak's insistently sunny, Bernanosian conviction that it is always possible to find "in every moment of history, in every culture, and in every place and time the workings of divine grace."[70] Perhaps this clash of sensibilities explains how Novak could transform Bell's account of fatally conflicting social spheres into a triumphant defense of "democratic capitalism," a system in which politics, economics, and culture consistently reinforce and strengthen one another for the benefit of all. In Novak's Panglossian view, Christianity, modern democracy, and modern capitalism arose from and continue to share "the same logic, the same moral principles, the same set of cultural values, institutions, and presuppositions."[71] Although Bell deserved credit for highlighting the pluralistic character of democratic capitalism, Novak maintained that he had failed to take account of its "underlying spiritual power . . . and its capacities for self-renewal." The system contains its own "powerfully self-transforming, creative, and inventive" spirit, if only we would train ourselves to detect it.[72]

The Spirit of Democratic Capitalism (1982), which would become Novak's most influential book, contains the "theology of economics" he had been aspiring to write since the mid-1970s. Much of the book's content overlaps with one of the seminal works of neoconservatism, Irving Kristol's *Two Cheers for Capitalism* (1978), which had offered a forceful, if pragmatic, defense of the free market against its many detractors. Capitalism creates wealth that over time improves economic conditions for everyone; it limits the power of the state by empowering the private sector; it makes possible and inspires widespread private charity; it encourages (by rewarding) the virtues of hard work, self-reliance, and entrepreneurial creativity. Kristol's aim in pointing out these and other benefits of the free market was to make a modest case for capitalism as the best economic system in comparison to the available alternatives. In publishing the book when he did, he inadvertently provided the future Reagan administration with a series of powerful arguments in defense of its economic agenda.

If *Two Cheers for Capitalism* served as prospective justification of Reaganomics, *The Spirit of Democratic Capitalism* was its catechism. Nearly every one of Kristol's pragmatic arguments could be found in its pages. Yet Novak considered them to be merely starting points. The market economy also required a spiritual justification—one that highlighted its providentially guided beauty and balance—and that is what he aimed to provide. Opening a business doesn't just potentially enrich yourself and marginally increase the wealth of society; it does God's work by creating jobs, and thus wages, for others. A business career isn't merely an enjoyable and possibly lucrative line of work; it is a "vocation" in the sense of a calling from God. The invention and marketing of innovative products doesn't just provide a creative outlet; it expresses your essence as a being made in the image of the divine Creator. Markets don't simply produce economic growth; they mirror the divine Trinity in the way they enable many diverse individuals to function as one, in perfect harmony.[73] Corporations aren't merely large, profit-seeking businesses; they "mirror the presence of God" in seven sacramental ways and even offer publicly accessible "metaphors for grace."[74]

Ever since Adam Smith's eighteenth-century *Wealth of Nations*, admirers of capitalism have recognized that the self-interested decisions of individuals in a free-market system can have unintentionally beneficial social consequences. In a capitalistic system what was once considered a vice (the selfish pursuit of personal wealth) sometimes produces outcomes (like the alleviation of poverty) that were traditionally associated with acts of virtue (self-sacrifice for the greater good). But Novak went much further than this, to claim—or at least strongly imply—that the entire system of capitalistic exchange, in which (supposedly) everyone involved miraculously benefits, is itself an expression of divine beneficence. For Novak, Smith's "invisible hand" guiding the market was quite simply the hand of God—and the rise and spread of democratic capitalism in the world the Greatest Story Ever Told, albeit retold in a distinctly late-twentieth-century American accent.

Novak's boosterism was not limited to the American present. Indeed, in *The Spirit of Democratic Capitalism*, and even more so in the months and years following its publication, Novak attempted to ground his theological account of democratic capitalism in American and Western European history. The American political, cultural, and economic achievement was, he claimed, an outgrowth of an infinitely syncretic "Whig tradition," which included (among many others) Thomas Aquinas, Thomas Hooker, Montaigne, the Jesuits of Salamanca, Montesquieu, Adam Smith, nearly every one of the American founding fathers, Macaulay, Alexis de Tocqueville, Lord Acton, Edmund Burke, Abraham Lincoln, Ludwig von Mises, Yves Simon, John Courtney Murray, Jacques Maritain, Friedrich Hayek, and Pope John Paul II. Most educated readers had to admit that these thinkers and writers had little, if anything, of substance in common and thus fell far short of constituting a coherent tradition. Yet this mélange became the imagined source of everything Novak approved of in modern American life. In Novak's hands, these Thomists, deists, skeptics, humanists, monarchists, republicans, and orthodox believers were transformed into unproblematic defenders of the precise mixture of capitalism, democracy, and traditional religious faith that Novak himself advocated—they were transformed, in other words, into theocons.[75]

From the time of his earliest writings, Novak had been inspired by a vision of a catholic synthesis—between modernity and Catholicism, church and state, sacred and secular, the sexual and the spiritual, theism and atheism. At its most extreme, during the heyday of the counterculture, the urge to synthesize led the young Catholic thinker into heterodoxy, if not outright heresy, as he blurred fundamental distinctions, dissolved significant differences, and ended up with a thoroughly muddled revolutionary agenda. Just over a decade later, in the era of Reagan and Thatcher, Novak envisioned a very different—and only somewhat less questionable—synthesis, this time combining conservative religiosity, liberal democratic politics, and free-market capitalism. Like his earlier attempt at synthesis, this one was very far removed from traditional Catholic teaching, which since the late nineteenth century had endorsed a moderate form of socialism in order to tame what the church considered to be the materialistic excesses of the market. But in Reagan's America, the idea of a capitalist theodicy was much less controversial. Indeed, it seemed to distill and express the hopes of many of the new president's most devoted followers, who fervently believed in the fundamental compatibility between—and even the providential imperative of—unleashing the market on the one hand and defending traditional moral and religious values on the other.[76]

In his writings of the early 1980s, Novak made the case for this agenda in the most sweeping terms possible, and it gained him the widest audience of his career. Yet his greatest influence would come indirectly, in future years—when Neuhaus, his old friend and colleague on the far left, incorporated key elements of Novak's synthesizing project (first, in the mid-1980s, on the religious character of the American founding; later, in the late 1980s and early 1990s, on the compatibility of this religiosity with capitalism) into a new radical ideology for the emergent religious right.

The Failed Messiah and the Final Metamorphosis

By 1976 the first stage of Neuhaus's ideological evolution was complete. The one-time advocate of revolutionary populism had become an even more radical populist, advocating the overthrow of the nation's liberal secularist elite in the name of the traditionalist Judeo-Christian piety supposedly affirmed by ordinary Americans. Despite the theological radicalism of this new agenda, its practical implications were relatively benign. Neuhaus himself had declared in 1975 that he did not intend his "reaction" against public secularism to be "reactionary."[77] And indeed, his statements on public policy from the mid-1970s show that he had merely become a conservative Democrat. As late as 1978, Neuhaus would argue that his proposed religious revitalization of the country would entail a greater commitment to fight world hunger, support universal health care, restrict the right to private firearms, and push for other generally liberal policies.[78] To be sure, his insistence on grounding these proposals in his Christian faith made Neuhaus a somewhat unusual Democrat. But once Jimmy Carter received the party's nomination for president in 1976, Neuhaus's combination of devout Christian piety and political moderation came to seem oddly fashionable.

It is hardly surprising that Neuhaus's identification with the Democrats peaked during Jimmy Carter's presidential campaign. After all, like Neuhaus, Carter was a faith-based Democrat. What's more, like Neuhaus's hero Martin Luther King Jr., Carter had come out of the rural South to challenge the nation's political establishment in the name of a higher moral and religious ideal, which appealed to Neuhaus's persistent suspicion of temporal authority and intense longing to bring politics into conformity with divine authority. In fact, this longing is perhaps the only plausible explanation of Neuhaus's astonishing enthusiasm for Carter, which is quite simply impossible to exaggerate. Reading Neuhaus's effusive statements about Carter in the run-up to the 1976 election, it is clear that he viewed the Georgia governor's candidacy in eschatological terms—as the likely fulfillment of a lifetime of political and theological hopes. When these hopes were dashed, the resulting disappointment would propel Neuhaus into his second and final lurch to the right.

In a remarkable essay from the fall of 1976, Neuhaus declared that a Carter presidency would mark a "real watershed" in American history. Concerned that his readers might not appreciate the full implications of the metaphor, he explained that "a watershed involves a point of parting, a new configuration, a redirection of history into a different course."[79] In an America divided between "the secularism of the elite and the most deeply held beliefs of most of the American people," Carter held out the possibility of bridging the gap. Yet he would do so not by imposing an alien religious vision on the country from above—not by replacing "the secular definition of America with a religious definition"—but rather by making possible "a marriage, or a remarriage," of politics and religion "that is beyond the divorce." Neuhaus employed this striking image to illustrate Carter's "ominous responsibility," which concerned nothing less than "a comprehensive rethinking of . . . present clichés about [the] 'separation of Church and State.' "[80]

But the consequences of a Carter presidency were not limited to the boundaries of the United States. In the most far-reaching passage of the essay, Neuhaus detected signs of a "major cultural shift" in the rise of Jimmy Carter—a shift "not only in the definition of the American experiment but in Western culture's understanding of modernity." Going even further, Neuhaus proposed that "the Carter era could signal the end of the public hegemony of the secular Enlightenment in the Western world."[81] Having thus expressed his world-historical hopes for a Carter victory, Neuhaus shifted into a biblical cadence for his conclusion. Gesturing toward providence, he mused about how "wondrously strange" it would be if "after two hundred years, it is Jimmy Carter from Georgia who is raised up to signal the way in renewing the [American social] contract," and, even more fundamentally, in encouraging the nation to recommit itself to "the covenant."[82] Neuhaus clearly believed that Carter would be the vehicle for instituting his own ideas for the religious renewal of American public life—and that in doing so the president would also be fulfilling God's plans for the United States and the world.

Neuhaus's monumental hopes for Carter continued well into his presidency, right up until the president repaid Neuhaus's lavish endorsement by appointing him to the newly formed White House Conference on the Family in 1979. The decision to ask Neuhaus to join the conference made a great deal of policy sense. Three years earlier, Michael Novak had invited Neuhaus and his old friend Peter Berger (who was in the process of making his own much less dramatic trek across the political spectrum from left to right) to host a series of meetings at the American Enterprise Institute in Washington, D.C., on the importance of such subpolitical "mediating institutions" as families, businesses, and churches for the health and vitality of democratic civil society. In those meetings and in the resulting book *(To Empower People* [1977]), Berger and Neuhaus argued that government's role in dealing with such institutions should be minimal—basically getting out of the way so that they could thrive in freedom. When it came to families, for example, both authors believed that parents were in a much better position than the state to make decisions about how to raise and educate children. To the extent that the state had any role to play at all, it should act in such a way as to perpetuate and strengthen the structures of the traditional two-parent family.

Given President Carter's moral and religious conservatism, Neuhaus had every reason to believe that the White House Conference on the Family would follow these suggestions. But his faith was misplaced. In order to placate criticism from feminists and gay rights activists who feared that the executive branch would be holding up a single form of family life as legitimate and therefore denigrating "alternative lifestyles," the Carter administration quickly moved to pluralize the title of the conference (from "Family" to "Families")—an action that inspired Neuhaus to immediately resign.[83] The American people, he believed, agreed with him about the importance of strengthening the traditional family. For the president to turn against them and side with secular elites who had nothing but contempt for this essential cultural institution was an enormous betrayal—of American democracy no less than of the substantial religious hopes that Neuhaus had invested in him.

Neuhaus was far from being the only person to abandon the president as a result of the "Families" debacle. Today it is widely recognized that many things contributed to Carter's defeat in 1980—the endless Iran hostage crisis, the botched attempt to rescue the hostages using military force, persistent economic "stagflation," Ronald Reagan's skills as a campaigner. A factor rarely mentioned is the hostility Carter faced from his fellow evangelicals, who in the year leading up to the election withdrew their support and even actively campaigned against him. The ill-fated Conference on Families played a crucial role in fostering this evangelical disaffection. For the members of the New Christian Right—and above all for the Moral Majority, founded by Jerry Falwell in 1979 in order to prosecute a campaign against the spread of "secular humanism"—President Carter had done far too little to oppose the moral crisis they perceived in the country.[84] Reagan, they came to believe, would be much more effective at combating the growing secularism and immorality of American life since the 1960s. The decisive shift of the evangelicals to the GOP in 1980 would spark a series of further changes in American politics over the next twenty-five years—changes that our nation's political culture has only recently begun to absorb and understand, the most consequential of which has been the religious polarization of the parties, with the Republicans increasingly becoming the party of intense piety and the Democrats the party of more casual faith and thoroughgoing secularism.

As for Neuhaus, his second significant political disappointment since 1972 led to another period of ideological reevaluation. Carter's choice to embrace the secular liberals in his party after he had indicated an intent to turn back their advance in the culture convinced Neuhaus that his desired reforms were unlikely to be taken up by the Democrats anytime soon. Nevertheless he was unprepared to publicly embrace the Republicans, despite having quietly supported Reagan during the 1980 campaign.[85] Surprisingly enough, it was the evangelicals who inspired Neuhaus to keep his distance from the GOP. In some ways the rise of the evangelicals to political prominence seemed to fulfill Neuhaus's hopes for and predictions about the role of traditionalist religious populism in America's future. Yet many aspects of evangelical culture and belief offended his style and sensibility. As he would admit in a candid interview over two decades later, several years after forming a potent political and theological alliance with several prominent evangelicals, Neuhaus intensely disliked their "overly confident claims to being born again," not to mention their "forced happiness and joy," and even their "awful music."[86] Far more significant, though, he thought that Falwell and his followers were being unrealistic in supposing that their idiosyncratic faith, based on highly subjective "born again" experiences, could serve as the religiously based public philosophy the country so desperately needed. And then there was their uniformly reactionary outlook on everything from abortion to pornography, the sexual revolution to gay rights. Neuhaus shared many of their cultural and moral concerns, but he also understood why their stridency alienated so many mainstream Americans. The evangelicals risked tearing the country apart and, in the process, discrediting Neuhaus's goal of using a vibrant public religiosity to unify the nation.

Yet the evangelicals made great strides during the early 1980s, helping to determine the outcome of a presidential election, working to influence the Republican agenda, and promising to push the terms of debate in the country in a more religious direction (however slowly and marginally at first). As the evangelicals began to organize for Reagan's 1984 reelection campaign, Neuhaus reluctantly concluded that the religious right was the only game in town. His political instincts and ambitions, his public spiritedness, and his religious faith all told him that it couldn't be ignored. On the contrary, it needed to be engaged, hopefully moderated, certainly educated, but also, at some level, joined—and perhaps even, behind the scenes, at the level of ideas and ideology, led. In 1970 he had aspired to act as a moral tutor for the revolutionary left; now, just over a decade later, he would offer to perform a similar service for a religious insurgency of the right, despite the fact that the right defined itself, at least in part, by its opposition to everything the 1960s (and in his youth, Neuhaus himself) had stood for.

THE THEOCON MANIFESTO

Neuhaus would stake out his new position as the sage of the religious right in a book that would present a sympathetic critique of the evangelicals and lay out his vision of a more politically responsible, intellectually respectable, and theologically informed approach to amplifying the influence of religion in American politics and culture. That book—*The Naked Public Square: Religion and Democracy in America* (1984)—would come to serve as the manifesto of the nascent theoconservative movement.

The Naked Public Square instantly brought Neuhaus more public attention than he had ever received. Largely favorable reviews appeared in the country's leading newspapers and magazines, and for a brief period the book's argument was widely debated in the mainstream press.[87] Neuhaus's timing was impeccable. Published in the run-up to the 1984 election, when journalists were focusing increasingly anxious attention on conservative evangelicalism and its influence on Ronald Reagan's reelection campaign, Neuhaus's book raised the controversial topic of the relation between religion and politics and addressed it with originality and intelligence. And then there was the book's rhetoric, which disarmed many of the author's would-be critics. Indeed, in his brief preface and at key moments throughout the text, Neuhaus portrayed himself as a moderate, irenic defender of civility, mutual understanding, and the beleaguered "vital center" of American politics against extremists of various stripes, including and especially Jerry Falwell's moral majoritarians.[88] No one could have taken him to be a liberal, but Neuhaus did seem to go out of his way to speak to the concerns, and to employ the language, of liberalism.

At least in some passages. In many others, the old revolutionary Neuhaus of the 1960s came to the surface, revealing his radical intent. Strangely, few critics appeared to notice, amidst all the rhetorical sweetness, the author's warnings of an impending dark age—a time of civil war and imminent totalitarianism in America—let alone his eschatological assertion that "only a transcendent, a religious, vision can turn this society from disaster and toward the fulfillment of its destiny" as a "sacred enterprise."[89]

Neuhaus's argument was extremely subtle—even, in places, contradictory—but it was also quite powerful. The rise of the Moral Majority, he claimed, had "kicked a tripwire" in the United States, alerting all thoughtful citizens to a fundamental, and potentially fatal, tension in modern American life. "We insist," he claimed, that "we are a democratic society, yet we have in recent decades systematically excluded from policy consideration the operative values of the American people, values that are overwhelmingly grounded in religious belief."[90] The cause of this antidemocratic trend was the rise of the idea that the United States is a secular society. Drawing on and amplifying the arguments and rhetoric of conservative philosopher Alasdair MacIntyre, Neuhaus described the cultural elites who had promulgated the secularist thesis as "barbarians" who had emancipated themselves from the moral and religious truths that all "civilized people consider self-evident." These barbarians exercise enormous influence on the country, demanding that religious Americans "produce evidence for the self-evident" or else withdraw from public debate and discussion.[91] Neuhaus described this withdrawal in several ways, but the most potent was the image that provided his book its title: America's decline would be complete when the secularists had succeeded in creating the "naked public square"—a public square that had been thoroughly stripped of religiously based moral arguments.

Neuhaus went on to argue that in advancing the naked public square the secularists had been abetted by the (theological and demographic) decline of the mainline Protestant churches since the early 1960s. Together the Episcopal, Congregationalist, Presbyterian, and Methodist denominations had once provided the country with a unifying religious vision, but in recent years they had begun to shirk their civic and religious duties. Here Neuhaus drew on an argument he had been making since 1975, when he had persuaded eighteen prominent church leaders (including his old partner in left-wing activism William Sloane Coffin) to sign the Hartford Appeal for Theological Affirmation, which denounced the mainline National Council of Churches (NCC) for acquiescing to the secularism of the "white, middle-class cultural elite."[92] Nearly a decade later, Neuhaus was even less forgiving in his evaluation of the mainline, which he now charged with having accommodated itself to explicitly antireligious trends in American culture and thus also with having deliberately distanced itself from the deep religious convictions of the vast majority of the American people—all for the sake of remaining "useful" in progressive political circles, which were now dominated by the ideology of secularism.[93] The effect of this accommodation had been to transform the mainline churches into liberal special interest groups lacking any distinctive theological teaching. No wonder, then, that these once culturally dominant denominations were in freefall, being rapidly overtaken by a populist evangelical and fundamentalist insurgency.

In Neuhaus's view, this populist religious uprising demonstrated beyond a shadow of a doubt that, despite its influence and public prominence, secularism could never prevail in the United States—that, in fact, Americans were and would remain "a Christian people."[94] Yet throughout the book Neuhaus also insisted that the triumph of secularism was an active possibility to be struggled against at all costs—one that might very well lead to the moral collapse of the nation. At times this tension nearly derailed his argument. In the end, he avoided incoherence by making a series of clarifying (and explosive) assertions and predictions. Relying on the writings of the Jesuit John Courtney Murray, and perhaps projecting his own craving for divine authority onto the world at large, Neuhaus argued that the public affirmation of some kind of absolute authority was inevitable because "transcendence abhors a vacuum." The attempt to expunge traditional religious faith from public life would thus end up empowering an "ersatz religion" of the state (most likely a "distinctly American form of Communism").[95] Hence the *true* danger of the advance of secularism was not that it would succeed in creating a society without religion but rather that "it will lead—not next year, maybe not in twenty years, but all too soon—to totalitarianism." Unless, that is, the country first experienced a violent rebellion on the part of those traditionalist believers who refused to go along with the establishment of the substitute state religion.[96] Regardless of whether or not the naked public square was an actual possibility, America was surrounded by cataclysmic futures on every side.

The country's only hope of avoiding these nightmare scenarios was for it to embrace the reinvigoration of public religiosity—or, in the language of Neuhaus's chosen metaphor, to reclothe the public square. Yet it was far from clear how this should be accomplished. On the one hand, expressing a perennial sentiment, Neuhaus indicated that "populist resentment against the logic of the naked public square is a source of hope." On the other hand, however, simply allowing each and every religious group to bring its own distinctive truth claims to bear on public questions would not yield the authentic "voice of Christian America."[97] It would instead produce a cacophony of divergent divine claims, each based on private revelation or parochial tradition. The case of the Moral Majority demonstrated this more vividly than any other. However justified their grievances against the creeping secularism of American life, Falwell and his followers had understandably alienated their fellow citizens, even those who sympathized with their aims. The reason was obvious: the religious agenda of the evangelicals was based almost entirely on publicly unverifiable subjective experiences of being "born again" in Jesus Christ—experiences that were incapable of persuading nonbelievers or people of other faiths. Even if the moral majoritarians were to become a genuine electoral majority, their faith-based policies would justly be viewed by nonevangelical Americans as an illegitimate and coercive imposition of private moral and religious views onto the nation as a whole by force. The public comportment of the evangelicals thus threatened to set back the cause of revitalizing public religion by confirming the warnings of liberal secularists about the inevitably private character of religious faith—and about how the very attempt to bring religiously based moral arguments into the public sphere produces a rancorous politics that amounts to "civil war carried on by other means."[98]

The Naked Public Square contains Neuhaus's first attempt to solve the problem of the evangelicals by developing an alternative way for them to talk about religion in public. Instead of referring to their personal religious experiences, they would have to adopt a nondenominational "public language of moral purpose," like the one Neuhaus and Novak had begun to use in their writings, and learn to make more sophisticated, intellectually respectable arguments about American society and history, democracy and justice, culture and the law. In his work on the syncretic "Whig tradition" in America, Novak had already developed a novel account of the country's history that could be employed by thoughtful religious believers to engage advocates of secularism, placing them on the defensive.

In some of the most provocative and influential passages of *The Naked Public Square* Neuhaus expanded on these efforts by portraying the American founding in explicitly religious terms. Flatly rejecting several decades of Supreme Court jurisprudence, Neuhaus denied that the First Amendment contains two religion clauses pitted against each other—one forbidding the "establishment" of religion, and the other permitting its "free exercise." In Neuhaus's view, this interpretation, which developed in a series of postwar cases that culminated in the 1963 decision outlawing school prayer *(Abington v. Schempp),* broke from established tradition on relations between church and state. The traditional stance of the American government toward religion, according to Neuhaus, was certainly not outright hostility. But neither was it neutrality, which would have led to the de facto "establishment of a religion of secularism." Rather, American tradition had maintained that the state should actively encourage public religiosity, as long as it did not officially establish any one church. It is thus more accurate to say that the First Amendment contains one religion clause with two provisions, both of which are intended to empower the nation's churches, not to cordon them off into the private sphere. Only in the midtwentieth century did secularist judges begin to turn religious freedom against public religious observance.[99] Before then, the state sided emphatically with religion, which is what it was intended to do by the nation's founders.

Unlike appeals to private revelation or parochial tradition, these and other (highly questionable) assertions about the place of religion in the American past and present could be effectively deployed in public argument not just by evangelicals but by any Protestant, Catholic, or Jewish opponent of secularism. They could even be used to engage and (at least potentially) persuade open-minded nonbelievers.[100] Here, then, was a language of public piety that promised to make a politically significant difference—by neutralizing the negative fallout from the rise of the Moral Majority, by providing evangelicals and other conservative believers with the means to advance a right-wing cultural and political agenda on a whole range of issues (including abortion, education, and the role of women in society and the family), and by challenging liberal secularist claims about the inevitably private character of all religious arguments. Most of all, this strategy showed how it might be possible to construct an interdenominational electoral coalition on the basis of shared disaffection with the secularist drift of American life since the 1960s. These were—and they remain—the core ambitions of theoconservative ideology.

In the years following the publication of *The Naked Public Square*, Neuhaus, Novak, and a growing circle of like-minded intellectuals would revise and refine many aspects of this ideology. Some of these changes would prove to be quite significant—perhaps none more so than Neuhaus's decision during the late 1980s to recast it in explicitly Catholic terms.[101] And much work remained to be done to ensure that the ideology achieved a maximum degree of influence. Still, by the mid-1980s the fundamentals of theoconservatism were in place. The theocons would provide evangelicals and other culturally alienated Christians and Jews with ideas and rhetoric to challenge secular politics at a fundamental level—and to contend, for the first time, for political and cultural power. For these wayward sons of the 1960s, it was the chance of a lifetime—finally to lead, after so many futile struggles and crushing disappointments, what they considered to be a morally and democratically legitimate populist revolution in the United States.

2

THE PATH TO POWER

I N *THE NAKED PUBLIC SQUARE*, Richard John Neuhaus proposed an ambitious and intellectually rigorous ideological program whose goal was the overthrow of secularism in American public
life. This aim would be accomplished by equipping newly politicized
Protestant evangelicals with arguments and rhetoric that would enable them to contend more effectively for political power. In the
months following its publication, the book had a substantial impact
on public debate, adding a great deal of depth and urgency to the ongoing discussion of the role of conservative evangelicals in President
Reagan's reelection campaign. Yet, predictably, the media's attention
soon turned to other issues, leaving the question of the relation between religion and politics in America for another day. Over the next
several years, Neuhaus and his allies would push their agenda on several fronts, while generating remarkably little public attention. This
chapter traces the theocons' path to power and influence in the
decade between 1984 and 1994—years during which they engaged in

a stealth campaign to build the institutions and form the alliances that would ultimately propel their ideas into the White House.

In their effort to inject a fiery religiosity into the country's politics, the theocons pursued three distinct strategies that overlapped one another in time. First, they founded magazines, institutes, and think tanks, as well as secured reliable funding for their writing, as a way of influencing public opinion in Washington and around the country. Second, they allied their movement with powerful conservative forces within the Catholic Church, the largest and most intellectually rigorous religious group in the nation. Third, they engineered a potent theological and ideological alliance between conservative Catholics and Protestant evangelicals. All of these initiatives would prove to be enormously successful. Together they provided the theocon movement with the means to capture cultural and political power in the United States.

THE INFRASTRUCTURE OF INFLUENCE

In seeking to put their ideas into action, the theocons followed the example of their ideological cousins, the neoconservatives. Throughout the late 1970s and early 1980s, the neocons perfected the art of political pressure and persuasion, constructing a potent network of think tanks, institutes, journals, and foundations to spread their ideas among policy makers in Washington. In order to have a similar impact, the theocons piggybacked on this neocon network; they also used neocon connections to begin the long and arduous process of building their own independent infrastructure of influence.

The ideological and institutional synergy between the neocons and theocons was made possible by a remarkable convergence between the two groups during the 1980s—a convergence that would have seemed highly unlikely just fifteen years earlier. At the end of the 1960s, when Neuhaus and Michael Novak embraced religious and political radicalism, the men who would become the neocons (primarily the social scientists associated with Irving Kristol's quarterly journal *The Public Interest*) were moderate liberals with a distaste for ideological stridency. Indeed, it was largely the political extremism of men like the young Neuhaus and Novak—as well as what Kristol and his associates perceived as liberal capitulation to this extremism—that inspired the proto-neocons to drift rightward in the first place.

On the theocon side, the convergence was accomplished largely by Novak, whose writing during his transitional decade drew very heavily on the arguments of the neocons—Nathan Glazer on ethnicity, Daniel Bell on democratic pluralism, and Irving Kristol on capitalism. Yet Novak's overtly Catholic conclusions—not to mention Neuhaus's eschatological speculations about America's historical destiny and his advocacy of a radical religious populism—showed that on a deeper level the neocons and theocons remained very far apart. The forging of an enthusiastic and productive alliance between the two groups would require that the line of influence begin to run in the other direction as well—that the neocons adopt key theocon assumptions about the proper role of religion and populist politics in American life.

The story of how and why the neocons became sympathetic to theocon arguments begins in the early 1970s, with neocon attempts to understand and respond to the radicalism of the New Left and the counterculture. In their earliest efforts to make sense of the massive cultural changes wrought by the 1960s, Kristol and his colleagues drew on the work of such writers as Joseph Schumpeter, David Bazelon, and Milovan Djilas. All three authors pointed out that when modern societies reach what Daniel Bell called a "postindustrial" level of development, they tend to become increasingly dependent on a "new class" of highly skilled intellectuals, including scientists, teachers, journalists, lawyers, psychologists, social workers, and other professionals.[1] Since all societies are dominated by some elite, the rise of this new class would be unremarkable were it not for one troubling fact: intellectual elites differ from others in their tendency to adopt an adversarial, even subversive, relation to their own societies. As literary critic Lionel Trilling noted in an important essay of the mid-1960s that significantly shaped the political imagination of the neocons, the modern intellectual stakes out and occupies "a ground and a vantage point from which to judge and condemn . . . the culture that produced him."[2] Using the concepts of the new class and the adversary culture to understand the country, the neocons concluded that the tumult and turmoil of the late 1960s and early '70s could be traced to the destructive influence of a decadent and subversive intellectual elite.

It was an interpretation quite similar to the antielitist theory that Neuhaus began to develop in the same period, shortly after his break from the radical left. There was, however, a crucial difference between the two theories—a difference that could be traced to the distinctive traditions from which each theory derived. Whereas the influence of C. Wright Mills's radical attack on the unjust and illegitimate rule of a "power elite" in American society led Neuhaus to advocate a (sometimes literal, sometimes symbolic) populist revolution to overthrow the "regime" of the country's ruling intellectuals, Kristol at first refused to propose a political response to recent developments in the country. Adopting Trilling's deeply ambivalent stance toward the adversary culture of the intellectuals, Kristol explicitly rejected a "populist perspective" that portrayed new class elites as "usurp[ing] control of our media" and using "their strategic positions to launch an assault on our traditions and institutions." Such a simple-mindedly polemical view was, for Kristol, "misleading and ultimately self-defeating." The rise of the new class and the adversary culture could not simply be willed or wished away, since they had emerged out of and had their roots in the extraordinarily complicated dynamics of modern, urban civilization itself. The early neocons maintained that the appropriate response to these troubling trends was careful study and reflection on the complexities of contemporary American life—not futile and destructive calls to stamp them out through political action.[3]

The moderation and detachment championed by the neocons

would soon come to an end, however. While some, like Glazer and
Bell, continued to keep some distance from the political fray, Kristol
and several regular contributors to *The Public Interest* and Norman
Podhoretz's *Commentary* magazine grew increasingly frustrated with
the political and cultural drift of the country during the late 1970s.[4]
Believing that the adversary impulses of the new class were leading
the nation into paralyzing self-doubt and uncertainty, the neocons
began to fight back—to act as a class of nonadversary counterintellectuals.[5] Instead of criticizing capitalism, they began to defend it. Instead of capitulating to urban crime and decay, they began to
advocate harsh penalties for lawbreakers as well as the radical reform
or elimination of failing Great Society social programs. Instead of
treating American military power as a moral burden, they began to
portray it as a beacon of hope for a world threatened by totalitarian
tyranny. They made these arguments in the pages of their own journals, but they also branched out into other publications, including
Robert L. Bartley's *Wall Street Journal* editorial page. A Washington
think tank, the American Enterprise Institute (AEI), became a vibrant
center for neoconservative public policy research, providing a home
for refugees from the adversary culture of the universities, fostering
like-minded young scholars, publicizing their findings on Capitol
Hill, and, eventually, serving as an intellectual bull pen of would-be
bureaucrats, ready and eager to staff the executive-branch depart-
ments of Republican presidential administrations. The neocons' quest
for influence even led them to build an exceedingly unlikely alliance
with the Unification Church of the Reverend Sun Myung Moon,
which at the time was seeking to found a right-wing daily newspaper,
The Washington Times, in the nation's capital.

With the election of Ronald Reagan in 1980, the neocons tasted
genuine political power for the first time—and any lingering admiration for disinterested reflection on social and cultural complexity
quickly vanished. By the mid-1980s, Kristol would repudiate his earlier aversion to populism and even begin to endorse an explicitly reli-

gious culture for the United States. In an important essay from 1985, he acknowledged that political philosophers from Aristotle to the American founding fathers had assumed that populism was an example of "democracy at its least rational, its least sensible." Yet for Kristol the new populism of the religious right—the populism that had catapulted Reagan and a coterie of neocon advisers to power—was somehow different. Instead of arising from irrational passions and resentments, the populism of the early 1980s was "not at all extreme"; it was merely an expression of the "common sense" of the American people against the "un-wisdom of their governing elites—whether elected, appointed, or (as with the media) self-appointed."[6] Two years later, Kristol would assert that defending the American way of life against foreign and domestic enemies required that citizens develop a "religious attachment" to their country.[7] In future years he would go even further, to claim that modern conservatism should be based on a synthesis of religion, nationalism, and economic growth—and that Republicans should give up their resistance to the transformation of their party into an explicitly religious organization—all for the sake of banishing liberalism, now flatly described as the "enemy," from American political life.[8]

Whatever the reasons for Kristol's dramatic ideological evolution, the fact was that by the mid-1980s the neocons had come to share several key theoconservative assumptions and goals—most importantly, the conviction that a religious-populist insurgency on the part of the American people would make it possible to retake cultural territory lost since the 1960s.[9] In pursuing these goals, Kristol and the other neocons came to see Neuhaus and Novak as crucial allies. At first the theocons were invited to organize panels and conferences at AEI, where Novak soon became a permanent fellow; then they were given control of their own Washington think tank, the Ethics and Public Policy Center, which would explore religious and cultural issues full time. Neocon magazines opened their pages to theocon

authors and arguments. Then, in late 1984, Kristol approached
Neuhaus to ask if he would be interested in editing his own magazine.
Kristol regretted having recently taken on responsibility for the quarterly journal *This World*, and he was looking to pass it along to someone in the "family." With Neuhaus enjoying unprecedented publicity
with *The Naked Public Square*, he seemed like the perfect choice.

But Neuhaus had something more ambitious in mind. Ever since
he had given up his full-time parish duties in 1978, Neuhaus had
been looking to direct a think tank in New York City that could serve
as an institutional home and provide an outlet for his boundless intellectual and political energy. At the same time, he was also concerned that his own project not become too closely identified with the
neocons, who despite their recent warmth toward public piety continued to view religion purely in instrumental terms, as something
good for the country rather than as something true. Neuhaus thought
it would be more useful for his project to serve as a bridge between
the urbane world of the largely secular and Jewish neocons and a very
different group of right-wing intellectuals—the so-called "paleoconservatives," whose rural, deeply Christian outlook derived from the
antimodern Southern Agrarians and the stodgy traditionalism of Russell Kirk.

Keeping both sides happy would be difficult. Not only did the
two camps differ profoundly about everything from immigration to
the welfare state (with the neocons at least moderately in favor of
both and the paleocons sharply opposed), but they also had a history
of bitter public acrimony. In the early days of the Reagan presidency,
the administration considered appointing paleoconservative M. E.
Bradford to head the National Endowment for the Humanities—a
choice that alarmed the neocons, who quickly set out to publicize
Bradford's opposition to the 1964 Civil Rights Act, his two-time endorsement of George Wallace for president, and his tendency to refer
to Abraham Lincoln as a criminal for his actions during the Civil War.

Fearing public scandal and an embarrassing confirmation fight in the Senate, the new administration quickly withdrew Bradford's name and settled on Kristol's choice (a young academic named William J. Bennett) as an alternative. It was a humiliating experience for Bradford and his paleoconservative allies, who from that point forward considered the neocons their mortal enemies.[10]

Despite the many challenges involved, Neuhaus made a bold proposal to one of the premier paleoconservative organizations, the Illinois-based Rockford Institute. Neuhaus would serve as the president of a small nonprofit Manhattan think tank to be called the Center on Religion and Society. It would be run under the auspices of Rockford but funded almost entirely by the neocon Bradley and Scaife Foundations. In addition to sponsoring conferences and lectures that would explore the intersection between religion and politics, the center would publish the quarterly *This World*, with Neuhaus acting as editor in chief, as well as a monthly newsletter *(The Religion and Society Report)* written entirely by Neuhaus. The journal would run scholarly essays on the kinds of issues raised in *The Naked Public Square*, and the newsletter would apply its ideological framework to practical issues facing the country, offering clever and at times lacerating commentary on the follies and half-hidden antireligious prejudices of the country's secular liberal elite. It was an arrangement that could only benefit the paleocons, who would gain considerable exposure at little cost. Neuhaus, meanwhile, would enjoy the satisfaction of knowing that he had pulled off the most significant act of right-wing intellectual diplomacy since William F. Buckley's *National Review* managed to bridge the traditionalist and libertarian factions of the nascent conservative movement during the 1960s. After some hesitation and negotiation, all the parties agreed to go forward with the plan, and for the next several years the neocons and paleocons observed an uneasy truce overseen by Neuhaus, whose think tank and publications influenced the terms of discussion and debate among conservative intellectuals in Washington and around the country.

By 1989, however, long-suppressed tensions began to surface. In March, the Rockford Institute's flagship journal, *Chronicles,* ran a lead article by its editor, Thomas Fleming, which amounted to a nativist polemic against open immigration. Another article in the same issue openly attacked the influence of the neocons in Washington using anti-Semitic innuendoes, while yet another portrayed the arguably anti-Semitic Gore Vidal as an ideal American conservative. The neocons were furious and strongly urged Neuhaus to break publicly from Rockford. Neuhaus's first move was to write a strongly worded memo to Fleming in which he accused the editor of being insufficiently vigilant about avoiding classically anti-Semitic rhetoric. While he awaited a response from Fleming, Neuhaus began discussions with the center's financial backers about options for keeping it afloat if the relationship with Rockford deteriorated. These talks didn't get very far. On the morning of May 5, 1989, the staff of the center arrived at their Manhattan offices to find a group of men ("thugs" is how Neuhaus described them) demanding in Rockford's name that they immediately vacate the premises with all of their belongings. Before long Neuhaus and his coworkers were left standing on the sidewalk in the rain, clutching plastic garbage bags filled with the few files they could grab before being forcibly escorted from the building.[11]

It was a key moment in the self-marginalization of the paleocons—and an unexpected opportunity for the theocons. The story made the front page of the *New York Times* and was widely discussed in the conservative press, where Neuhaus's side received nearly unanimous support.[12] Over the coming months, the neocon Olin Foundation joined with the Bradley and Scaife Foundations in providing Neuhaus with several generous grants. The Center on Religion and Society would be reconstituted as the Institute on Religion and Public Life, and Neuhaus's quarterly journal and monthly newsletter would be combined to form a new monthly magazine, *First Things,* which would serve as the flagship journal of the growing theoconservative movement.

THE CATHOLIC MOMENT

By the end of the 1980s, Neuhaus and Novak were enjoying considerable success in following the example of the neocons—in spreading their message using foundation money and a growing network of think tanks, institutes, and magazines. But whereas controlling institutions of public policy was sufficient for the neocons, the theocons needed to adopt a broader strategy. Neuhaus and Novak hoped to motivate and lead a grassroots religious insurgency, not simply provide it with an intellectual justification from inside the Washington beltway. As Neuhaus put it in the inaugural issue of *First Things*, "religion's contribution to the renewal of democracy depends, first, upon the renewal of religion."[13] And in order to inspire that fundamental religious renewal, the theocons needed to exercise influence—or at least forge alliances with like-minded clergy and lay people—within established churches.

Mere Orthodoxy

In seeking to build an interdenominational religious ideology and electoral coalition, Neuhaus and his colleagues took full advantage of trends that were already well under way in American religion. As sociologist Robert Wuthnow has noted, in the latter half of the twentieth century historical animosities between Catholics and Protestants in America began to give way to a new division separating politically liberal and politically conservative believers of every faith.[14] Whereas differences in ethnic background and religious practice and doctrine once determined the religious identity of Americans, it was now far more common for this identity to be determined by one's position on issues tied to the nation's burgeoning "culture war": abortion, euthanasia, the breakdown of order and authority in the family, the banning of school prayer and other expressions of public piety, and the rise of a popular culture saturated with sex and violence. By opposing these trends one automatically placed oneself in the traditionalist bloc within a given church, while by reacting to them with resignation, in-difference, or enthusiasm one aligned oneself with modernist ele-ments in the same church.

The classic example of this development could be seen in the Catholic Church in America, which had been riven by rancorous theological and doctrinal disputes since the conclusion of Vatican II, with some Catholics seeking to expand on the council's call to engage (and perhaps even embrace) the modern world and others re-jecting the reformist spirit of the council altogether. If anything, these debates had intensified since the beginning of Pope John Paul II's pontificate in 1978, as he and his trusted lieutenant, Joseph Cardinal Ratzinger (now Pope Benedict XVI), took strong stands in favor of a tra-ditionalist interpretation of Vatican II and set out to enforce it by pub-licly reprimanding theologians who challenged their authority.[15]

Along with polarization within churches, the restructuring of Amer-ican religion led to the formation of new and unexpected alliances among members of formerly antagonistic faith communities, as groups of traditionalists in different denominations began to perceive common-alities with one another.[16] At the level of theology, traditionalists shared the conviction that God is real and that his moral teachings are true. While it might seem that such basic assumptions are necessary for any religious belief, it is not uncommon in the modern world for people to ground their faith in something other than the reality of God—whether it be tradition, history, community, subjective feeling, or psychological comfort. Passionately rejecting such human-centered religious founda-tions, traditionalists advocated a radical submission to divine reality and truth—and to the way that that reality and truth gets authoritatively in-terpreted within each individual church. Traditionalist Catholics thus submitted to the authority of the Vatican on faith and morals, evangeli-cals accepted biblical literalism and the necessity of being born again in Christ, Pentecostals gave themselves over to the holy spirit, and so forth. Whereas such differences were once a source of conflict and division among religious groups, they had come to be a source of unity, as traditionalists viewed the mere fact of their upholding orthodoxy (in whatever form) as a reason to join together against common modernist and secularist enemies.

Since the early 1980s Neuhaus had been working to exploit this trend—to intensify it, to give it form and direction, and to supplement it with political content around which traditionalists within any and every denomination could rally. Hence his contribution to the 1981 founding of the Washington-based Institute on Religion and Democracy, an ecumenical nonprofit organization that works to discredit theological and political liberals within the Protestant mainline, as well as to encourage the mainline's few remaining traditionalists to advance a conservative theological and political agenda. Hence also his efforts in *The Naked Public Square* and elsewhere to help evangelical Protestants to broaden their own traditionalist political project.

Yet Neuhaus knew that he could not pin his political hopes entirely on disaffected Protestants. His doubts about the ability of the mainline to influence the culture in a positive direction began in the mid-1970s, and they deepened over time, as membership in the denominations represented by the National Council of Churches shrank, and the council's bureaucratic leadership drifted deeper into leftist politics, with each passing year. As Neuhaus would quip with increasing frequency during the 1980s and '90s, the mainline had already become the "oldline," and was well on its way to becoming the "sideline," of American religion. As for the evangelicals, their contribution to fashioning a political agenda based on mere orthodoxy was crucial but far from sufficient. There simply were not enough conservative Protestants to ensure the victory of a theocon political movement. At 25 to 30 percent of the electorate, evangelicals could make—and in Reagan's presidential victories they had made—an important, even a decisive, difference. But Reagan had won by combining evangelical votes with the support of groups (above all, moderate Democrats and the GOP's libertarian wing) whose members were largely uninterested in, and even openly hostile to, the core theocon issues. To inject a vibrant religiosity into the nation's politics, it would be necessary to motivate and inspire traditionalists within other religious groups as well.

The Road to Rome

The largest and most powerful of these groups by far was the Catholic Church. Neuhaus first broached the possibility of a Catholic-theocon alliance in the concluding pages of *The Naked Public Square*, where he briefly paused in his ongoing discussion of the Moral Majority to reflect on the place of Catholicism in America. Taking into account the Catholic Church's demographic power, its "rich tradition of social and political theory," and "Vatican II's theological internalization of the democratic idea," Neuhaus declared that, far more than evangelicals, "Catholics are uniquely posed to propose the American proposition anew"—and in the process to transform the late twentieth century into "the Catholic moment." The only question remaining for Neuhaus in 1984 was whether American Catholicism had the will and the wherewithal to transform itself into "a public force of culture-forming influence" in the United States.[17]

It would take the still nominally Lutheran Neuhaus less than three years to put his doubts to rest. As the title of his 1987 book *The Catholic Moment* makes clear, he now firmly believed the time had come for the church to assume "its rightful role in the culture-forming task of constructing a religiously informed public philosophy for the American experiment in ordered liberty."[18] While the evangelicals would continue to serve as vital members of the theocon coalition, and a handful of traditionalists within the Protestant mainline would contribute to it as best they could, Neuhaus had become convinced that the movement's ultimate success depended on the participation, and even the leadership, of the Catholic Church.

As Neuhaus was well aware, recruiting the Catholic Church (or at least significant numbers of Catholics) to the theocon cause posed several challenges and risks. Over the past few decades, Catholics had arguably done more than any other Christian group in the United States to reinforce what Neuhaus called the naked public square. This pattern had been set by John F. Kennedy in a 1960 speech to the Baptist ministers of Houston, Texas, in which the Catholic presidential candidate attempted to defuse widespread concern that he would take his moral and political direction from the Vatican:

> I believe in an America where the separation of church and state is absolute—where no Catholic prelate would tell the president (should he be a Catholic) how to act and no Protestant minister would tell his parishioners for whom to vote—where no church or church school is granted any public funds or political preference. . . .
> I believe in an America . . . where no religious body seeks to impose its will directly or indirectly upon the general populace or the public acts of its officials. . . . I believe in a president whose views on religion are his own private affair, neither imposed by him on the nation nor imposed by the nation upon him as a condition to holding that office.[19]

However politically necessary such a declaration might have been in the era before Vatican II, Neuhaus considered it a profound betrayal of the Christian imperative to bring religious truth claims to bear on matters of public import. And to the extent that American Catholic laypeople had become accustomed to treating Kennedy's wholly privatized faith as a model of how they should conduct themselves politically, the effort to mobilize the church for the theocon project would be exceedingly difficult.

The political sensibility of the Catholic clergy was very different— and yet it ended up producing similarly apolitical results. During the past few decades, the American bishops had begun to practice a "prophetic" mode of leftist politics, which had the effect of ensuring that they would be excluded from responsible political debate. A pair of recent pastoral letters (*The Challenge of Peace* [1983] and *Economic Justice for All* [1986]) vividly demonstrated the point. In these statements, the bishops staked out positions so far to the left—advocating a foreign policy of unilateral nuclear disarmament and a socialist economic policy—that next to no one in political power took them seriously. These documents thus showed that a large segment of the American Catholic hierarchy was ready and eager to follow the Protestant National Council of Churches into political irrelevancy.

Even more troubling than these unhelpful political habits was the likely influence of a Catholic-theocon alliance on the character of the theocon movement itself. Tying the theocon project to Catholicism would seemingly connect the health and vitality of the nation not merely to traditionalist religion as such (which was already controversial enough) but to the fate of one church in particular. While Neuhaus's diplomatic instincts led him to sidestep this crucial issue and its practical implications in *The Catholic Moment*, a recent recruit to the theocon cause proved to be much less cautious. Through the mid-1980s George Weigel devoted most of his intellectual and spiritual energies to defending Ronald Reagan's anti-Communist foreign policy using concepts derived from the Catholic "just war" tradition.[20] But inspired by Neuhaus's call to theological arms, the intensely pious Catholic set out to expand on the bold proposals of his Lutheran friend and ideological ally. In *Catholicism and the Renewal of American Democracy* (1989), Weigel indicated that the success of the theocon project would depend on whether it was possible to realize the baldly sectarian vision of John Ireland, the late-nineteenth-century archbishop of St. Paul, who believed that Catholics in the United States were called by God "to make America Catholic."[21] While admitting that Ireland's project would have to be adjusted to take account of the "confessional pluralism that is the native and ongoing condition of American life," Weigel nonetheless insisted that the goal of Catholicizing the United States remained "an essential task for the Church in America"—for the good of the country no less than for

Catholic clergy and laity.[22] This was, quite obviously, a vision of the theocon movement that threatened to alienate and antagonize its Protestant members, and perhaps fatally so.

For all these potential problems, Neuhaus believed that the promise of uniting the theoconservative movement with the Catholic Church was so great that the effort had to be attempted. Catholics were, first of all, the single largest religious group in the country, making it exceedingly difficult if not impossible to launch a successful program for political and religious reform in the country without significant support from within the ranks of the Catholic faithful. Then there was the church's long history of theological and political reflection, which made Catholics far more competent than evangelicals and other Protestants to take the lead in pressing religiously based moral arguments in the nation's political life.

But most promising of all was the Vatican's robust defense of ecclesiastical authority. Unlike the Protestant mainline, whose leadership had come to preach unorthodox, antitraditionalist views, the heads of the Catholic Church in Rome (Pope John Paul II and Cardinal Ratzinger) refused to compromise with or capitulate to blatant theological deviancy. Neuhaus spent a large portion of *The Catholic Moment* defending the Pope and his aide against the charge that they were power-hungry authoritarians out to crush dissent. Actively endorsing Ratzinger's self-interpretation, Neuhaus argued that vigorously upholding orthodoxy appears to be authoritarian only to those who begin by making unorthodox assumptions. Once one accepts what the church has always asserted about itself—namely, that it was established by Christ for the sake of spreading his gift of salvation throughout the world, and that it is prevented from lapsing into fundamental error in matters of faith and morals by the ministrations of the holy spirit—then "dissent" begins to look like active rebellion against the will of God. Whether the challenge to ecclesiastical authority came from quasi-Marxist "liberation theology" in Latin America or from liberal theologians in Europe and America such as Hans

Küng and Charles Curran, the Vatican was right to reprimand "apostates" and call them back to "the way, the truth, and the life" proclaimed by Christ and embodied in his church.[23] In doing so, Rome taught an indispensable spiritual and political lesson to a modern world deeply hostile to every form of authority, regardless of its proclaimed source or foundation.

Gazing across the Atlantic to St. Peter's Basilica, then, Neuhaus believed he spied enormously powerful allies in his struggle against secularism in the modern world—Christian intellectuals who had undertaken their own theoconservative project within the church and who longed to engage the enemies of Christian truth wherever they were found, including in the political realm. *The Catholic Moment* was Neuhaus's application to serve as the Pope's emissary to the United States, his special representative in making the case for Christian truth claims in American public life. As an alternative to both JFK-style disengagement from public debate and the effectively apolitical stance of "prophetic" engagement adopted by the American bishops, Neuhaus issued a call to "repoliticize" Roman Catholicism in America.[24]

Saving America's Catholic Soul

What it would mean to repoliticize American Catholicism remained somewhat vague in *The Catholic Moment* itself, but Neuhaus and Weigel would go a long way toward clarifying it over the coming years. Both men denied that they envisioned the literal conversion of large numbers of Americans to the Catholic Church, let alone the adoption of Catholicism as the American state religion. Conversion implied the radical replacement of one set of views and beliefs by another. In keeping with the kinds of arguments that Neuhaus and Novak had been making since they first began to drift away from the left in the early 1970s, the theocons proposed instead to reveal the numerous ways in which the political system of the United States *already* presupposed and drew on Catholic-Christian assumptions.

Greatly increasing the public role of conservative Catholicism in the nation's public life would then be portrayed as a necessary corrective to the relatively recent and unprecedented secularist assault on the country's default quasi-Catholic religiosity. In this way, the theocons would portray their advocacy of a novel American-Catholic synthesis as a return to a prior condition of harmony from which the nation had only recently fallen away. Simply put, the country's political institutions and principles would remain what they always had been, but our understanding of their meaning, function, and intent would be spiritualized—Catholicized.

In furthering this project, Neuhaus and Weigel drew heavily on the writings and example of one of American Catholicism's most important twentieth-century thinkers, John Courtney Murray, S.J. (1904–1967). Murray had been notorious in church circles in the years leading up to the Second Vatican Council for arguing that the Vatican's historic opposition to democracy, toleration, and liberalism arose in (understandable) reaction to the anticlericalist cast of continental European politics since the French Revolution, not from disinterested reflection on the political possibilities opened up by modernity as such. In Murray's view, American history showed that another political arrangement was possible under modern conditions— one that was far more accommodating to religion in general and to Catholicism in particular. The church thus owed it to the world to moderate its stance and to begin explicitly defending American-style liberal democracy. In the words of historian Patrick Allitt, Murray aimed to convince the Vatican that "it need have no fears of Americanism but rather should acknowledge the United States' constitutional system as the ideal modern setting for the Church."[25] In Catholic circles this was a highly controversial contention at the time Murray advanced it—first in a series of academic articles during the 1950s, and then in his now-classic book *We Hold These Truths: Catholic Reflections on the American Proposition* (1960). His argument was so divisive, in fact, that it caused him to be omitted from the U.S.

delegation to the first session of Vatican II. The intervention of a handful of American bishops produced an invitation to the second session, however, where his views were eventually vindicated in the council's "Declaration on Religious Freedom" *(Dignitatis Humanae),* in which the church embraced democracy and human rights for the first time in its history.

The theocons thoroughly endorsed the Vatican's Murray-inspired thaw with regard to democracy and human rights, as did most Catholics in America and around the world. But equally important were a different and even more contentious set of arguments that Murray made about the character of the American political system itself. In Murray's view, the reason the United States had proven to be such an accommodating place for religion was that it "had preserved the political-philosophical heritage of medieval Christendom better than any European nation, even the ostensibly Catholic monarchies of France and Spain." Unlike European systems that embraced political absolutism, the American founders upheld an "older wisdom" rooted in the political limits prescribed by Catholic "natural law." As improbable as it sounded, Murray insisted that, despite its incorrigible Protestantism, the United States was the Western nation that more than any other had "faithfully carried the heritage of Catholic Christendom into the mid-twentieth century."[26]

It was a breathtaking act of historical revisionism—one in which Catholicism was portrayed not as the enemy of modern liberalism but rather as its true source and indispensable foundation.[27] Indeed, Murray maintained that from the country's seventeenth-century origins, the American people had tacitly adhered to a Catholic-Christian consensus on moral matters. John Winthrop gave voice to this consensus when he described the Puritans as constructing a "city on a hill." Thomas Jefferson drew on it in the Declaration of Independence, when he enumerated certain "self-evident" truths and God-given rights to "life, liberty, and the pursuit of happiness." Abraham Lincoln gestured toward it in his second inaugural address, when he meditated on the providential meaning of the Civil War. Updating the point, the theocons suggested that Ronald Reagan translated this same consensus into twentieth-century terms when he claimed that the United States was engaged in a world-historical struggle to defend freedom against the "evil empire" of atheistic totalitarianism. Even America's embrace of religious toleration and the disestablishment of religion could be traced to the nation's underlying Catholic-Christian heritage, for as Neuhaus put it in a Murrayan passage, "it is not chiefly a secular but a religious restraint that prevents biblical believers from coercing others in matters of conscience."[28]

And yet, despite the utterly essential role it has always played in providing the nation with a moral and theological foundation, America's religious consensus had recently come under attack by a rabid secularist ideology. Earlier in the century the responsibility for defending the country's moral and religious consensus against its assailants would have fallen to the Protestant churches, but now that the mainline had ceased to perform its appointed function, the time had come for the Catholic Church to take on this responsibility—to accept the task of preserving and even reconstituting America's theological essence. And the stakes, as usual for the theocons, were extremely high. As Weigel wrote in a striking sentence that nicely summarizes the theocon position on Murray and the contribution of his ideas to their project: "The issue, Murray boldly claimed, was not whether Catholicism was compatible with democracy; it was whether American democracy could survive unless it reconstructed a public consensus around those 'elementary affirmations' upon which it was founded—affirmations whose roots Murray believed were not the original product of the Enlightenment and its American deist heirs, but of the Catholic medieval theory of man and society."[29] Either the United States would return to its medieval Catholic roots or the very existence of its democratic order would be imperiled—those were America's only options.

When it came to the question of precisely how the Catholic

Church should seek to inspire or lead this renewal, the theocons made a pair of proposals. Murray himself had suggested that Catholicism's tradition of natural law theorizing could serve as a potentially universal vocabulary that could be invoked in public debate about the profoundest moral questions facing the nation. As Weigel put it, whereas evangelicals and fundamentalists resorted to citing "proof-texts from-Scripture," which convinced no one who was not already a believer in biblical literalism, Catholic natural law promised to serve as "a philosophical foundation on which virtually all men and women of good will could participate in the ongoing argument about the American experiment and its foundational consensus."[30] Even more promising than natural law, however, were the church's social encyclicals, especially those published during the pontificate of John Paul II. These book-length statements, which touched on various political and moral questions, were addressed not only to members of the church but also to open-minded readers of all faiths, provided that they were willing to engage in moral reflection without prejudice or antireligious (i.e., anti-Catholic) animus. Neuhaus and his colleagues hoped that these encyclicals—of course properly interpreted, edited, and recast for an American audience by the theocons themselves—might be used to ground the country's foundational consensus and ultimately serve as an interdenominational "public philosophy capable of sustaining the American experiment into its third century."[31]

Catholic Capitalism

Fashioning an ideology that synthesized the often conflicting outlooks and sensibilities of the United States and the Catholic Church was, to put it mildly, a daunting challenge—and in no area was it more difficult than in economics. Ever since Novak published *The Spirit of Democratic Capitalism*, the theocons had been trying to make a case for the easy compatibility of free markets and Christian ethics. As certain passages of *The Catholic Moment* make clear, Neuhaus experienced significant embarrassment over the Vatican's habit of issuing often strident condemnations of capitalistic exchange along with occasional warm words for the expansive welfare states of continental Europe.[32] For the theocons, such statements needlessly alienated large numbers of American Christians, as Weigel explained in a 1990 essay in which he pondered the spiritual plight of a hypothetical chief executive officer of a major American corporation. As a good Catholic, this businessman supports the church and numerous charities. But what does the church have to say about the morality of his efforts to "create wealth"? About the virtue of his "entrepreneurial energies," which have "made jobs available for others"? About how his payment of taxes and his work on behalf of philanthropic organizations make a "significant contribution to the common good"? "If truth be told," Weigel answered, the church "probably doesn't have much to say at all" about any of these profoundly moral activities. And when it does pronounce on them, the Vatican too often speaks from ignorance, falsely asserting that the capitalist acts solely out of selfish and materialist motives.[33] According to Neuhaus, this was a significant problem: "It is spiritually eviscerating that what millions of men and women do fifty or seventy hours of most every week is bracketed off from their understanding of their faith."[34] If Catholicism was to fulfill its promise of spiritualizing every aspect of modern American life, it would have to adopt a far more positive and affirmative outlook on capitalism.

Frustrations with the Vatican on these questions significantly diminished with the publication of the first papal encyclical after the fall of Communism, *Centesimus Annus*, which the theocons went out of their way to ensure would be interpreted as a vindication of their own procapitalist position. On April 28, 1991, Neuhaus obtained an advance copy of the encyclical, probably leaked to him by a sympathetic American bishop. On the morning of May 2—hours before the document's official release in Rome—*The Wall Street Journal* ran a lengthy op-ed by Neuhaus under the title "Pope Affirms the 'New Capitalism.' " The column portrayed the encyclical as "a ringing endorsement of the market economy," claimed that its central message was that "capitalism is the economic corollary of the Christian understanding of man's nature and destiny," and chided left-wing American bishops for being out of step with "the Church's authoritative teaching." The following day, Weigel published a similar statement in the *Los Angeles Times*. As the theocons intended them to, these opinion pieces succeeded in setting the tone for coverage of the encyclical in the mainstream media and in putting Catholic critics of the free market, including many members of the American hierarchy, on the defensive.[35]

Centesimus Annus did mark a modest change in the Vatican's outlook toward the market economy. Whereas previous statements by John Paul had emphasized the spiritual degradation wrought by consumerism and materialism, and such injunctions could still be found in the 1991 encyclical, the statement struck a different note overall. In one passage in particular, the Pope highlighted "the positive role of business, private property, and the resulting responsibility for the means of production, as well as free human creativity in the economic sector"—provided, that is, that the economic sector is "circumscribed within a strong juridical framework which places it at the service of human freedom in its totality, and which sees it as a particular aspect of that freedom, the core of which is ethical and religious."[36] If the theocons had merely pointed out this shift of emphasis, their interpretation on the encyclical would have been relatively uncontroversial. Yet in characteristic fashion, they went further—to insist that the U.S. economy was already sufficiently regulated by such a "strong juridical framework." They thus managed to imply that the Vatican had endorsed American-style capitalism (with its relatively low rates of taxation, its minimum of regulation, and its absence of universal health insurance) as the Catholic economic ideal.

In the two years following its publication, the theocons fully incorporated their interpretation of *Centesimus Annus* into their overarching ideological vision. In *Doing Well and Doing Good: The Chal-*

lenge to the Christian Capitalist (1992), Neuhaus expanded on his earlier claims, to argue that the Pope had effectively endorsed Novak's
spiritualized vision of "democratic capitalism." (Neuhaus even hinted,
without providing evidence, that Novak's work had directly influenced the change in John Paul's views of the market.)[37] As for Novak
himself, he was inspired by the encyclical to build on his earlier arguments about the inherent morality of the free economy. In *The
Catholic Ethic and the Spirit of Capitalism* (1993) he challenged Max
Weber's classic theory about the connection between a "Protestant
ethic" and the emergence of markets in early modern Europe. Drawing on the work of political scientist Samuel Huntington on the
"third wave" of democratization around the world since the mid-1970s,
Novak argued that Weber's thesis was simply wrong, since many recently democratized countries were Catholic. Far from developing
out of the harsh asceticism of Protestant piety, democratic capitalism
was more closely tied to the unleashing of the "creative subjectivity of
the human person," which the Catholic Church did far more than
Protestantism to support and encourage. Hence not only does capitalism perfectly harmonize with Catholicism, but Catholics are
perfectly suited to be the best capitalists of all. Indeed, a capitalist
economy dominated by a generally Catholic outlook would be one in
which its members spontaneously acted to maximize their own benefit as well as the common good, through private charity and the creation of jobs and wealth—the only effective means of alleviating the
suffering and degradation of poverty. Such a Catholic system—which
Novak believed already existed in the United States—would thus also
achieve the moral moderation advocated by the Pope without having
to rely on government regulation, whose influence inevitably stifles
humanity's creative subjectivity. In this way, the theocons made it
clear that America's religious consensus was perfectly compatible with,
and even entailed, free-market capitalism.

Abortion and the "Culture of Death"

Yet economics was far from being the most important component of the newly Romanized theocon ideology. At the core of that ideology would be absolute opposition to legalized abortion. By the late 1980s, Neuhaus's moral ambivalence about the issue in the decade following *Roe v. Wade* had vanished. Where he once believed that abortion was one area of public policy in which there could be "little expectation" of finding a solution that was "absolutely just," he now regularly described the procedure as an unambiguous moral evil—one that rivaled slavery in the purity of its immorality and in its fundamental incompatibility with the nation's highest principles.[38] In Neuhaus's view, the American experiment had always been based on the self-evident truth of innate human dignity (grounded in man's status as a being created in the image of God) and the rights that flow from that dignity. Moreover, American history was a story of how the dignity of ever-greater numbers of people had gradually been recognized and their rights protected by the authority of the state. Until 1973, that is. With the *Roe* decision, the Supreme Court summarily excluded the innocent, unborn child from such protection, and in doing so it placed American culture at the top of a very slippery slope. Adopting the apocalyptic rhetoric for which he has had such a weakness since his days as a radical pastor, Neuhaus declared that legalized abortion fosters such a profound disrespect for human life that it could very well lead to everything from "infanticide to eliminating the inconvenient elderly to, perhaps, genocide" in the United States.[39]

In making this incendiary argument, Neuhaus drew once again on the writings of John Paul II, who frequently referred to an incipient "culture of death" in the Western world—a culture in which concerns about efficiency and the drive toward individual autonomy increasingly trump the absolute, inviolable rights of individuals.[40] Concerns about possible tensions or conflicts between the good of the fetus and the good of the woman in whose body it develops were simply irrelevant. For the pontiff, the obvious, unquestionable truth was that "procured abortion is the deliberate and direct killing, by whatever means it is carried out, of a human being in the initial phase of his or her existence."[41] When a woman fails to recognize this plain fact, it is a sign that a monstrous feminist ideology has insinuated itself into her consciousness, convincing her that her desire for a career or self-fulfillment should outweigh the innocent life of her child. Likewise, when a society fails to recognize murder for what it is and act accordingly (by outlawing and punishing it), this is evidence of "an extremely dangerous crisis of the moral sense, which is becoming more and more incapable of distinguishing between good and evil, even when the fundamental right to life is at stake."[42] Once this crisis becomes advanced, society begins to permit and even encourage the taking or manipulation of life for any number of trivial and egoistic reasons. First euthanasia, cloning, and research on human embryos are legalized; then these practices become commonplace; and finally the society begins to mandate death for the weakest and most vulnerable. In order to prevent this slide toward a new Holocaust, governments must begin to (re)orient themselves toward absolute moral truths. They must intervene to prevent the taking of innocent life—to forestall the culture of death and foster a culture of life. When they fail to do so, these states—even otherwise liberal states—begin to resemble the worst totalitarian tyrannies of the twentieth century.[43]

By the early 1990s, the Catholic Church (including the American bishops) and most evangelical Protestants were already united in staunch opposition to the "right to choose."[44] But the theocons recognized that John Paul II's uniquely sweeping attack on legalized abortion—which portrayed it as the leading edge of a much broader trend toward nihilistic despotism—could serve to galvanize members of both communities, convincing them of the dire necessity of toiling together to redeem the nation from its dalliance with death. All orthodox Christians, regardless of their historical, theological, and doctrinal differences, were called to witness to the unspeakable evil taking place in their midst, in hospitals and abortion clinics, in every city, in every state, on every day of the year—with the supposed sanction of the U.S. Constitution, and thus with the tacit consent (and approval) of every American citizen. Such Christians owed it to God, to their country, to the defenseless victims of constitutionally protected lethal violence, and to the mothers who inexplicably inflict that violence, to do everything in their power to build a culture in which every human being, from conception through natural death, is "protected by law and welcomed in life."[45] At the very least, orthodox Christians of every denomination were called to vote exclusively for prolife politicians— which meant, in practice, to vote exclusively for the Republican Party.

The theocons did not endorse John Paul's uncompromising moral position in all of its aspects. His insistence on linking capital punishment to the culture of death, for example, received remarkably nuanced and critical treatment in the pages of *First Things*. Likewise, his claim that birth control contributes to modern moral degradation by denying the intrinsic connection between love and life was usually passed over in silence.[46] Each of these positions would alienate members of the interdenominational coalition the theocons were attempting to build, and so neither of them could be incorporated into a politically salient religious ideology. But on a range of other issues— from abortion, euthanasia, and embryonic stem-cell research to the dangers of gay marriage—the theocons sought to enact policies that conformed to the Vatican's position in nearly every respect. In the view of Neuhaus and his colleagues, the Catholic Church of John Paul II had provided traditionalists of all Christian denominations with a unifying agenda that could be used to transform the United States into a homogeneously traditionalist Catholic-Christian nation.

Outside of Catholic America

If the theocons could bring about this transformation, they would have gone a long way toward realizing Archbishop Ireland's dream of converting the country to Catholicism, albeit to a form of the faith that the nineteenth-century cleric might not have recognized. Their ideal America would be a nation ruled by a form of Catholic ideology, not confessional or doctrinal Catholicism. Many members of the Catholic Church would affirm this ideology, but so would many non-Catholics, including large numbers of evangelical and fundamentalist Protestants, and perhaps even a handful of sympathetic Jews.

The only people certain to reject this ideology and thus automatically to exclude themselves from the country's Catholic-Christian consensus would be atheists—and hence they would be the only ones whose status as citizens in such an America would be uncertain. "An atheist can be a citizen" of the United States, Neuhaus wrote in a revealing essay from 1991, but it was impossible on principle for an unbeliever to be "a good citizen." Adopting Lincolnian rhetoric and eliding the distinction between the moderate deism of the nation's founders and his own intense Christian piety, Neuhaus flatly denied that the American political order was "conceived and dedicated by atheists" and thus also that it could be "conceived and dedicated anew by atheists." The godless were simply incapable of giving "a morally convincing account" of the nation—a necessary condition for fruitful participation in its experiment in ordered liberty. To be "morally convincing," Neuhaus insisted, such an account must make reference to "reasons that draw authority from that which is higher than the self, from that which is external to the self, from that to which the self is ultimately obligated." No wonder, then, that it is "those who believe in the God of Abraham, Isaac, Jacob, and Jesus [who] turn out to be the best citizens."[47]

To his credit, Neuhaus fully acknowledged the blatant circularity of his argument—the way it excluded atheists from the category of good citizenship by appealing exclusively to the assumptions of those traditionalists who believe that good citizenship requires the affirmation of divine authority. Yet in his effort to defend this circularity, Neuhaus made a startling admission. Establishing standards of good citizenship on the basis of exclusionary theistic assumptions is thoroughly justified, he claimed, because such assumptions are made by "a majority" in American society. The implication of this appeal to raw majoritarian power was plain. Neuhaus often portrayed himself as a defender of the "civil public square." He and his allies frequently insisted, against evangelicals and others, that public debate should take place using reason and that it should employ categories derived from universal principles of natural law accessible to all. But in his remarks on atheism, Neuhaus made it very clear that the country's moral and religious consensus is actually the imposition of the beliefs of one part of a highly diverse community onto its other parts. In theocon America, might would by definition be synonymous with right.[48]

EVANGELICALS AND CATHOLICS TOGETHER

By the early 1990s, all that remained of the theocons' quest for influence was for the traditionalist religious alliance they advocated to be formalized. Preliminary discussions along these lines between Neuhaus and several prominent evangelicals had been initiated by Charles W. Colson in 1985, shortly after the publication of *The Naked Public Square*. Colson—Watergate felon, born-again Christian, and founder of Prison Fellowship Ministries, a successful nonprofit organization that uses evangelical Christianity to reform jailed convicts—had been greatly impressed by Neuhaus's book and its vision of conservative Christians contributing to the revitalization of public religiosity in America. At their initial meeting, Colson and Neuhaus were joined by their mutual friend, evangelical theologian Carl Henry, along with "members of the House and Senate and Cabinet," as well as "distinguished preachers, writers, and activists"—all of whom "reflect[ed] and pray[ed] together about what we believed to be a historic moment of responsibility for Christians in America."[49] Over the next several years, additional meetings and conversations generated interest but no concrete results beyond the confirmation that conservatives within several denominations shared a common list of concerns about the drift of American culture since the 1960s.

Yet even these ongoing informal discussions were thrown into disarray when Neuhaus announced in 1990 that he was converting to Catholicism and would soon be ordained as a priest. Viewed in retrospect, Neuhaus's conversion seems thoroughly overdetermined. There was, of course, his 1987 declaration of a "Catholic moment," which included his claim that the Roman Catholic Church "can and should be" the world's leading church "in proclaiming and exemplifying the Gospel."[50] After such a statement it was hard to imagine him remaining a Lutheran for long. Then there was his lifelong craving for divine—and persistent hostility to earthly—authority. By the end of the 1980s, Neuhaus had come to believe that the Catholic Church, as the concrete institution that proclaims itself to be the embodiment of divine authority within the world, would provide much-needed discipline for his restless intellect and unruly political and spiritual passions. This is clear from an autobiographical account of his conversion in which he himself posed the question of authority: "Do I have a felt need for authority, for obedience, for submission? But of course. Obedience is the rightly ordered disposition toward truth, and submission is subordination of the self to that by which the self is claimed. Truth commands, and authority has to do with authorship, the origins, of commanding truth." The only alternative to such radical submission to transcendent truth as it was embodied and proclaimed by the extra-earthly authority of the Vatican, he had come to believe, was "making it up as we go along, and, by acting in God's name, taking His name in vain."[51]

On September 8, 1990, with his close friend New York's Archbishop John Cardinal O'Connor by his side, Neuhaus entered the Catholic Church.[52] Precisely one year later, in a ceremony attended by bishops, archbishops, and cardinals from around the United States, as well as by Novak, Weigel, and such prominent conservative intellectuals as William F. Buckley Jr. and Judge Robert Bork, he was ordained a priest.[53] The leadership of the theocon movement was now uniformly Catholic—a fact that made ecumenical conversation more difficult than ever. For all of the political polarization in American religion, historic anti-Catholic prejudice remained a significant force among conservative Protestants, many of whom were still taught as children that the Pope is the Antichrist. It was one thing for Catholics, evangelicals, fundamentalists, and Pentecostals to engage in an interdenominational discussion headed up by a nonevangelical Lutheran minister; it was quite another for the discussion to be led by a priest.

After several months of cautious diplomacy, the conversation resumed—this time with a greater intensity and sense of purpose. At a series of discreet meetings beginning in September 1992, Neuhaus, Weigel, Jesuit theologian Avery Dulles, and four other Catholics worked on drafting a statement of common cause with Colson and seven other conservative Protestants, including representatives of the Southern Baptist Convention, the Pentecostal Assemblies of God, and the World Evangelical Fellowship. After eighteen months of work, the group announced on March 29, 1994, that they had completed a declaration to be titled "Evangelicals and Catholics Together: The Christian Mission for the Third Millennium" (hereafter, ECT).[54] Published in the May 1994 issue of *First Things,* the final draft was signed not only by the fifteen participants in the meetings that produced the statement but also by two dozen supporters of the initiative, including Michael Novak, Bill Bright of the fundamentalist Campus Crusade for Christ, and the Reverend Pat Robertson.

Although much of the statement sought to find common ground on theological and doctrinal matters, the document's longest section— titled "We Contend Together"—set out an ambitious political agenda using concepts, terms, arguments, and rhetoric unmistakably derived from the writings of Neuhaus, Weigel, Novak, and Pope John Paul II. Looking out at contemporary America, the authors saw a culture

"laid waste by relativism, anti-intellectualism, and nihilism"—a culture that denies "the very idea of truth." "Americans," they claimed,
"are drifting away from, are often explicitly defying, the constituting
truths of this experiment in ordered liberty."⁵⁵ Above all, the revitalization of American democracy depended on the recognition that "religious freedom is itself grounded in and is a product of religious
faith." The separation of church and state did not mean and could
not be construed to mean the "separation of religion from public life."
On the contrary, religion was the "foundation of our legal order"—a
fact recognized by the great majority of Americans, for whom "morality is derived, however variously and confusedly, from religion."⁵⁶

The authors of the statement then went on to list a series of policies that they insisted flowed directly from the recognition of religiously grounded "moral truth." First and foremost, it was necessary
to "secure the legal protection of the unborn," since legalized abortion
is an assault on innocent human life as well as a "massive attack on
the dignity, rights, and needs of women." It is, moreover, the "leading edge of an encroaching culture of death" that includes euthanasia,
eugenics, and "population control." On the subject of education, a
"comprehensive policy of parental choice" should be enacted, and the
public schools must engage in "moral education," including a defense
of "chastity" and the inculcation of a "readiness for marriage, parenthood, and family." Going further, they opposed "pornography . . .
along with the celebration of violence, sexual depravity, and antireligious bigotry in the entertainment media." At the same time they
also encouraged a "vibrant market economy," since a free economy
"accords with a Christian understanding of human freedom" and
"makes possible patterns of creativity, cooperation, and accountability that contribute to the common good." And all of this flowed from
the conviction that our "one nation under God" is "a nation under
judgment, mercy, and providential care of the Lord of the nations to
whom we alone render unqualified allegiance."⁵⁷

The ECT statement was an enormous triumph for the theocons,

bringing the intellectual heft of Catholicism together with the zealous religiosity of the evangelicals, and overcoming a great deal of mutual suspicion and animosity between the two communities—all for the sake of empowering the ideological agenda that Neuhaus, Novak, and Weigel had long considered the best hope for a vibrant American future. Not that reaction to the declaration was universally positive. Bestselling evangelical author Dave Hunt, for example, described ECT as "the most significant event in almost five hundred years of church history" and denounced it as "the most devastating blow against the Gospel in at least one thousand years."[58] This hyperbolic response was echoed by one hundred evangelical leaders who signed a statement attacking the initiative.[59] On the other hand, Neuhaus volunteered that "one of America's most prominent evangelical scholars told me that, upon receiving the declaration, he stayed up all night reading and rereading it, and fell on his knees to thank God that something so long prayed for was at last happening."[60]

What was obvious to critics and supporters of the initiative alike was that it stood as an unprecedented and dramatic example of what Colson aptly described as the "ecumenism of the trenches."[61] Large numbers of Catholics and evangelical Protestants clearly believed that the country faced "a cultural crisis of historic magnitude"—one that threatened "to unravel the moral consensus" that for the past two centuries had enabled the American people, in spite of all their differences, "to live together in freedom."[62] In their shared alarm at the prospect of the country descending into moral anarchy, these Catholics and evangelicals perceived themselves to be allies and friends stationed on the same side of a cultural chasm, arrayed against the well-armed forces of secular liberalism. Given the political, moral, and theological stakes, it was essential that historic and doctrinal differences be overlooked and that the members of each faith community fulfill the imperative to work together on the goal of turning the tide in the nation's culture war.[63]

But Neuhaus and his colleagues had not only forged a historic theological and political alliance. They had also provided a vision of America's religious and political future. It would be a religious future in which upholding theological orthodoxy and moral traditionalism overrode doctrinal disagreements. And it would be a political future in which the most orthodox and traditionalist Christians set the public tone and policy agenda for the nation. At subsequent gatherings over the coming years, the participants in ECT would solidify and strengthen their alliance as they awaited a presidential candidate around whom they could rally—a candidate who would use the theo-con political coalition to catapult himself to the pinnacle of American political power and from that position seek to enact its moral and re-ligious agenda.

FROM DESPAIR TO REDEMPTION

THE PUBLICATION OF "Evangelicals and Catholics Together" in the spring of 1994 was a tremendous achievement for the theocons—the culmination of several years of effort at building an interdenominational coalition of traditionalist religious believers to turn back the advance of secularism in the United States. The next and final step in their project—finding a politician to champion theo-conservative ideas, win the White House on the back of the theocon coalition, and then use the power of the presidency to enact its agenda—would take considerable discipline and patience, as there was simply no way to know how long it would take for the right Republican to appear on the scene.

Yet exercising discipline and patience in Bill Clinton's America would prove to be impossible for the theocons. While most Americans enjoyed a decade of relative peace and unprecedented economic prosperity, Richard John Neuhaus and his theocon colleagues grew increasingly frustrated by the cultural and moral direction of the country and their own seeming incapacity to change it. By the fall of

1996—with Clinton coasting to easy reelection against a Republican challenger (Bob Dole) who kept his distance from the restless religious faction of his party—the theocons had had enough. In a special issue of Neuhaus's magazine *First Things*, the theocons let out a cry of ideological fury, suggesting that a morally corrupt "regime" was usurping democracy in America—and that a morally justified revolution on the part of the country's most religious citizens might very well be just around the corner.

This reversion to the rhetoric of revolution was inspired by several developments in the country during the early and mid-1990s, but the most important were a series of court rulings on abortion, religious expression, gay rights, and euthanasia—all of which convinced the theocons that the judiciary was actively seeking to foist an un-American ideology of militant secularism on the country through antidemocratic means. It was outrage at these efforts to transform the nation—and even more so, the apparent indifference of the American people to these blatant acts of "judicial usurpation"—that provoked their theologically inspired temper tantrum. Reaction to the *First Things* symposium was swift and severe, causing an explosion of controversy among conservatives and nearly wrecking the theocon-neocon alliance that Neuhaus and his colleagues had worked so hard to cultivate over the prior two decades. In the end, the alliance was saved—and the theocons' faith in American democracy redeemed—by the rise of a presidential candidate (George W. Bush) who promised to reverse the country's slide toward secularism once and for all.

PROVOCATIONS

In many ways, the 1990s were years of triumph for the theocons, even beyond the success of their ecumenical initiatives. The circulation of *First Things* quickly grew to rival that of the much older *Commentary* magazine (roughly 30,000 subscribers), and it managed to publish numerous stimulating and rigorous articles, including (at the journal's intellectual peak) a fascinating debate between Neuhaus and literary theorist Stanley Fish on the challenge of religious pluralism in a free society.[1] Michael Novak won the million-dollar Templeton Prize for Progress in Religion in 1994.[2] George Weigel served as president of the influential Ethics and Public Policy Center in Washington from 1989 to 1996 and spent the latter half of the decade researching and writing a thousand-page biography of Pope John Paul II, *Witness to Hope* (2000), which received largely favorable reviews and went on to be translated into nearly a dozen languages.

When it came to political influence, things were equally encouraging. A growing cadre of congressmen and senators—including Henry Hyde of Illinois, Rick Santorum of Pennsylvania, and Sam Brownback of Kansas—embraced the theocon agenda and worked to enact it into law. Supreme Court justices Antonin Scalia and Clarence Thomas increasingly staked out positions in their opinions and dissents very close to those of the theocons. And within the broader conservative intellectual universe, theocon ideas grew more influential with each passing year. In 1997, leading neocon strategist William Kristol would declare that if Republicans were serious about becoming a "majority party" and a "governing party," then "*Roe* and abortion are the test." In words that could have been written by Neuhaus or Weigel, Kristol insisted that abortion was where "judicial liberation," "sexual liberation," and "women's liberation" came together; it was thus "the focal point for liberalism's simultaneous assault on self-government, morals, and nature." No wonder then that "challenging the judicially imposed regime of abortion-on-demand is key to a conservative reformation in politics, in morals, and in beliefs."[3]

Yet despite these numerous signs of progress for their cause, the 1990s were a time of frustration and discontent for the theocons, as a series of developments in the country seemed to betray and even to mock their efforts. There was, first of all, the end of Republican presidential rule in 1992, which came as a brutal shock to many on the right. Up until the last minute, Neuhaus had been confident that his fellow Americans "would sober up . . . turn away from Clinton, and reelect George Bush."[4] When this hope turned out to be misplaced, the theocons confronted the painful reality of being locked out of positions of direct power and influence in Washington for the first time in twelve years. Even more difficult to face, however, was the prospect that their movement was somehow out of step with the American people. How could the nation have elected a draft-dodging serial adulterer who had insisted, against the core theocon belief in the political primacy of culture, that the election was all about "the economy, stupid"? It defied explanation in theocon terms. And so Neuhaus and his colleagues chose at first to assume they had been wrong about Clinton and that the American people had been right. Giving the president-elect the benefit of the doubt, they hoped against hope that his campaign's talk of a "new covenant" signaled that the incoming administration would stake out a moderate to conservative position on social and religious policy.[5]

But such hopes were quickly dashed. In the opening days of the Clinton administration, the president set out to overturn the ban on homosexuals serving in the military. Worse, at a news conference on the twentieth anniversary of the *Roe v. Wade* decision (a mere two days after his inauguration), Clinton announced that he was rescinding a series of executive orders under Presidents Reagan and Bush that had placed modest restrictions on government support for abortion. Neuhaus watched the announcement from a hospital bed where he was recovering from emergency surgery to remove a cancerous tumor. Lifting his head from the pillow, he pronounced, "Mark my words: We are watching a man stumbling through the rubble of a ruined presidency."[6] Six months later, in a keynote address to the nation's largest antiabortion group (the National Right to Life Committee), Neuhaus gave vent to his bitter disappointment by likening Washington under the Clinton administration to the political environment in the years leading up to the Civil War, when "all three branches of government were in the hands of pro-slavery forces."[7]

Over the next few years, President Clinton would demonstrate again and again that he was the enemy of everything the theocons stood for. He nominated safely prochoice candidates to the judiciary. He vetoed a series of bills intended to restrict late-term abortions. He attempted to have abortion-on-demand declared a fundamental human right at the 1994 Cairo World Conference on Population and Development. His surgeon general, Jocelyn Elders, advocated including a discussion of masturbation in public school sex education. His attorney general, Janet Reno, ensured that there would be no "recriminations" about the deadly conflagration at the Branch Davidian compound in Waco, Texas, which Neuhaus considered to be "the single most violent government assault on religious freedom in American history."[8] To be sure, the so-called Gingrich revolution of 1994 momentarily raised theocon spirits, convincing some that a populist revolt against Clinton was under way. But the president survived the insurrection—and even managed to rebound in the polls as he headed toward his 1996 campaign for reelection.

As disheartening as were these political developments, even more distressing to the theocons were a series of court decisions, the first and most devastating of which was announced in the summer of 1992. After twelve years of Republican rule—a period during which Presidents Reagan and Bush had named five justices to the Supreme Court—the theocons (as well as many abortion-rights advocacy groups) fully expected the judiciary to overturn or at least substantially curtail the scope of *Roe v. Wade*. The only question for the theocons was which case would provide the opportunity to set things right. By the Court's 1991–1992 term, it was clear that the case would be *Planned Parenthood of Southeastern Pennsylvania v. Casey*. What no one predicted was that the nation's highest court, while somewhat weakening *Roe* itself, would use *Casey* to affirm a woman's constitutional right to an abortion—and on a new, more secure, and more morally radical basis than before.

The theocons reacted to the decision with blind rage. In a blister-

ing essay published in the *Wall Street Journal* just three days after it
was announced, Neuhaus declared that *Casey* would go down in history as "the *Dred Scott* [decision] of our time"—that is, a profoundly
unjust ruling that in the very act of seeking to resolve a highly contentious issue managed only to highlight and exacerbate an underlying and perhaps fatal division in the nation. Just as *Dred Scott*
precipitated the Civil War of the 1860s, so *Casey* threatened to spark
another conflagration 130 years later. The fact was that the United
States was now really two nations:

> one concentrated on rights and laws, the other on rights and
> wrongs; one radically individualistic and dedicated to fulfillment to
> the self, the other communal and invoking the common good; one
> viewing law as the instrument of the will to power and license, the
> other affirming an objective moral order reflected in a Constitution
> to which we are obliged; one typically secular, the other typically
> religious; one elitist, the other populist.

Whereas secular America greeted *Casey* with everything from indifference to elation, religious America reacted to the decision with
"anomie" and "anger," refusing to accept it as "the law of the land"
and viewing it as fundamentally illegitimate—merely "one wrong decision of the Court affirming an earlier wrong decision of the Court."
Just as the country began to divide over the issue of slavery in the
1850s, so America in 1992 was a nation in which "the fragile bonds
of civility" were beginning to unravel. Neuhaus even went so far as to
quote Lincoln's first inaugural address, delivered on the eve of the
Civil War, in which the new president described a nation in which the
people had "ceased to be their own rulers," having surrendered their
government to the "eminent tribunal" of the Supreme Court. The
point was as obvious as it was ominous: just as it had during the nineteenth century, the judicial branch of government was leading the
country to the brink of violent social and cultural conflict.[9]

The severity of the theocon response to the *Casey* decision was a product not only of disappointment at the Court's refusal to overturn *Roe* but also of outrage that the majority had chosen to ground the constitutional right to abortion in a comprehensive theory of human autonomy. In a crucial passage of their plurality opinion, Justices Kennedy, O'Connor, and Souter (all Reagan-Bush appointees) asserted that "at the heart of liberty is the right to define one's own concept of existence, of meaning, of the universe, and of the mystery of human life." Most Americans would likely find nothing shocking in this statement—what, after all, is so objectionable about the notion that individuals have the right to determine the meaning of life for themselves, without state interference?—but for the theocons it was a grotesque assertion of atheistic impiety. George Weigel spoke for his colleagues when he railed against the passage for expressing the "imperial" ideology of the "autonomous, unencumbered self" who is allowed to do "whatever he or she deems necessary to the 'satisfaction' of his or her 'needs.' " Such a view of human beings simply could not serve as "the *telos* of the American experiment." On the contrary, the Court's attempt to tie this libertarian anthropology to the nation's fundamental law raised "the most serious questions" about the "moral continuity of the present constitutional order with the constitutional order ratified in 1788–89."[10] Far more than any previous ruling, *Casey* convinced the theocons that the Supreme Court was out to transform the Constitution into something very different from what the nation's founders intended—into a set of laws that expressly mandated moral decadence.

Over the coming years, a series of further rulings intensified theocon alarm about the moral and religious collapse of the country—and even more so about the judiciary's role in encouraging it. In *Lee v. Weisman* (1992), the Supreme Court held that exposing a junior high school student to an officially approved nondenominational graduation prayer constituted undue psychological coercion of religious practice. In *Romer v. Evans* (1996), the Court declared a Colorado

statute opposing gay rights to be unconstitutional on the grounds
that it expressed rationally unjustifiable "animus" against homosexuals. And in the same year, the Ninth Circuit Court of Appeals claimed
to find a "right to die" in the U.S. Constitution.[11] That the eight-to-
three decision was based in large part on the "mystery of life" passage
of *Casey* only augmented the horror of the theocons, since they had
every reason to believe that the Supreme Court would uphold the
Ninth Circuit's ruling on appeal.[12] In an anguished editorial in the
May 1996 issue of *First Things*, Neuhaus contemplated the possibility and expressed his view of what it would portend for the future of
the nation:

> If the decision of the Ninth Circuit is declared the law of the land,
> our public life will move from widespread alienation and protest
> to open insurrection. No sensible person should welcome that
> prospect. But if it comes, the guilt will surely fall on judges who ar-
> rogated to themselves the political and moral authority that once
> belonged to the people of this democratic republic. History will
> show that, with that arrogation, the compact was broken, the con-
> sent of the governed was nullified, and this constitutional order was
> undone.[13]

With these words, Neuhaus walked a very fine line between describing an imminent populist revolution against the judiciary and seeking to incite one. Yet even this statement proved to be an insufficient
expression of righteous indignation. With the May issue of *First
Things* still on newsstands, the theocons decided that something even
bolder and more radical was called for.

THE END OF DEMOCRACY

Seated around a conference table in a cigar-smoke-filled room of the
Union League Club on East Thirty-seventh Street in Manhattan were

the core members of the theoconservative movement. In addition to Neuhaus and Weigel, several more recent recruits to the cause had traveled to New York for the annual May meeting of the *First Things* editorial board. There was Hadley Arkes, professor of jurisprudence at Amherst College. Arkes was one of the few Jews in the theocon inner circle, though his opposition to abortion, his rationalistic faith in the power of moral principles to "plant premises" that mold public opinion, and his tireless appeals to natural law absolutes made him an honorary Catholic.[14] Robert P. George of Princeton University's government department made similarly broad claims for reason's powers. As a student of ultraconservative Catholic theologian Germain Grisez and Oxford natural law ethicist John Finnis, George was unshakably convinced that it was possible to provide a rational justification for the moral teachings of his beloved Catholic Church, including its bans on abortion, euthanasia, and contraception. Russell Hittinger of the School of Philosophy at the Catholic University of America made nearly identical claims, though he was more likely than his practically minded colleagues to justify his assertions with the metaphysical arguments of medieval theologians.

Over the past several years, each of these men had become convinced that America had crossed an ominous threshold, with elite hostility to Judeo-Christianity and the natural law principles of the American founding growing ever bolder and more destructive. But now, as the group discussed the series of recent court rulings, the rationalists became radicalized. Over the course of the day, the assertions grew fiercer, the language more extreme, the panic more palpable. The theocons were convinced that the judiciary was behaving in a way that could only be described as tyrannical, usurping the sovereignty of the people, leading the country into moral degradation, and bringing democracy in America to the brink of extinction. Failing to distinguish between the state's *permitting* private citizens to procure abortions and practice euthanasia on the one hand and its *acting* to put innocents to death against their will on the other, the theocons began to describe the United States in terms usually reserved for totalitarian states. By the time the meeting drew to a close, the group had whipped itself into such a moralistic frenzy that it had decided to publish a "wake-up call." *First Things* would run a special issue on the subject of encroaching "judicial tyranny," with contributions from the leading theocons, in the hopes of lighting a fire under the American people and sending a warning to the country's judges.

At a heated meeting several days later in the magazine's editorial offices, *First Things* editor James Nuechterlein attempted to persuade Neuhaus and the rest of the staff not to go forward with the planned special issue. By temperament more of a mid-1970s neocon than a theocon, Nuechterlein worried that, however necessary it might have been for the participants in the recent gathering of the editorial board to blow off steam by talking of revolution, civil war, and tyranny, expressing such sentiments in print, and sustaining them on page after page in the magazine, would make the journal look extremist and irresponsible. Neuhaus considered the concerns of his more moderate friend and colleague, and he listened to the arguments of the rest of the staff, every one of whom was eager to run the special issue. In the end, Neuhaus decided to proceed with the symposium as planned. After briefly entertaining and then rejecting the possibility of resigning in protest, Nuechterlein prepared to accept the duty of putting out the special issue and facing the consequences, which he suspected would be severe.[15]

As it turned out, the contributions to the symposium were every bit as alarmist as Nuechterlein feared. Concerns about judicial aggrandizement of power were nothing new in American history, going back at least as far as the debates surrounding the adoption of the U.S. Constitution. They had been voiced by many in the years leading up to the Civil War, partisans of the New Deal frequently expressed them in the 1930s, and conservatives had raised them numerous times in more recent years in response to the expansive rulings of the Warren and Berger Courts. What made the *First Things* special issue unique was its incendiary rhetoric. Titled "The End of Democracy? The Judicial Usurpation of Politics," the symposium was at bottom a call to arms—an expression of fury and dread at what its contributors considered to be the advent of tyranny on American shores. Reading through the pages of the symposium, it was difficult to avoid the conclusion that the country was on the verge of civil war, revolution, or totalitarianism—or perhaps all three. But whatever awaited the country, it was bound to be bloody.

Neuhaus set the tone. In an unsigned introduction to the symposium that made use of the same radical concepts and rhetoric he had employed twenty-six years earlier during his most militant period, Neuhaus announced that the question explored in the November issue, "in full awareness of its far-reaching consequences," was nothing less than "whether we have reached or are reaching the point where conscientious citizens can no longer give moral assent to the existing regime." Neuhaus then assured his readers that the question raised by the title of the symposium was in no way hyperbolic, for the subject explored in its pages was nothing less than "the end of democracy" in America.[16] After all, the "founders called this order an experiment, and it is in the nature of experiments that they can fail." And recent events showed that "the government of the United States of America no longer governs by the consent of the governed"—the most fundamental precondition of democratic politics. Adopting the revolutionary language of the Declaration of Independence, Neuhaus lamented the judiciary's "long train of abuses and usurpations," and warned darkly about "the prospect—some might say the present reality—of despotism" in America. "Still more sobering," Neuhaus claimed, was the fact that "law, as it is presently made by the judiciary, has declared its independence from morality."[17]

Yet the country would not simply sit back and watch as "the citizens of this democratic republic are deemed to lack the competence for self-government." Indeed, one of the most "elemental principles of Western Civilization is the truth that laws which violate the moral law are null and void and must in conscience be disobeyed." The country's founders understood this, so did the "antislavery movement" and Martin Luther King Jr., and in our time the principle had been invoked by Pope John Paul II, who declared that "laws and decrees enacted in contravention of the moral order, and hence of the divine will, can have no binding force in conscience." Having quoted the Pope's encyclical on the "culture of life" *(Evangelium Vitae),* Neuhaus pointed out that the document's footnotes referred to "papal statements condemning the crimes of Nazi Germany." Lest he be misunderstood, Neuhaus insisted that America "is not, and, please God, will never become Nazi Germany." Yet he also reminded his readers that "it is only blind hubris that denies that it can happen here and, in peculiarly American ways, may be happening here."[18] Seeking to clarify his point, Neuhaus suggested that "what is happening now is the displacement of a constitutional order by a regime that does not have, and will not obtain, and cannot command the consent of the people."[19] To deny this fact was a "recklessly myopic response." Hence the stark and radical options confronting American citizens, ranging "from noncompliance to resistance to civil disobedience to morally justified revolution."[20]

The intensity of Neuhaus's argument and rhetoric was matched, if not surpassed, by the other contributors to the special issue—beginning with the symposium's first titled essay, by Judge Robert H. Bork. Since being rejected by the Senate in 1987 for a spot on the Supreme Court, Bork had gained a reputation for being an embittered reactionary, and in his *First Things* essay he showed that he had also become a theocon fellow traveler. Bork began by suggesting that Americans were currently being "ruled by an oligarchy" of judges who intended to radically alter the country for the worse.[21] Not only had the First Amendment's speech clause "been made a guarantor of moral chaos," but its "religion clauses have been reshaped to banish religious symbolism from public life." Broadening his attack, Bork traced the recent "arrogantly authoritarian" behavior of judges—their tendency to act as a "band of outlaws" who "coerce others without warrant in law"—to flaws in the nation's Constitution itself. He therefore concluded that "as our institutional arrangements now stand, the Court can never be made a legitimate element of a basically democratic polity."[22]

Russell Hittinger continued the assault on the American political system, asserting that the country now lived "under an altered constitutional regime" whose laws were "unworthy of loyalty."[23] Turning his attention to public officials whose faith brings them into conflict with the new constitutional order, Hittinger posed a stark alternative: "Either right-minded citizens will have to disobey orders or perhaps relinquish offices of public authority, or the new constitutional rulers will have to be challenged and reformed." While the first option pointed to withdrawal from politics or to civil disobedience, the second implied, among other things, direct confrontation with the powers that be. Such confrontation must not "play within the game imposed by the Court, in the hope of incrementally improving the situation issue-by-issue," since doing so would "actually deepen rather than mitigate the authority of the new order." Rather, issues must be chosen for the purpose of "prompting a constitutional crisis," which, given the reality of the country's lapsing into "despotic rule," was clearly "the responsible thing to do."[24]

Charles W. Colson similarly maintained that events in America might have reached the point where "the only political action believers can take is some kind of direct, extrapolitical confrontation of the judicially controlled regime." While Christians should not hope for a "showdown between church and state," such a clash may in fact be inevitable, and so it is something for which they "need to prepare."[25] Reminding his readers that "revolution can be justified from a Christian viewpoint," Colson announced that, "with fear and trembling, I have begun to believe that . . . we are fast approaching this point."[26] After all, it was already "hard to imagine that a Christian in good conscience could swear to uphold the Constitution or laws of a nation that practices" abortion and euthanasia. And the future seemed likely to bring even worse—namely, a "regime in which the courts have usurped the democratic process by reckless exercise of naked power."[27]

Finally, in a contribution titled "The Tyrant State," Robert P. George asserted that "the courts . . . have imposed upon the nation immoral policies that pro-life Americans cannot, in conscience, accept," creating what is "truly a crisis" for the United States.[28] Quoting from Pope John Paul II, George insisted that *there is a grave and clear obligation to oppose by conscientious objection"* laws that legitimate abortion and euthanasia. This duty is not merely a suggestion, and it is not something that can be fulfilled merely by personally refraining from the immoral acts themselves. On the contrary, the Pope's teaching is a public "call to *action"* to "overcome these 'crimes against life' and create a new 'culture of life' " by "working in various spheres— including the political sphere."[29] Given this moral imperative, "the refusal of the courts over more than twenty-three years to reverse *Roe v. Wade* must . . . be accounted a failure of American democracy"—a failure whose practical political implication George did not explicitly spell out for his readers.[30]

While all of the contributors to the symposium agreed about the gravity of the situation facing the country, there was a significant, though unexplored, fault line running through the essays concerning whether the American people should be considered part of the problem or part of the solution. Bork and Hadley Arkes, for example, concluded their contributions with expressions of frustration and dismay at the apathy of American citizens in the face of impending tyranny. Bork proposed solutions to judicial despotism that were so radical— making decisions of the courts subject to modification or reversal by majority vote of Congress and stripping the courts of the power of judicial review entirely—that they would be enacted only if the nation's elites were confronted by a widespread populist uprising against judicial tyranny. And yet, no such grassroots campaign was in sight. On the contrary, a "supine" people appeared willing to lazily and passively observe "democracy slip away."[31] Arkes was equally dismayed, as he pondered incredulously "what it would take in this country—what would have to happen?—before serious Christians and Jews would recognize, at once, that a critical line has been crossed?"[32] In the end, Arkes concluded that "something in the religious sensibility" of Americans had been deadened by "the ethic of modernity."

Neuhaus and Colson, by contrast, expressed far more confidence that, in the end, the American people would do the right thing and rise up against their robed oppressors. Detecting "a growing alienation of millions of Americans from a government they do not recognize as theirs," the symposium's introduction predicted that "Americans, perhaps even a majority," would not stand idly by as unelected judges forced believers to choose between loyalty to the country and devotion to God—to give up the patriotic slogan "God and country" for the tragic division embodied in the motto "God *or* country."[33] Colson shared Neuhaus's faith in the American people and his conviction that they would resist the elite imposition of secularist ideology. In Colson's view, American Christians would soon conclude that the government had become "sufficiently corrupt that a believer must resist it." And short of revolution, there was always the hope that the Republican Party would notice that "believing Protestants and Roman Catholics . . . represent a viable political majority in this country."[34]

Only George managed to sidestep the issue entirely, by appealing to an understanding of democracy that transcended politics altogether. Relying on the writings of Pope John Paul II to outflank Supreme Court justice Antonin Scalia from the right, George denied that overturning *Roe v. Wade* and returning the question of abortion to state legislatures would be sufficient to put the country back on moral track, since many of those legislatures would likely vote to keep abortion legal and thereby betray the "substantive principle of equal worth and dignity that is the moral linchpin of democracy."[35] For George, whether the people acted (democratically) to outlaw abortion

by constitutional amendment or the Court banned the practice by
ruling (undemocratically) that the unborn must be included among
those protected from lethal violence by the Fourteenth Amendment's
Equal Protection Clause was a matter of relative indifference. Far
more important was whether America would take a stand consistent
with its founding Catholic-Christian principles by denying that the
Constitution included a right to commit wrongful homicide.

RECRIMINATIONS

Nuechterlein had predicted that the symposium would generate more
controversy than Neuhaus had bargained for, though even he was sur-
prised by the ferocity of the early morning phone call from neocon
Midge Decter. The special issue of *First Things* (November 1996) had
been dropped in the mail by the printer only a few days earlier, so he
was unsure if anyone outside of the editorial office had seen the magazine. But Decter's tone of voice instantly told him that her copy
had already arrived. For much of the magazine's first six years of production (from 1991 to 1995), Decter had served as an editor at the
journal (albeit one uncredited on the masthead). But now, with her
husband (neocon founding father and longtime editor of *Commentary* magazine Norman Podhoretz) ranting furiously in the background, Decter expressed dismay and disgust to her friend and former
colleague. As she went on to write in a letter to the editor of *First
Things*, "When I first read the editorial introduction to the symposium presumably devoted to the subject of judicial usurpation, I
could hardly believe my eyes." The rhetoric of revolution had stunned
her and her husband, but they thought they understood perfectly well
where it came from. As Decter put it in her letter, addressing her
supposed ideological allies directly: "I presume in the name of
friendship . . . to accuse you of growing impatient with your labors,
and in your impatience, reckless."[36] And such recklessness, she claimed,

was inexcusable for intellectuals purporting to be conservatives, of whatever stripe. By the time the phone call was over, Nuechterlein realized that he and his colleagues were going to be facing a firestorm.[37]

Over the coming days, the theocons received far more mainstream media attention than ever before. The *New York Times* ran a total of three articles touching on the symposium.[38] Every leading conservative magazine and newspaper ran at least one editorial or major article addressing the special issue.[39] Even Neuhaus's old antagonists at the Rockford Institute weighed in, clearly delighting in what they took to be the new, more radically right-wing "paleoconservative tendency" at *First Things* that, while "welcome," was also "just a few decades too late."[40]

But the most intense reaction came from the neocons, several of whom publicly denounced the symposium and sought to distance themselves from the journal. Neocon political theorist Walter Berns resigned from the *First Things* editorial board in a tersely worded note.[41] He was joined by historian Gertrude Himmelfarb, who in her letter of resignation described the symposium's "apocalyptic conclusions" as "absurd and irresponsible."[42] David Brooks chimed in with an article on "The Right's Anti-American Temptation."[43] William Kristol was less accusatory than many, though he worried that the "radicalizing mood" of the symposium would serve as a needless distraction from the "truly radical task" of building a "conservative governing majority in this country."[44] And Norman Podhoretz wrote a private letter to Neuhaus in which he described the symposium as resembling nothing so much as "the extremist hysteria of the old counterculture of the 1960s." The theocons had thus given "aid and comfort" to the "bomb-throwers among us." In Podhoretz's view, "nothing less than a frank and forthright recognition of error" would suffice to repair the damage. Two months later he would claim to detect no sign of such an act of contrition.[45]

Although several participants in the controversy went out of their way to deny it, the theocon-neocon split over the symposium clearly grew out of a deeper tension between Catholic-Christian and Jewish writers over issues of moral and intellectual responsibility. As Jacob Heilbrunn noted in an important essay on the dispute, the Jewish neocons were much less willing than the Christian theocons to issue absolute condemnations of the American political system, fearing that doing so would (in Decter's words) "only end by strengthening the devil's hand."[46] On one level, this difference could be traced to Jewish gratitude to the United States for providing a safe refuge in the modern world. The neocons were thus particularly offended by the parallel that Neuhaus had drawn between modern America and Nazi Germany. As Jews they could personally testify to the categorical difference between the two "regimes." But as Himmelfarb implied in her letter of resignation, the theocons had actually gone beyond moral equivalence—to insinuate (most likely unintentionally, through shoddy moral reasoning) that the evil of the United States might actually be worse than Germany under Hitler. After all, Neuhaus and his colleagues had questioned the legitimacy of the American government even though the Catholic Church had never declared "Nazi Germany or the Soviet Union illegitimate, despite the genocide and mass murders."[47] To many of the neocons, the theocons had begun to engage in politically dangerous and intellectually sloppy moral posturing.

More fundamentally, the Jewish neocons had numerous historically grounded reasons to feel uneasy about the dark and paranoid style of Catholicism so vividly displayed in the symposium. A mere half-century removed from the Holocaust and the long history of virulently anti-Jewish violence that preceded it in Christian Europe, the neocons may have feared that they were witnessing the reappearance in the United States of a profoundly threatening form of Catholic piety. That the neocons had helped to empower the very thinkers who now expressed such volatile religious passions no doubt contributed to the disgust and sense of betrayal that marked their responses to the symposium.

For their part, the Catholic-Christian theocons wondered whether the largely Jewish neocons were serious in claiming to uphold traditional morality. Arkes asserted that "in their heart of hearts," the neocons "don't think people are being killed" when abortions are performed.[48] Paul Weyrich, head of the evangelical Free Congress Foundation and a powerful theocon ally, announced that he resented the "political correctness of some of the neocons who suggest that you can't discuss something."[49] And in the same issue of *First Things* containing the highly critical letters of Decter, Himmelfarb, and Berns, James C. Dobson, of the influential evangelical organization Focus on the Family, struck back against the neocons, praising the symposium for making an "indisputable case for the illegitimacy of the regime now passing itself off as a democracy." Placing himself and the other theocons in "a long tradition of Christians who believe that rulers may forfeit their divine mandate when they systematically contravene the divine law," Dobson angrily dismissed critics who failed to recognize the "accumulation of evidence" that "our judiciary has . . . stepped out from under the moral law upon which governing authority depends." Dobson thus concluded by asking whether "clergy and laity alike [will] be willing to face cultural ostracism, imprisonment, or worse" in doing their duty to reform the country by any means necessary.[50]

For all the fireworks between the neocons and theocons, the most intellectually challenging response to the symposium came from Neuhaus's old (Lutheran) friend and compatriot Peter Berger, who followed Himmelfarb and Berns in swiftly resigning from the *First Things* editorial board. Perhaps recalling Neuhaus's incendiary contribution to the book they coauthored in 1970 *(Movement and Revolution)*, Berger wondered whether his one-time collaborator would soon revert to "the 'Amerika' language of the 1960s, this time in a Right translation." More incisively, Berger posed a potent thought experiment to the symposium's contributors—one intended to expose the true motivations behind the special issue:

> Imagine that abortion in the United States had achieved its present legal status through an act of Congress rather than a Supreme Court decision. Imagine further that the Supreme Court had then ruled this act to be unconstitutional. I doubt very much that most of the *First Things* contributors would have viewed the latter action as a serious usurpation of power, let alone a reason to question the legitimacy of the American polity.[51]

Far more decisively than even Robert George's contribution to the symposium, Berger's thought experiment revealed that the real issue for the theocons was not so much the "judicial usurpation" of democracy as America's imperfect conformity to the moral teachings of orthodox Catholic-Christianity. As long as a large segment of the American people opposed the judicial imposition of abortion-on-demand, euthanasia, and other socially libertarian policies, the theocons could pose as defenders of democracy for its own sake.[52] But as Berger's thought experiment implied, the moment it became clear that the American majority was unwilling to stand against the judiciary, the theocons would likely be led by their intense moral and religious passions to abandon their populism and embrace political authority—so long as that authority promised to turn back the decadent secularist tide.

In an essay written largely in response to Berger's thought experiment, George effectively conceded the point. Brandishing his rationalism with pride, George asserted as an uncontestable fact that "human beings come to be and become persons at the same time" (at the moment of conception), and pointed out that the Fourteenth Amendment guaranteed the equal protection of all "persons." It therefore followed with perfect logic that by ratifying the amendment "the

American people have . . . committed themselves to a proposition that is inconsistent with the regime of abortion-on-demand."[53] Once again following the lead of Pope John Paul II, George insisted that pressing this point in American public life inevitably amounted to a defense of "democracy," regardless of whether the American people affirmed it or it was imposed on the nation from above by a Supreme Court remade in the theocon image. This highly flexible notion of democracy—synonymous with majoritarianism one moment and bold acts of countermajoritarian authority on the part of Catholic-Christian judges the next—was based on what George called the "moral principle of the equality-in-dignity of all human beings." In George's view, it was this conception of democracy that he and "others connected with *First Things* believe was operative in the central proposition of the Declaration of Independence ("all men are created equal") and enshrined in our Constitution (particularly, though not exclusively, in the Equal Protection Clause of the Fourteenth Amendment)."[54] In these passages it was clear that the theocon attempt to blur the distinction between the political system of the United States and the moral teachings of the Catholic Church had now yielded a full-blown (and distinctively American) Christian political theology.

As the confident tone and far-reaching claims of George's essay suggested, the theocons responded to their numerous critics with defiance. Arkes once again drew parallels between the 1860s and the 1990s, even quoting Lincoln to demonstrate that the participants in the *First Things* symposium deserved credit for showing restraint in not explicitly counseling their fellow citizens to break the law.[55] Weigel, who had been present at the editorial board meeting that gave birth to the symposium but did not contribute to the special issue, reiterated the dangers of the moral trends that the magazine had highlighted, claiming that they made a "lethal ideological cocktail" that would lead directly to "totalitarianism."[56]

As for Neuhaus, he was equally unrepentant. In a lengthy essay in which he responded to nearly every critic of the symposium and then

restated his own position on the issues, he showed that he believed
that America's crisis was, at bottom, a crisis of authority:

> A nation under God . . . means a nation under judgment. The po-
> litical, cultural, moral, and spiritual crisis of our country is that
> those who dominate our public discourse, whether on the left or on
> the right, are unwilling, and perhaps incapable, of acknowledging
> a higher authority than procedural rules and partisan agendas. This
> circumstance is what I have elsewhere called "the naked public
> square," and it is not sustainable. That is why our social and cul-
> tural order, along with our constitutional order, is unraveling.[57]

Ever since the days of his youthful radicalism, Neuhaus had challenged political authority in the name of divine authority, arguing
that the legitimacy of the first depended on its conformity to the second. And now, as a priest determined to uphold the absolute authority of the truths proclaimed by the Roman Catholic Church, he was
convinced that the United States had been brought to the verge of destruction by its failure to live up to its own Catholic-Christian ideals.
As he wrote in the final pages of his essay, summing up his considered
view of the country, "The American experiment began with the declaration of self-evident truths, and it may well be ending with the exclusion of those truths from the public square under the iron rule of
'the separation of church and state.' " The imminent failure of the
American experiment in self-government might lead to "totalitarianism" in the United States, or it might not. What was certain was that
once the experiment had come to an end, it would mean "the end of
democracy" in America.[58]

Such conclusions—easily as extreme as anything found in the
original symposium—certainly did nothing to mend fences with the
neocons, who continued to wonder what had gotten into their former
allies. Relations with the evangelicals, by contrast, only improved as a
result of the controversy. Indeed, the special issue of *First Things* suc-

ceeded in energizing and inspiring the conservative Protestant participants in Evangelicals and Catholics Together, convincing them that their Catholic partners were serious about challenging the rule of secularism in American public life. In the months following the symposium, Neuhaus and Colson sought to capitalize on this evangelical excitement by restating its main points in a new document that could be widely disseminated, reaching a much broader audience than the readers of Neuhaus's magazine.

The resulting declaration—"We Hold These Truths: A Statement of Christian Conscience and Citizenship"—received little attention from the mainstream media, but through churches, newsletters, radio programs, lobbying organizations, and the Catholic press (where it was widely reported) its message reached millions of devoutly religious Americans.[59] Signed by forty-six Catholic, Protestant, and Eastern Orthodox leaders—including fifteen Catholic bishops, archbishops, and/or cardinals, as well as James Dobson, Gary Bauer of the Family Research Council, and Ralph Reed of the Christian Coalition—the document brought the theocon message to an enormous and largely sympathetic audience in several faith communities. These readers learned that "the great threat to the American experiment today is not from enemies abroad but from disordered liberty" and that the kind of freedom defended by recent Supreme Court jurisprudence was "the very antithesis of the ordered liberty affirmed by the founders" and upheld by the American people for the past two hundred years. Political power in the United States was thus being wielded by the judiciary "without the consent of the governed."[60] While the restatement of the theocon position refrained from explicitly raising the prospect of morally justified revolution as the original symposium had done, the document did draw the familiar comparison between the current "crisis" and the one that precipitated the Civil War, as well as declare that the American experiment was "imperiled" by recent undemocratic Court rulings.[61] By the end of the statement, readers had been alerted to what sounded like a grave threat facing the country—and were left with few concrete suggestions about how they should respond.

DEMOCRACY REDEEMED

The special issue of *First Things* produced mixed results for the theocons. On the one hand, the Catholic-evangelical coalition was strengthened by the symposium's expression of righteous anger, and the resulting publicity contributed to a significant spike in circulation at *First Things*. On the other hand, the alliance with the neocons—cultivated and nurtured for years—had been shattered. It would take several years and plenty of discreet diplomacy on the part of the theocons to dissolve all the bad blood built up by the symposium and its aftermath. Over time, however, the participants in the controversy would learn once again to work together on common goals—to ensure that intellectual and moral differences took a back seat to political expediency.

But beyond the near-fatal conflict with the neocons, the symposium had exposed an intellectual rift among the theocons themselves—a divide that only widened over the coming years, as Neuhaus and his colleagues joined with other conservatives in working, and failing, to bring down the presidency of Bill Clinton. On one side, Hadley Arkes was inclined to view Clinton's persistent popularity as a sign of national corruption. As he wrote shortly after the president's reelection in 1996, "It becomes more and more apparent that Bill Clinton is a reflection of something in the American character, and the public reaction to Clinton offers a precise reflection, at this moment, of the national soul."[62]

Neuhaus shared the dismay of his friend and ally regarding Clinton's remarkable resiliency, but he refused to draw any conclusions about the "national soul" from the president's political success. To concede that Clinton's moral laxity expressed something profound about the state of the country in the 1990s would be to admit that the American people were very far away from rising up against elite moral corruption—and thus that the theocon hope of leading a populist insurgency against secularism was profoundly misplaced. And so Neuhaus chose to blame the influence of the "prestige media" and the lackluster Dole campaign, which had been far too "eager not to seem nasty." Together the media and the leadership of the Republican Party "decided that [Clinton's] wretched character [was] a political non-issue," and the result was that the Democrat coasted to reelection.[63] In a different world—one in which the press and the GOP campaign had focused more incessantly on morals and character, thereby informing Americans about the depth of their president's degradation—the American people would have decisively rejected him. But as it was, the media and the Washington establishment got their way, manipulating the country into ignorantly reelecting a man who perfectly mirrored the decadence of the nation's secular elite.

Neuhaus's effort to defend the virtue of ordinary Americans against conservative critics was made far more difficult by the failure of congressional Republicans to remove Clinton from office in early 1999 for lying under oath about a sexual affair with an intern—and even more so by the fact that the president's job approval rating surged during the impeachment proceedings. That a large number of Americans seemed to rally around the president, even after the extent of his moral transgressions became widely known, inspired widespread anger and despair on the right, leading a slew of self-described conservative populists to turn on the American people with a vengeance. Robert Bork intensified his denunciations of a nation he now considered to be "slouching toward Gomorrah."[64] William J. Bennett railed against the "death of outrage."[65] The critic Roger Kimball pronounced that "the hedonistic, self-infatuated ethos of cultural revolution has triumphed to an extent unimaginable" just a few years earlier.[66] And Paul Weyrich announced in disgust that the time had come for serious Christians to withdraw from political engagement altogether.[67]

Neuhaus maintained an uncharacteristic silence about the entire

impeachment proceeding as it unfolded in late 1998 and early 1999.
While he fully supported the effort to remove Clinton from office, he
decided to withhold public judgment of the events and the vociferous
reaction to them among conservatives until the entire drama had
played itself out.[68] It was not until the summer of 1999 that Neuhaus
weighed in—with a tortured, and tortuous, fifteen-thousand-word
essay on the subject of "Bill Clinton and the American Character." If
his fellow conservatives were right to conclude that elite degradation
had finally managed to corrupt the American population as a whole,
then the entire theocon project was doomed to failure—and perhaps
Weyrich was justified in defending withdrawal from public life in favor of private study and prayer, as the nation descended ever deeper
into barbarism.

But Neuhaus refused to concede the point. In his essay he sifted
through the Starr Report on Bill Clinton's sordid activities in the Oval
Office, the president's efforts to cover them up, Congress's failure to
remove him from office, and the impassioned reaction of his fellow
conservatives to the whole debacle. And when it was all over, he concluded that Clinton had managed to survive not because of the genuine approval of a corrupt American citizenry—let alone because
those citizens were disgusted at the simultaneously prudish and pruri-
ent pursuit of the president by the Republican Party leadership—but
rather because of the insidious influence of the nation's media and
cultural elite. Employing precisely the same argument he had been
making since the mid-1970s, Neuhaus exhaustively enumerated all
the elite forces that had conspired to ensure that Bill Clinton would
be protected from just punishment for his transgressions of the law
and his oath of office:

> Put together the numbers: feminists and those intimidated by
> them, for whom the only issue is abortion; die-hard liberal Demo-
> crats and leftists on the commanding heights of culture for whom
> conservatism is pure evil; big labor, especially in education and

other parts of the public sector, for whom the alternative to Clinton is catastrophe; and blacks who are pitiably grateful for the assurance that Master feels their pain. Add in the very large number of sensible Americans who found the whole thing repugnant and just wanted it to go away, and you ended up with those high "approval" ratings.

In other words—and in sharp contrast to the antidemocratic sentiments of his fellow right-wingers—Neuhaus concluded that "what happened beginning in January 1998 does not tell us much that is worth knowing about 'the American people.' "[69] It merely confirmed what morally righteous Americans already knew about the stakes in the culture war—namely, that allowing the "other" side to gain political power produced an ignoble spectacle of nearly boundless immorality.[70]

Unlike so many of his allies on the right, then, Neuhaus continued to put his faith in the common sense and moral traditionalism of the American people, hoping that at some time in the near future this faith would be tested and vindicated by the rise of a successful theocon candidate for president. As it turned out, Neuhaus had just such a candidate in mind when he penned his lengthy rumination on the ruins of the Clinton presidency. Back in May 1998, Neuhaus had been contacted by the governor of Texas, George W. Bush, who invited him to Austin for a meeting. In their conversation, Bush told Neuhaus that he was contemplating a run for president in 2000 and wanted to establish connections with "writers and pro-life leaders in the East" in order to "provide assurances" that he shared the concerns and goals of the religious right.[71] Above all, he wanted Neuhaus to know that he accepted the notion, expressed in the pages of *First Things*, that "human life was to be protected by law from its beginning to its close."[72]

The two men would talk again over the next several months. Neuhaus provided the governor with "tutorials on Catholic social teaching" and the "culture of life."[73] Bush declared that he was firmly "committed to the goal of every unborn child protected in law and welcomed in life."[74] They discussed how the church "connected opposition to abortion, euthanasia, family planning, stem-cell research, and cloning."[75] Then, as the presidential campaign got under way, Bush and his political advisor Karl Rove hired an evangelical speechwriter (Michael Gerson) who had "consumed the works of Neuhaus, Novak, and their comrade George Weigel."[76] Before long, Bush had incorporated distinctively theocon rhetoric and ideas into his policy agenda and stump speech. It has even been suggested that Bush's core campaign theme of "compassionate conservatism" ultimately derived from the Catholic concept of "subsidiarity"—the idea, championed by Neuhaus and Novak for years, that social problems are best solved by subpolitical, private organizations such as churches and private charities.[77]

By the time of the first primaries in the winter of 2000, Neuhaus was convinced that his hopes would finally be fulfilled—that the theocons had at long last found their political champion. Ronald Reagan had been an important early ally, but he was a divorced man who rarely went to church, and he deliberately kept his distance from the front lines of the culture war. His pragmatic successor, George H. W. Bush, was even less inclined to push an overtly religious agenda; he limited his support for the religious right to key government appointments and left it to his vice president, Dan Quayle, to raise issues of pressing concern to social conservatives. George W. Bush promised to be something else entirely—a politician whose support for the theocon cause was grounded in his own evangelical piety and whose closest advisors recognized the enormous untapped electoral potential of appealing directly to millions of disaffected traditionalist Catholics and Protestants (and those moderates who were receptive to the same faith-based rhetoric).

If Neuhaus and his powerful allies within the Bush campaign were right about the size and extent of the theocon coalition, then the

Republican candidate would easily win the general election—indeed, it would be a landslide, with Bush triumphing over Al Gore by "at least a ten point margin in the popular vote and 330 or more in the electoral college." This, at any rate, is what Neuhaus, relying on "inside information from the Bush camp," believed would happen.[78] That such predictions were wrong became painfully apparent by early evening on election night. Over the following weeks, Bush and his advisors would become convinced that the outcome (a virtual tie in the popular vote and the electoral college, capped by a statistical tie in the deciding state of Florida) resulted from the decision of approximately four million evangelicals to stay home on election day—and that this decision had in turn been inspired by the story of a drunk driving arrest in Bush's past, which dominated media coverage during the final weekend of the campaign. Thus, as far as the Republicans were concerned, the theocon electoral strategy had fallen short of expectations only because of the dirty tricks of the Gore campaign (which, it was assumed, had leaked the DWI story) and its allies in the liberal media.

It is hardly surprising that the Bush campaign asked the U.S. Supreme Court to stop the Florida recount, ordered by the Florida State Supreme Court, since it threatened to reverse the Republican's infinitesimal lead in the popular vote and throw the state's electoral-college votes to Gore. It is even less surprising that much of the right momentarily abandoned its stated opposition to judicial activism and rejoiced at the Court's highly partisan five-to-four decision in *Bush v. Gore* that ensured Democratic defeat. What is remarkable is that Neuhaus, who a mere four years earlier had denounced the judicial usurpation of democracy in such extreme and unconditional terms, not only did not criticize the disturbing precedent set by the Supreme Court's breathtakingly bold act of usurpation in *Bush v. Gore* but actually praised it, describing the decision as "the right one."[79] As Peter Berger had implied in his response to the 1996 symposium, the theocons were perfectly willing to endorse a little judicial tyranny, as long

as it empowered their side in the culture war—even if it meant having to live with the irony that "democracy" in America had been redeemed by a blatantly antidemocratic act.

Despite its messiness, the election of George W. Bush realized
long-standing theoconservative hopes. By December 2000, all the despair of the 1990s had vanished, replaced with a rebirth of energy,
confidence, and excitement. For years Neuhaus and his colleagues
had been working to unite Catholic ideas for the ordering of American public life with the faith and fervor of the evangelical Protestant
world—all for the purpose of capturing political power. And now
they had finally succeeded. With Bush in the White House, the theocons were certain that cultural ground lost to liberalism since the
1960s would finally be retaken, democracy in America would be re-
vitalized, and secularism would, for the first time in nearly forty years,
be put on the defensive. It was a time for rejoicing. And yet, just nine
months into the Bush presidency, events would conspire to give their
cause more momentum than any of them had ever imagined.

4

THEOCONS AT WAR

THE FIRST SEVERAL MONTHS of 2001 were a time of celebration for the theocons. After nearly a decade in exile, they and their ideas were swept to the pinnacle of public power and influence by George W. Bush's victory, with the new administration going out of its way to ensure that Richard John Neuhaus and his ideological compatriots enjoyed unprecedented political access. Neuhaus was invited to the White House to discuss strategy with the president. Peter Wehner, the White House director of strategic initiatives and a top aide to Karl Rove, kept the theocon Institute on Religion and Public Life "in the loop" on all pertinent administration business. Rove and members of the Republican National Committee planned Catholic outreach in weekly conference calls with Deal Hudson, editor and publisher of *Crisis* magazine, a theocon journal started by Michael Novak back in the early 1980s.[1] Evangelical theocon Michael Gerson directed the administration's speechwriting office.[2] The White House even employed a full-time liaison to conservative Christians, Timothy Goeglein, whose responsibilities included formulating policies that would advance the theoconservative agenda.[3] By the summer of 2001, the theocons had every reason to expect that the Bush administration would devote the bulk of its time and energy toward realizing their vision of a vibrantly religious America.

Yet these expectations were shattered on the morning of September 11, 2001, when it became immediately apparent that prosecuting the culture war would take a back seat to waging an actual war against the perpetrators of that morning's massive terrorist attacks. During President Bush's first term, the theocon agenda dominated domestic policy, but after September 11 domestic policy in general (aside from "homeland security") received considerably less attention than foreign policy. Instead of succumbing to disappointment and frustration in the face of this development, Neuhaus and his colleagues quickly came to consider the prospect of George W. Bush leading Christian America in a global war as an unanticipated opportunity to advance their domestic goals. Such a war would likely lead to a series of decisive victories on the battlefield, thereby greatly strengthening the president's popularity and, in turn, empowering him to push the theocon agenda at home with greater potency. Moreover, as a battle fought in the name of national self-defense as well as for transcendent ideals of freedom and justice, the war would also have the probable effect of nudging the country in a more conservative direction overall. An America committed to fighting an open-ended "war on terror," as well as morally self-confident enough to launch a preemptive attack, invasion, and occupation of a sovereign nation in defiance of worldwide public opinion, would be far more likely to embrace the theoconservative message than the pathologically self-absorbed country that President Bush had inherited from Bill Clinton nine months earlier. Or so the theocons believed.

Not that the theocons exercised much direct influence on the making of the Bush administration's foreign policy. On the contrary, the line of influence ran far more in the other direction, with the theocons serving as freelance propaganda ministers for the president, providing moral and theological justifications for his policies in order to sell them to conservative religious believers. It took the theocons a matter of weeks to declare the "war on terror" a just war pitting Christian civilization against its enemies. Just over a year later, they defended the Bush administration's plan for the invasion of Iraq and the overthrow of its government. The effort to support that policy continued long after the primary cause for war (eliminating Saddam Hussein's stockpile of weapons of mass destruction) had collapsed and the security situation under American occupation deteriorated. Then, with the war in Iraq going badly, the theocons proposed that succeeding in the wider war required the initiation of a (nonmilitary) confrontation with Europe—a continent seemingly unwilling to defend the Christian essence of Western civilization against the challenge of militant Islam. Standing up to European decadence and even seeking to project America's Christian beliefs across the Atlantic would, they claimed, increase the likelihood of American victory in the war on terror as well as prepare the country to embrace more fully the theoconservative agenda at home.

CHRISTIAN AMERICA AT WAR

When the first plane slammed into the side of the World Trade Center on the morning of September 11, 2001, Neuhaus was on his way out the door of his apartment for the short walk to Immaculate Conception Church on Fourteenth Street and First Avenue, where, as on most mornings, he was scheduled to celebrate nine o'clock Mass. Moments after the collision, he passed a crowd of people on a street corner, gazing at the large plume of smoke rising from the North Tower less than three miles to the south. Assuming it was simply a catastrophic fire, Neuhaus said a brief prayer for the people trapped in the building and continued on his way to church. Only after Mass did he discover what had happened—a terrorist attack so spectacular that it would "inaugurate a time of national unity and sobriety in a society that has been . . . on a long and hedonistic holiday from history."[4]

September 11 and America's Mission

Nine days later, on the evening of September 20, President Bush addressed Congress and the nation to discuss the coming American response to the attacks. Much of the president's speech was unremarkable. Once it had been determined that the attacks had been encouraged, orchestrated, and funded by Osama bin Laden's Al Qaeda organization, which had been given refuge and support by the Taliban government in Afghanistan, a military campaign to kill or capture Bin Laden, depose the Taliban, and destroy Al Qaeda's terrorist training camps in the country was all but inevitable.

Yet President Bush also indicated that the country would go far beyond pursuing such limited goals. Declaring that "our war on terror begins with Al Qaeda, but it does not end there," the president explained that "our mission" was not merely to bring to justice the men and the groups that had attacked the country but also to "defend freedom" in a world where "freedom itself is under attack." This battle for freedom would be "civilization's fight," led by the United States. As it had so many times in the twentieth century, "the advance of human freedom" depended on America doing its duty by standing up to—and facing down—the forces of evil. In this struggle—both military and metaphysical—"the outcome is certain," since "freedom and fear, justice and cruelty, have always been at war, and we know that God is not neutral between them."

In choosing to cast the American response to the attacks in such broad, even spiritual, terms, the president showed how much he had already been influenced by the arguments of the many neoconservative intellectuals working in the White House, the Department of Defense, and the National Security Council. Long before September 11, the neocons had sought to construct a militaristic ideology of national mission. In an important essay from 1996, neocon writers William Kristol and Robert Kagan quoted John Quincy Adams's famous caution against Americans going abroad "in search of monsters to destroy," and they responded by asking, "But why not?" Unlike liberal humanitarians, who advocated the use of American military force abroad primarily in order to protect the victims of such monsters, Kristol and Kagan were much more concerned with how a stance of military assertiveness would affect the United States. Yet unlike foreign policy "realists," who developed strategies to maximize America's international interests, the neocons emphasized domestic considerations above all others. Failing to act against evil, they claimed, was a policy of "cowardice and dishonor," and as such it could not help but be morally degrading to the nation. A policy of aggressive military intervention to oppose tyranny and spread democracy, by contrast, would have morally beneficial results. Kristol and Kagan even went so far as to claim that "the remoralization of America at home ultimately requires the remoralization of American foreign policy." It was thus possible for the United States to reverse what the neocons considered to be the nation's moral decline while also benefiting the victims of unjust aggression around the globe. In the words of Kristol and Kagan, a militaristic-moralistic foreign policy would be "good for conservatives, good for America, and good for the world."[5]

Given their view of war as morally salutary, it was understandable that the neocons surrounding Kristol's *Weekly Standard* magazine (and its sister lobbying organization, the Project for the New American Century) supported Bill Clinton's military interventions in the Balkans during the late 1990s. Somewhat more surprising was their extraordinarily harsh attack on President Bush when, during his first few months in office, the new administration negotiated a peaceful resolution to a standoff with China after an American spy plane was forced to land by a Chinese fighter jet. The *Weekly Standard* editorial on Bush's handling of the standoff, titled "A National Humiliation," clearly implied that the new president should have been willing to go to war with a nuclear-armed nation of 1.2 billion citizens for the sake of saving face.[6] On the eve of September 11, the neocons showed every sign of craving military conflict, regardless of the cause or the cost.

With the startling late-summer attacks on New York and Washington, the neocons finally got their war—along with an administration shocked by events into an appreciation of acting boldly and thinking big. In his September 20 speech—with its highly spiritualized and moralized account of the attacks and the coming American response to them—President Bush indicated that from then on he would be taking his foreign policy cues from the neocons. That the speech was so well received—and especially that the president's audacious call to wage war in the name of "civilization" itself resonated with large segments of the country—was a sign that his earnest rhetoric touched something deep in the national psyche. As Andrew Sullivan wrote at the time, America's national myth includes the idea that the country exists as "the place apart, the city on the hill, the eternal elsewhere"—a place of safety and refuge from the bloodshed and suffering that mark so many pages of human history. Americans have always believed that "whatever horrors lay out there, there was always this place, where no external force could harm them, where no foreign threat could ever intrude." And the remarkable fact was that this myth had been reinforced and seemingly confirmed over the course of the twentieth century—decades during which the United States engaged in a series of wars and police actions around the globe without ever suffering "an attack on America itself—its soil, its cities, its land."[7] In these manifold conflicts, only the distant military outpost of Pearl Harbor ever experienced the horror of aerial bombardment. Through two world wars, the deadly skirmishes of the Cold War, and the grossly lopsided interventions of the 1990s, American civilians remained secure in their homeland, unscathed by the indiscriminate violence of modern warfare, untouched by the uniquely potent experience of existential threat that comes from living with the ever-present possibility of violent death at the hands of a powerful national enemy.

Until September 11, that is. In his address to the country nine days later, President Bush acknowledged and encouraged the national longing to right the wrong that had been done to America that morning—not just the particular wrong of the attacks on the World Trade Center and the Pentagon, but even more so the generalized assault on the country's sense of its own mythical invincibility. Hence the president's proposal to return the country to a state of absolute safety. Accomplishing that goal would take a monumental effort and a massive military campaign. Eviscerating the terrorist organization that had attacked the nation would be a necessary first step, but it would be far from sufficient. The coming "war on terror" would not end, the president told the country, "until every terrorist group of global reach has been found, stopped, and defeated." Months later, after the (partial) success of the war in Afghanistan, he would go on to add "rogue states" seeking to develop "weapons of mass destruction" to the list of enemies that would have to be defeated before the United States could once again feel secure. The "war on terror," then, would be no ordinary war; it would be a series of wars—a worldwide crusade with an indeterminate, even eschatological, end point. Providing moral and theological justification for such a war was a task for which the theocons were uniquely qualified.

America's War of Religion

When the staff of *First Things* gathered in early October to discuss how the magazine should respond to the traumatic events of September 11, Neuhaus indicated that he intended to go beyond even the president's sweeping conception of the war. As he leaned back in his chair, staring pensively into the distance and drawing slowly on his cigar, Neuhaus explained to his staff in a tone of grave authority that Samuel Huntington's controversial thesis about an impending "clash of civilizations" was America's surest guide to the coming years and decades of violent conflict with militant Islam.[8] The United States was the most powerful nation in the Christian West and the only one with sufficient self-confidence to lead a potentially victorious campaign against its enemies in the Muslim world—which was what the so-called "war on terror" was all about. Even if diplomatic considerations prevented the president from speaking truthfully about the civilizational scope of the struggle that awaited us, it was imperative that someone do so with intelligence and force. That, he asserted, would be a task for *First Things.*

In the lengthy unsigned editorial that he penned for the magazine, Neuhaus made it very clear that the theocons considered Bush's open-ended "war on terror" to be an obvious example of a "just war." And in the "Great Tradition of Christian thought," a "just war, although occasioned by evil, is not itself an evil; nor is it even, as it is commonly said today, a necessary evil." On the contrary, a just war is, for all of the suffering it may entail for combatants and civilian victims of collateral damage, an unambiguous good.[9] Hence, unlike the taking of life in abortion or stem-cell research, which is always an evil absolutely prohibited by the innate dignity of all human beings, killing in war is perfectly acceptable—even, once again, a positive good—provided that the war is just.[10]

Giving free reign to his populist convictions, Neuhaus praised the American people for their acuity in realizing that in the good war that awaits us "America must unapologetically take the lead." Indeed, the only people likely to "dissent from our national purpose in this war" were members of "our morally debilitated professoriat," who are "inveterate complexifiers, offering detailed analyses of the seven sides of four-sided questions while declaring their achingly superior sensitivities that make them too sensitive for decent company." "Ordinary Americans," by contrast, "view reality from the moral pinnacle of common sense," and they were unshakably convinced of the righteousness of the nation's cause.[11]

Having established to his satisfaction the justice of the war and the good sense of the American people, Neuhaus took a moment to comment on the positive domestic consequences of the terrorist attacks. Just as the neocons had taken to highlighting the social and moral benefits of military conflict, so Neuhaus noted that "in a time of grave testing, America has once again given public expression to the belief that we are 'one nation under God.' "[12] Pointing to the spontaneous display of American flags and the significant surge in church attendance in the days and weeks following the attacks, Neuhaus declared that the country was simply "giving public expression to what has been there all along in an overwhelmingly Christian nation." It was also significant, he claimed,

> that following the attack, the first gathering of national leadership and the first extended, and eloquent, address by the president was in a cathedral. And that Irving Berlin's "God Bless America" is getting equal time, at least, with the less religiously explicit national anthem. And that children in public schools gather in the classroom for prayer. And that the fallen beams of the World Trade Center, forming a cross, are blessed as the semi-official memorial to the victims.

All these and countless other signs of instinctive public religious expression revealed the "real America" for which "intellectuals are forever in search."[13] Challenged by tragedy, America had overcome its recent bout of self-indulgence and begun to reacquaint itself with its core theological convictions.

And such sobriety was essential if the United States hoped to muster the strength and resolve that would be needed to triumph in the coming conflict—a battle that, Neuhaus asserted, could be defined in many ways, but was "also and inescapably a war of religion."[14] In the weeks following the attacks, Andrew Sullivan, too, had suggested that the war on terror should be understood as a religious war, albeit one that pitted Western secular modernity against the atavistic, antimodern form of faith currently fighting for dominance in the Islamic world.[15] But Neuhaus refused to accept Sullivan's secular description of the West. Taking his cues, instead, from the way that Muslims typically view Europe and America, he claimed that when they "speak of the West, they mean the Christian West. They mean Christendom." And in doing so, Muslims demonstrated that they understood us better than we often understood ourselves. "Many in the West want to believe that ours is a secularized culture," but, in fact, most Muslims rightly view secularization itself "as a form of specifically Christian decadence." One positive domestic consequence of the coming war might therefore be a growing recognition that "we are . . . who they think we are, namely, the Christian West," fighting a just, unambiguously good religious war in the name of Christian civilization against its mortal enemies.[16]

Just Wars

In describing the conflict in these morally charged terms, Neuhaus built on a distinctive theocon approach to dealing with questions of war and peace going back nearly twenty years. Until the mid-1980s, the theocons were nearly indistinguishable from the neocons when it came to questions of foreign policy. Both groups of writers emphasized the need for America to regain its confidence after the demoralizing experience of defeat in Vietnam, and both also supported Ronald Reagan's policy of aggressive confrontation with the Soviet Union.[17] It was not until 1983 that the theocons first began to develop a unique approach to international relations. That was the year in which the American Catholic bishops released their pastoral letter *The Challenge of Peace,* which denounced the recently reinvigorated arms race in blunt and uncompromising terms. Michael Novak was so outraged by the statement that he responded with a lengthy letter of his own, "Moral Clarity in the Nuclear Age." First published in the small Catholic magazine he had recently founded with Notre Dame professor Ralph McInerny (*Catholicism in Crisis*),[18] Novak's essay so impressed William F. Buckley that he offered to reprint it in *National Review*, where it filled the entire issue of April 1, 1983. Later that year it was published yet again, this time as a book with an introduction by Buckley and a foreword by Billy Graham.[19]

Compared to the outlook of the Catholic conservatives surrounding Buckley's magazine in the 1950s—men who advocated the "rollback" of the Soviet Union and viewed the Cold War in explicitly religious terms—Novak's essay was a model of moderation.[20] Novak patiently reminded his readers of the two main categories of principles in classical "just war" reasoning: those governing when it is just to declare war, and those dealing with how war should be conducted once it is declared. In order to be considered just, a war had to be defensive. It had to be aimed at protecting the innocent against unjust aggression. It had to be undertaken with the intention of establishing a just peace and with a reasonable chance of success. It had to be declared and waged by a competent governing authority. And it had to be undertaken as a last resort. As for the rules of conduct within a war, they mandated that no more force than is necessary be used to vindicate the cause (proportionality) and that there be no intentional killing of innocent civilians (noncombatant immunity). In their pastoral letter, the bishops had argued that in an age when each superpower believed it could prevent its own defeat in a conflict by employing nuclear weapons—weapons that were wildly out of proportion to any cause and that would indiscriminately incinerate combatants and noncombatants alike, perhaps on a global scale—the concept of a "just war" had been rendered obsolete and the arms race profoundly immoral. In response, Novak argued that Cold War tensions had to be viewed in a moral context highlighting the Soviet Union's aggressive aims and its threat to humanity and freedom around the world. Given this context, a policy of deterrence—pursued with the intent to prevent either side from using nuclear weapons—was the least of the available evils.[21]

The theocons' most ambitious attempt to transform Novak's essay into a distinct doctrine of international relations came four years
later. On one level, George Weigel's magisterial *Tranquillitas Ordinis
[The Peace of Order]: The Present Failure and Future Promise of American Catholic Thought on War and Peace* (1987) was an angry polemic
against the Catholic bishops for abandoning the "just war" tradition
of the church in favor of what the author considered to be naïve pacifism and generically leftist anti-anticommunism. On another, more
edifying level, Weigel sought to recover and defend the importance of
the fifteen-hundred-year-old Catholic "just war" tradition—from St.
Augustine to John Courtney Murray—for crafting a foreign policy
firmly rooted in moral principle.[22] But the most noteworthy and original aspect of the book was its attempt to bestow the moral authority
of Catholicism on the foreign policy of the Reagan administration. In
Weigel's hands, supposedly disinterested "just war" theorizing managed to justify American policy vis-à-vis the Soviet Union during the
1980s in nearly every respect, including the administration's controversial interventions in Latin America.[23] Over the coming years,
Weigel and the other theocons would show time and time again that
this was precisely what they considered to be the most important contribution of the Catholic "just war" tradition to contemporary American politics—providing moral and theological imprimatur for the
foreign policies of successive Republican presidents.

This became abundantly clear in the debate surrounding the
1991 Gulf War, which Neuhaus, Weigel, and Novak all strongly endorsed and worked to defend in the media.[24] As the war commenced,
Weigel took to the pages of *First Things* to praise the administration
of George H. W. Bush for having done such an impressive job of justifying the war in terms derived from the "just war" tradition. Those
efforts confirmed that "the just war tradition was alive and well in the
American body politic."[25] In the tradition's true home, the churches,
the situation was far less encouraging, however. While the Bush administration had demonstrated its moral seriousness and sophistica-

tion, the Protestant mainline and the Catholic bishops had showed in their opposition to the war that they now embraced a "functional pacifism rooted . . . in a profound alienation from the American experiment and in a deep conviction that American power cannot serve good ends in the world."[26] In contrast, then, to Republican Party politicians, the churches had rendered themselves "utterly irrelevant to the public moral argument about the right ordering of our society and the definition of its role in the world."[27] This distinctive theocon approach to "just war" reasoning—ridiculing antiwar clerics for having forgotten the Catholic tradition and praising Republican administrations for keeping it alive—would be expanded and deployed with greater ferocity than ever before in the build-up to the second "war in the Gulf," the 2003 war to topple the government of Saddam Hussein.

ON TO BAGHDAD

Around the time of the January 2002 State of the Union speech— when President Bush broadened still further the scope of the "war on terror" to include an "axis of evil" consisting of Iraq, Iran, and North Korea—the mood on the American right began to grow fierce. What had been a uniform chorus of patriotic support for the president and the Afghanistan campaign quickly evolved into a frenzy of bellicosity. Some columnists denounced deterrence and stability in favor of unilateral preemptive war to overthrow hostile regimes.[28] Others openly advocated American imperialism.[29] Still others proposed that the United States act to topple the governments of a series of sovereign nations in the Muslim Middle East, including Iraq, Iran, Syria, Lebanon, Egypt, and Saudi Arabia.[30] And these were the intellectually respectable suggestions, published in mainstream newspapers and long-established journals of opinion. Farther down the media hierarchy, on cable news, Internet websites, and Web blogs, conservatives of all stripes closed ranks, unleashing a verbal barrage on any and all who dissented from a united front in favor of unapologetic American military muscle. The participants in this endless pep rally were insistent on open-ended war, overtly hostile to dissent, and thoroughly unforgiving of the slightest criticism of the United States abroad. They were dismissive of complication and analysis, defensive by default, worshipful of "manliness," admiring of swaggering bluntness, contemptuous of doubt and indecision, addicted to hyperbole, eager to expose "appeasement," and prone to paranoia. Self-congratulation and self-righteousness ruled the day.

The theocons contributed to this atmosphere of prowar hysteria in predictable ways. Neuhaus established himself as the rare priest who would grant interviews to National Public Radio in order to defend the justice of invading Iraq. Weigel spoke on college campuses about the administration's firm grasp of the "just war" tradition. And Novak traveled to Rome to lecture Vatican bureaucrats on the importance of deposing Saddam Hussein and transforming Iraq into a democratic oasis in the Middle East. But by far the most significant theocon statement on the invasion of Iraq was Weigel's "Moral Clarity in a Time of War," which he delivered as a lecture in the fall of 2002 at Washington's Ethics and Public Policy Center and at the Catholic University of America Law School before publishing it as a lengthy essay in the January 2003 issue of *First Things*. Although he would later deny it, the essay was clearly written to provide moral and theological justification for the Bush administration's Iraq policy in every one of its details.[31]

Weigel's case for war ran as follows.[32] In the post–September 11 world, the "peace of order" among nations is fundamentally threatened by international terrorist organizations and rogue states that traffic in weapons of mass destruction. In an ideal world, the United Nations would possess the means and the will to deal with these threats through the use of coercive military force. But, alas, the UN is deficient in both means and will. Luckily, the United States possesses both in abundance, just as it recognizes the unique responsibility for maintaining global order that flows from its status as the world's preeminent military power. America thus has the solemn duty to act as the worldwide enforcer of international justice—including the punishment of those who flout the peace of order—regardless of whether the other nations of the world recognize the legitimacy of such action. In serving as providentially appointed prosecutor, judge, jury, and executioner of international justice around the world, the United States furthers its own good (at home and abroad) as well as the good of all decent human beings on the planet. The unilateral overthrow of the government of Saddam Hussein is one example of such righteous American action, but it is hardly the only likely or defensible one to take place in the near future.

When Weigel provided the Bush administration with this moral and theological go-ahead for unilateral war with Iraq (as well as with many other rogue states around the world), he was well aware that most religious leaders and a great many public intellectuals both in the United States and abroad did not share his assessment of the situation. Based on any number of considerations—suspicion about administration evidence of the Iraqi threat, a desire to allow UN inspectors to complete their work, fear that an invasion would spark a regional conflagration, doubts about America's ability to manage an occupation and transition to a decent and stable post-Hussein political order—these writers had concluded that the coming invasion would fall far short of meeting the standards for a just war.

In response to such critics, Weigel insisted that the question of whether the war was just had to be bracketed off from the question of whether it was wise—and that the second question could only be answered by the political powers-that-be, who had access to privileged information and intelligence not possessed by private citizens. Going further, Weigel suggested that statesmen reached their final decision for war through the exercise of a "charism of political discernment" enjoyed by all "duly constituted public authorities." This charism—or gift of the holy spirit—is "not shared by bishops, stated clerks, rabbis, imams, or ecumenical and interreligious agencies"—all of whom should exercise "a measure of political modesty" in addressing questions of war and peace.[33] (Nowhere did Weigel indicate that modesty was a quality required of politicians and their foreign policy advisors.) It was difficult to read these words without concluding that the theocon message to critics of the administration's foreign policy was to keep their mouths shut and put their faith in the divinely inspired wisdom of the president of the United States.

Without expanding on Weigel's speculations about special political charisms, Neuhaus amplified his friend's point four months later, in an essay written just as the American invasion of Iraq began. On the one hand, Neuhaus had considerable "confidence in those responsible for making the relevant decisions" in the Bush administration. On the other hand, he viewed the many antiwar statements of church leaders, and especially those emanating from the Vatican, with "disappointment, and more than a little embarrassment."[34] As far as Neuhaus was concerned, the lesson to be drawn from the whole sorry episode was obvious:

> Ranking ecclesiastics took the time of U.S. decision-makers, badgering them about whether they had thought of this possible consequence or that. . . . The simple truth is that such consequences are unknowable and therefore unknown, except to God. I know that possible consequences have been considered, day and night for many months, by competent parties. . . . Religious leaders should bring more to the discussion than their fears. Nervous hand-wringing is not a moral argument.[35]

As American troops began their march to Baghdad, the theocons made it clear that the moral duty of religious leaders was to stop "badgering" the administration so that it could get on with waging its unquestionably just war to disarm Saddam Hussein.[36]

AFTER VICTORY

As the Iraq war got under way on March 20, 2003, Neuhaus grew no-
ticeably tense. On the Monday following the start of the invasion—
after a weekend during which millions of Americans entertained
themselves by watching U.S. missiles flatten the Baghdad skyline
while "embedded" television reporters swooned over their up-close-
and-personal views of the country's military machine in action—
Neuhaus appeared preoccupied but pleased. Quietly discussing the
progress of the war on the phone with Weigel, who conveyed inside
information from friends and allies in the administration, Neuhaus
felt reassured about his decision to support the war so emphatically.
Yet his underlying uncertainty and stress rushed to the surface as he
skimmed through a powerful antiwar essay by historian Tony Judt in
the *New York Review of Books*. In Judt's view, the United States under
George W. Bush was driven by "an eschatological urge to tear down a
frustrating international order," all the while exaggerating the threats
to its power and underestimating the risks of acting recklessly in the
world.[37] Reading these words, Neuhaus exploded in anger, lashing out
in acidic sarcasm at the suggestion that the president had acted out of
any motive besides his duty to protect the innocent against Iraqi aggression. As far as Neuhaus was concerned, Judt was just another
smug liberal, failing to acknowledge and appreciate America's obligation as the world's preeminent power to punish injustice and maintain order around the globe, regardless of worldwide public opinion.

Over the next few weeks, as the American invasion continued its
press toward Baghdad, Neuhaus's temper would flare again and again,
sparked by what he viewed as the defeatist coverage of the war in the
New York Times. The *Times* had been a constant source of annoyance,
and an inspiration for several snide remarks in nearly every one of his
monthly magazine columns, for many years. Not only was its influence unmatched by any other media outlet, but its reporting and ed-

itorial outlook perfectly expressed the elitist, secularist ideology that his own movement had been conjured to oppose. But now, perhaps egged on by several right-wing websites that had made a habit of accusing the paper of treason on a daily basis, he insisted that the bias in the *Times*'s coverage of the war was unprecedented. Each day Neuhaus entered the *First Things* office in a foul mood, threatening to cancel his subscription to the paper and fuming about the latest front-page story to imply that the war was already on the verge of becoming a quagmire: "Two weeks in and they're already calling it Vietnam!" For personal as well as political reasons, Neuhaus considered it indefensible to draw even the most casual comparison between the invasion of Iraq and America's ill-fated war in Southeast Asia.

These outbursts would stop very soon, replaced by pride and satisfaction as American troops entered Baghdad in early April nearly without a fight. Within days, Neuhaus's mood swung from defensive to euphoric, eventually leading him to give in to the temptation to gloat. At the May meeting of the *First Things* editorial board, just days after President Bush declared "mission accomplished" from the deck of an aircraft carrier, Neuhaus and Weigel invariably spoke of the war in the past tense and expressed open admiration for the manifest skill of the Bush administration in waging such an overwhelmingly successful military campaign. When questioned by a skeptical participant in the meeting about whether it was sensible for the nation's leaders to continue to craft policy under the assumption that all goods—the good of the United States at home and abroad, the good of the Iraqi people, the good of Israel, the good of Europe, and the good of the entire world—were compatible with one another, Neuhaus tersely replied that "it may very well be God's will that all good things *do* go together at this moment in history."

Adopting a similarly triumphant tone in his column for the August/September issue of *First Things*, Neuhaus confidently asserted that critics of the war had been "abysmally wrong on almost every point"—a fact that needed to be "clearly established on the public record" so that their concerns could be easily dismissed in the run-up to whatever military campaign might follow the liberation of Iraq. That American troops had thus far failed to find stockpiles of weapons of mass destruction was, he admitted, "troubling." Yet this (temporary) failure did not for a moment raise "questions about the liberation of Iraq." On the contrary, the invasion had been so successful—above all in combining military potency with precision targeting of weapons, thus keeping civilian casualties to a minimum—that the time had come to rethink a crucial aspect of the "just war" tradition. In future conflicts, Neuhaus suggested, it might become possible to conceive of "military action in terms not of the last resort but of the best resort."[38]

Neuhaus would not mention Iraq again in the pages of the magazine for over a year, as the hunt for chemical, biological, and nuclear weapons dragged on and conditions under the American occupation at first failed to improve and then began to deteriorate. It took many months for Neuhaus and the other theocons to acknowledge the truth of the situation, even in private. By this point, they were relying almost entirely on conservative opinion journals, editorial pages, and White House memoranda for their information, and these sources naturally went out of their way to highlight the little good news emerging from Iraq while attributing the seemingly endless stream of bad news in the mainstream media to liberal bias.

As the months passed and the number of insurgent attacks on American forces and Iraqi civilians multiplied, theocon confidence began to waver. Yet there was little the theocons thought they could do about the situation. Bush was heading into an election year, and they still considered the administration's domestic agenda to be far more crucial to their plans than the progress of the war; criticism of the president or members of his cabinet, which would only weaken him politically and antagonize theocon contacts in the White House, was therefore unthinkable. Although Neuhaus's spirits were buoyed after a May 2004 meeting at the White House, during which the president appeared calm and confident about the situation in Iraq, the effect was temporary.[39]

Over the next six months, as conditions in Iraq continued to worsen and the president ran a tight race for reelection against Democrat John Kerry, Neuhaus expressed public exasperation with the Bush administration only once—in response to stories of torture and abuse of detainees at the American-run Abu Ghraib prison outside Baghdad. Yes, he admitted to his fellow conservatives, much of the worldwide criticism of the United States in the wake of the torture scandal had been "motivated by opposition to American policy or generalized America-bashing." But the fact was that the United States had provided these critics with everything they needed to make the country look bad. Taking a strong stand against the abuse, Neuhaus declared flatly that torture was "never morally permissible" and that "we dare not trust ourselves to torture," which should be forbidden "absolutely."[40] Strangely, though, Neuhaus made a point of stepping back from this position five months later, several weeks after Bush had been safely reelected to a second term in office. Assuring his readers that he still believed that "we dare not trust ourselves to torture," he now "acknowledged" that such a stance was not "sufficient."[41] Whether his change of heart had come about through independent reflection or the influence of powerful friends who had taken offense at his criticism of the Bush administration was something about which readers were left to speculate.[42]

Other than his harsh words about Abu Ghraib in the October issue of First Things, Neuhaus and the other theocons kept silent about conditions in Iraq through the summer and fall of 2004. By late summer this silence had inspired one First Things reader—a program coordinator for the Mennonite Central Committee named Peter Dula—to pen a lengthy missive attacking the journal for its refusal to revise its prewar position in light of subsequent events. Writing from Jordan after having spent several months in postinvasion Baghdad, Dula understood that it was unlikely that the magazine would publish his criticisms, yet he submitted his essay nonetheless, perhaps in hopes that it might have some influence on Neuhaus's and Weigel's thinking. In the version of the essay eventually published as a cover story in the December 3, 2004, issue of *Commonweal* magazine, Dula accused the theocons of having gone out of their way to provide theological and moral justification for the administration's plans for Iraq—and then of succumbing to "moral muteness in a time of war." It was as if the theocons had given the president a green light and then neglected to acknowledge that doing so had led directly to a fatal multicar collision. As for the question of whether or not theocon claims for the justice of the war had been vindicated in light of events since the fall of Baghdad, Dula left no doubt where he stood: "The absence of weapons of mass destruction and the absence of compelling evidence of a link with Al Qaeda mean there was no just cause for this war." Moreover, "the incompetence and duplicity of the current administration mean that there was no competent authority for this war."[43] And no such war—one lacking a just cause and one waged by an incompetent authority—could be considered just.

Neuhaus never seriously entertained the possibility of publishing this attack on Weigel and himself (and the Bush administration). Yet behind the scenes, Dula's accusations struck a nerve, eventually inspiring Neuhaus to write an essay of his own in which he attempted to defend himself against the indictment. Published in the December issue of *First Things*, safely after the presidential election, the essay inadvertently illustrated the dangers of making moral judgments in a condition of self-imposed ignorance of the facts. Writing days after the release of the final report on Saddam Hussein's weapons programs by Charles Duelfer and the Iraq Study Group, Neuhaus chose to base his analysis not on the report itself but instead on a heavily redacted and deceptively interpreted version that had been provided to him by Karl Rove's White House deputy, Peter Wehner. Whereas the published report definitively showed that at the time of the invasion Iraq possessed no weapons of mass destruction (having destroyed them, as required by UN Security Council resolutions, many years earlier) and no active program to develop such weapons, Neuhaus nevertheless claimed to be convinced that "Saddam had the intention and, if America had dallied or left it to the UN, would have had the weaponry to dominate the Middle East and, in collusion with terrorist networks, inflict massive damage on America and the West."[44]

From this and several other statements in the essay, it appeared that Neuhaus had decided to reaffirm his prewar position—namely, that the "just cause" of the invasion was the attempt to disarm the profoundly dangerous regime of Saddam Hussein. That no weapons were ever found did nothing to undermine the justice of this cause, he claimed, since "leaders do not have the convenience of making decisions retrospectively," and the belief that Iraq possessed such weapons was thoroughly justified "on the basis of what was known" before the war.[45] With this assertion, Neuhaus chose to ignore the numerous postinvasion press reports that had uncovered the alarming extent to which Bush administration officials, along with a compliant media, had deliberately distorted intelligence in the run-up to the war, claiming that the administration knew far more than it did and greatly exaggerating the threat posed by Iraq, at every opportunity.[46] Far from seeking to undermine the invasion, as Neuhaus and other conservatives believed at the time, the *New York Times* and other mainstream news organizations had published several prominent stories that hyped administration claims (many of which later turned out to be false) without seeking independent confirmation of any kind.[47]

And these media outlets were far from being the only ones to create and perpetuate the illusion that the administration possessed greater knowledge of Saddam's weapons capabilities than it did. The theocons themselves had contributed to fostering the illusion, too—in their insistence on deferring to the "charism of political discernment" supposedly possessed by the president. As Anglican Archbishop Rowan Williams put it in an essay critical of theocon arguments in fa-

vor of the war, Weigel's extreme deference to governmental competence and authority encouraged a "weakening of . . . the self-critical
habit in [the] nation and its political classes." Williams went on to
point out that a country benefits when "lawyers, NGOs, linguists, an-
thropologists, religious communities, journalists, strategists, [and]
military and diplomatic historians" are encouraged to share what they
know with political leaders and their advisors—and when those leaders and advisors remain open-minded enough to listen to and learn
from the advice.[48] Yet the Bush administration took the diametrically
opposite approach, trumpeting its contempt for the "reality-based
community" and deliberately closing itself off from dissenting opinions.[49] And the theocons had treated such empty self-assurance as the
better part of wisdom.

As if tacitly acknowledging how unconvincing his argument
would appear to informed readers, Neuhaus did not simply reiterate
his prewar case for the invasion but actually added to it. Following
the lead of President Bush, whose defense of the war had similarly
evolved in the eighteen months since he prematurely announced the
end of major combat operations, Neuhaus now claimed that "success
in Iraq" followed not merely from disarmament but also from "having removed the regime of Saddam Hussein, thus ending the monstrous rule of a systematic perpetrator of crimes against humanity."[50]
Contrary to Dula's allegations, then, there was still a just cause for the
war, even though Hussein's weapons of mass destruction had proven
to be an imaginary threat. In shifting from one justification to another, however, Neuhaus unintentionally highlighted the disturbing
flexibility of the "just war" tradition, which now appeared to be quite
capable of sanctifying a remarkably wide range of conflicts.

Neuhaus's essay contained other noteworthy claims—among them
the denial that America's postwar policies in Iraq had been an "unmit-
igated disaster," which Dula and other critics had used to demonstrate
that President Bush was an "incompetent authority." Distancing

himself from his own role in advocating for the war, as well as refusing to render even the slightest judgment of the Bush administration's handling of the aftermath of the invasion, Neuhaus now insisted that "those who condemn the war because soldiers and innocent civilians are killed and maimed are not being serious. This is what happens in war, and is a very good reason for avoiding war."[51]

But perhaps the most extraordinary passage in the essay concerned President Bush's plan to use the American invasion and occupation to transform Iraq into a democracy that could then be exported to the rest of the Middle East—an aim that promised to serve as yet another retroactive justification for the war. Neuhaus expressed some skepticism about Bush's democratization project, wondering if it made sense to set the standard for success in Iraq quite so high. It would be far more prudent, he suggested, to judge success in Iraq by whether or not, "three or thirty years from now," Iraqis lived under a "reasonably decent and stable government."[52] Given the importance in the "just war" tradition of precisely defining the anticipated end point to military actions and intentions, this twenty-seven-year-long window for determining success was more than a little peculiar.

All told, Neuhaus's self-defense proved less than convincing. But by the time the essay appeared in print, it hardly mattered. By this point—with Bush about to begin his second term in office—the theocons had long ago traded in any intellectual respectability they once possessed on matters of war and peace for the opportunity to serve at the pleasure of the president. It was thus hardly surprising that, despite his published reservations about Bush's plans to democratize the Middle East, Neuhaus responded enthusiastically to the president's astonishingly ambitious second inaugural address, which committed the United States to the goal of "ending tyranny in our world."[53] Just minutes after the conclusion of the speech, Neuhaus received a call from Weigel, who was thrilled that some of the lines he had proposed to the president's speechwriting team had made it into the address. As for Neuhaus, savoring the moment and dreaming of the next four years with his friend and ally on the phone from Washington, he gave every appearance of being a man supremely satisfied.[54]

THE NEXT FRONT

With well over a hundred thousand American troops bogged down in Iraq, it was clear that, however loftily the president had spoken in his second inaugural address, neocon dreams of toppling governments from Cairo to Tehran were exceedingly unlikely to be fulfilled anytime soon. In Bush's second term, the worldwide "war on terror" (as opposed to the quite distinct and all-too-real war in Iraq) would increasingly come to be viewed as a metaphorical and rhetorical war, waged for the most part by intelligence services and police forces within sovereign nations. Unless another terrorist attack were traced directly to a nation-state—as the September 11 attacks had been linked to Afghanistan—there would be no new invasions and occupations in America's immediate future.

Which is not to say that the theocons were willing to abandon the ideological ambitions they had identified with (or projected onto) the war effort back in 2001. In their view, Christian America was embroiled in a long-term civilizational struggle with militant Islam, whether or not that struggle took an explicitly military form in its every phase. While the military component of the conflict dragged on in Iraq and, to a somewhat lesser extent, in Afghanistan, the United States needed to keep on the lookout for additional threats around the globe, opening other (nonmilitary) fronts in its battle with the Muslim world, whenever and wherever such actions were required. In what was perhaps the most original theocon contribution to thinking about the war, Weigel suggested that victory in the "war on terror" depended on the United States opening just such a "cold" front with our putative allies in continental Europe.

Hostility toward Europe, and especially France, was widespread in the United States during the months surrounding the start of the

Iraq war, especially on the right. Staunch French and German opposition to the American invasion provoked talk-radio personalities into
spasms of vituperation. One right-wing pundit (*National Review Online*'s Jonah Goldberg) dubbed the entire French nation "cheese-
eating surrender monkeys," while a conservative newspaper (Rupert
Murdoch's *New York Post*) took to describing the European members
of the UN Security Council who opposed the American push for war
in Iraq as the "Axis of Weasels." And in a historic act of national
pique, the U.S. Congress even went so far as to change the name of
French fries to "freedom fries" on the menu of the congressional cafe-
teria. Weigel shared his fellow conservatives' disgust at what was
widely thought to be European treachery, as well as their conviction
that recent tensions had nothing whatsoever to do with the actions of
the United States under President Bush and were instead the outgrowth of a distinctly "European problem." In typical theocon fashion, though, Weigel sought to examine this problem in the broadest
possible terms—that is, in "moral and cultural terms."[55]

In the *First Things* essay in which he first examined the European
threat to America, Weigel proposed to answer a dizzying array of
questions in just over six thousand words. Why were Europeans inclined to believe the "fiction" that the Kyoto Protocol on global
warming "would be observed by the nations that signed it"? Why
were European countries putting off "hard domestic political decisions" about the long-term viability of funding their welfare states?
Why had the leadership of the European Union failed to make reference to Europe's Christian heritage in its draft constitution? Why had
voters in Spain given "a de facto victory to appeasement in their
March 2004 elections" by voting against the party of the pro–Iraq
War José María Aznar, just days after a devastating terrorist attack on
a series of Madrid commuter trains? Why were European birthrates
so low, threatening the greatest continent-wide depopulation since
the Black Death of the fourteenth century? And then there was the
most far-reaching and deeply disturbing question of all: Why did

twentieth-century Europe produce "two world wars, three totalitarian systems, a Cold War threatening global catastrophe, oceans of blood, mountains of corpses, Auschwitz and the Gulag?"[56]

It was an extraordinarily wide range of questions, touching on very different problems with origins or causes in very different areas of European social life and history. Some questions were merely polemical, reflecting Weigel's transparently partisan agenda (Kyoto, the Spanish vote). Others were worth exploring but could be better understood in political and economic terms than moral and cultural ones (welfare state funding). Still others were important and clearly grew out of moral and cultural trends but were also extremely complicated, varying greatly from country to country and region to region (declining birthrates, religion in the EU constitution).[57] As for the final question, it was not only so broad that it bordered on the metaphysical, but it also pushed in the opposite direction from several of the previous questions. Weigel seemed to be looking for a single cause to explain why Europe had descended into an unprecedented orgy of violence in the first half of the twentieth century *and* why it was now so hesitant to take up arms—why it once gave birth to ideologies that inspired nations to pursue worldwide domination *and* why this delusional self-confidence had been replaced in our time by self-doubt so pathological that it was leading those same nations to commit "demographic suicide."[58]

Not only did Weigel propose a single comprehensive answer to this contradictory series of questions, but the answer was so simple that it could be easily compressed into a single sentence. In Weigel's view, "Europe's problem" was caused by a "profound, longstanding crisis in civilizational morale" that derived, in turn, from the ideology of "atheistic humanism," which had dominated the continent for the past century. Weigel maintained, in other words, that Europe was undergoing moral and cultural collapse—and that the collapse was the direct result of the fact that its citizens no longer believed in God. Quoting Catholic historian Christopher Dawson, Weigel insisted that contemporary Europe vividly demonstrated that "a secular society . . . is a monstrosity—a cancerous growth which will ultimately destroy itself."[59] This was the fate that the continent was fulfilling with its staggeringly low birthrates, which could eventually lead to the death of European civilization.[60] And also like cancer, European secularism threatened to metastasize around the globe, endangering the worldwide democratic project, from Central and Eastern Europe to Latin America, Asia, Canada, and even the United States, where the influence of European ideas could be seen in the 2003 Supreme Court decision *Lawrence v. Texas*, which struck down laws against sodomy on the basis of a "redefinition of freedom as personal willfulness."[61] An America ravaged by the cancer of European secularism would, like the Europe of today, lack the strength and the will needed to defend itself against, and ultimately triumph over, its fervently religious Muslim enemies.

Equally threatening, Europe's demographic collapse, combined with extremely high rates of Muslim immigration, meant that by the end of the twenty-first century the continent itself might very well be overtaken by Islam:

> Europe's current demographic trendlines could eventually produce a Europe in which Sobieski's victory at Vienna in 1683 [against the Ottoman Empire] is reversed, such that the Europe of the twenty-second century, or even the late twenty-first, is a Europe increasingly influenced, and perhaps even dominated, by radicalized Islamic populations, convinced that their long-delayed triumph in the European heartland is at hand.

Refusing to embrace and defend their Christian heritage and identity, unwilling to produce children who could keep the continent from being overrun by Muslim hordes, Europeans appeared to be well on their way to preparing a decisive victory for the enemies of the Christian West, and above all for the enemies of its military and cultural champion, Christian America. Recent trends in Europe thus posed several profound threats to the United States—threats to which the nation needed to respond with utmost urgency.

Weigel's proposed solution to America's European problem was perfectly predictable—merely an expansion of the domestic culture war to international relations—though this international dimension made it novel and uniquely disconcerting. In Weigel's view, Europe's only hope for survival was a "revitalization" of its "Christian roots and the rebirth of Christian conviction," leading to "something like a Great Awakening"—a "rebirth of life-transforming and culture-forming Christian conviction, especially Catholic conviction." And in fostering this rebirth of European Catholic-Christian religiosity, the United States had to play a decisive role. American public diplomacy, especially through its continental embassies, needed to engage European media, universities, research institutes, and voluntary organizations—all for the sake of challenging the hegemony of secularism in European culture. These efforts, which deserved to be "generously funded," might even require the founding of theocon versions of the Congress for Cultural Freedom and *Encounter*—the organization and journal established by the American government, and funded by the CIA, for the sake of defending anti-Communism in Europe during the early years of the Cold War.[62] In making this proposal, Weigel did not for a moment ponder the domestic or international implications of the United States taking on the role of a Christian missionary.

Leaving aside the numerous domestic obstacles to enacting such a policy, it is safe to say that none of Weigel's proposals to encourage a rebirth of Catholic-Christian piety in Europe would have any chance of changing the cultural outlook of the continent. For many Europeans, after all, it was precisely the religious quality of President Bush's rhetoric and self-presentation that had led to recent tensions with the United States. Having lived with the reality of vibrant public religiosity for well over a millennium—and having spent the better part of its bloody history since the sixteenth century attempting to find a humane alternative to it—Europeans were unlikely to seek the solution to their (real, though hardly fatal) problems in a return to the church.[63]

In America, however, the prospects for the expansion of public religiosity were far brighter. Guided by theoconservative ideas, empowered by a theoconservative electoral coalition, aided (since the 2002 midterm elections) by Republican majorities in both houses of Congress, the president of the United States had every intention of enacting a theoconservative agenda at home. Abortion and gay rights, stem-cell research and the right to die, sex education and the teaching of evolution in public schools, the power of the courts and the place of God in government—on these and a host of related issues touching on nearly every aspect of life and death, the theocons were on the march, leading a populist revolt against the rule of secularism in American public life, regardless of what transpired in the country's relations with the rest of the world. It was on the all-important domestic front that theocon ambitions would face their greatest test.

$=$ 5 $=$

THEOCON NATION

P RESIDENT GEORGE W. BUSH began to reward the theocons
for their support within hours of his inauguration. It took just
two days for him to issue an executive order banning government
funding of foreign organizations that perform legal abortions or provide information to the public about the availability of abortions.
Even after the September 11 attacks—when the administration's attention was diverted to seemingly more pressing issues of foreign policy, war, and homeland security—the president pushed the theocon
agenda wherever possible.

In 2002 the administration blocked $34 million in congression-
ally approved funding for the UN Population Fund on the grounds
that it encourages the practice of abortion in the developing world.
The Department of Education came out in support of "abstinence
only" sex education in public schools, barring discussion of condoms
and other forms of contraception, beyond pointing out the ways that
they can fail. The Food and Drug Administration—stocked with pro-
life presidential appointees—repeatedly refused to approve the so-

called "morning-after pill" (RU-486) for over-the-counter sales. The Federal Communications Commission began to levy massive fines against television and radio stations that broadcast "indecent" material. And perhaps most remarkable of all, there was the president's "faith-based initiative," which by 2004 had established offices in ten federal agencies and, under the direction of a centralized White House Office of Faith-Based and Community Initiatives, had begun to award $2 billion annually in federal grants directly to churches and other religious organizations.[1] Taken together, these policies were a vivid sign of theocon power and influence in George Bush's Washington.

For those opposed to the theocon project, these policies have inspired justified concern—about the influence of the religious right on the Republican Party, about the place of conservative evangelicals and Catholics in the nation's politics, and about the conservative drift of the country as a whole. Yet these were among the least troubling of the many theoconservative initiatives to emerge from President Bush's first term in office. The imposition of the so-called "global gag rule" against funding organizations that practice or promote abortion, for example, has been a matter of presidential prerogative since Ronald Reagan first imposed it in 1984 as part of his effort to drum up support among evangelicals for his reelection campaign. The rule was upheld by George H. W. Bush, overturned by Bill Clinton, and has now been reinstated by George W. Bush. And there is every reason to believe that the pattern will continue into the future—with Republicans imposing and Democrats lifting this relatively minor regulation on federal financing of abortion. The same holds for many other controversial theocon policies, which depend upon the presence of a champion in the Oval Office for their implementation and enforcement.

Far more alarming have been the theocons' efforts to spread their ideology beyond the executive branch of the federal government into Congress, the judiciary, state legislatures, the churches, and even the Constitution itself. Between 2001 and 2004, the president and his allies on the religious right made several attempts to guarantee that the unprecedented political power enjoyed by the theocons under the current administration produced long-lasting political and cultural gains. Some of these attempts—like the push to appoint staunchly conservative judges to the federal courts—have been widely reported and analyzed in the mainstream press. Others have been largely ignored. In the first of these efforts, theocon Hadley Arkes authored legislation—the Born-Alive Infants Protection Act, which Congress passed and President Bush signed into law in 2002—designed to "plant prolife premises" in the legal culture of the nation, thereby starting a process that the theocons believed would ultimately lead to the revocation or radical constriction of abortion rights. Second, Bush sought to change the terms of bioethical debate in the country by appointing theocon ally Leon Kass to chair a new President's Council on Bioethics—an advisory board that would soon be dominated by theocons and theocon sympathizers.

Third, Richard John Neuhaus and several of his colleagues urged President Bush to endorse an amendment to the U.S. Constitution (coauthored by theocons Robert P. George of Princeton University and Gerard V. Bradley of the University of Notre Dame) that would ban same-sex marriage. The president followed their advice and made his support for the amendment a centerpiece of his campaign for reelection—a strategy that not only contributed to the president's victory at the polls but also helped to inspire broad passage of anti-gay-marriage initiatives in twelve states throughout the country during the 2004 election cycle. Finally, Neuhaus (with the help of Joseph Cardinal Ratzinger, now Pope Benedict XVI) encouraged his allies in the U.S. Conference of Catholic Bishops to deny the sacrament of Communion to presidential candidate John Kerry and other pro-choice Catholic Democrats. It was the theocons' boldest attempt yet in their decades-long effort to persuade American Catholics to cut their historic ties to the Democratic Party and embrace a right-wing Republican agenda in its place. All these initiatives were designed to ensure that progress made in advancing the theocon agenda under George W. Bush would continue and expand over the years and even decades to come—ultimately transforming the United States into a theocon nation.

PLANTING PROLIFE PREMISES

Abortion was, as always, the most urgent issue for the theocons. From the moment *Bush v. Gore* was handed down, members of the movement began to dream of judicial nominations that would ultimately produce a decisive reversal of the *Roe v. Wade* decision and its "unlimited abortion license." The theocons were well aware that this strategy would likely take several years, as they waited, first, for Supreme Court justices to retire and be replaced by religious conservatives, and then for the right case to come along and wend its way to the nation's highest court.

There was, of course, another approach—the path of legislation—but it had produced deep disappointment in recent years. During the 1990s, bills outlawing late-term (so-called "partial-birth") abortion had passed the House of Representatives on four occasions. Two of the bills died in the Senate. The other two managed to pass both houses of Congress but were promptly vetoed by President Clinton. The theocons naturally expected that President Bush would eagerly sign a similar bill. Yet a federal law banning the procedure was unlikely to withstand judicial scrutiny. In *Stenberg v. Carhart* (2000), the Supreme Court had struck down a Nebraska state law banning late-term abortion on the grounds that it had taken insufficient account of possible consequences for the life and health of the mother. Not only had the ruling invalidated Nebraska's law, as well as similar laws in over two dozen other states, but it raised the distinct possibility that the Supreme Court would overturn any law—state or federal—that sought to restrict access to abortion at any point during a pregnancy. Once again the theocons concluded that their only hope was to wait patiently for the new president to bring about a slow-motion ideological shift on the Court. Only then could social conservatives hope to pass laws that would begin to reverse the "culture of death."

There was, however, an additional legislative possibility—one that theocon Hadley Arkes had been advocating since 1988. Asked to contribute material for the debating kit of President George H. W. Bush as he headed into his general-election contest with Michael Dukakis, Arkes made an extraordinary series of assertions. Abortion, he argued, could be considered a constitutional right only by denying the personhood of the baby prior to birth. But once this "premise" was implanted in the law, there was no principled way to outlaw any abortion at any time during pregnancy, right up to—and perhaps even beyond—birth. After all, biological science and sonogram technology both showed that the fetus in utero is substantially similar to—not at all different in kind from—a baby outside the womb. The "right to choose" therefore implied a right to infanticide—or as Arkes shockingly put it, a "right to a dead baby." And as a rationalist, Arkes was convinced that such an implication at the level of principle meant that the possibility could become a reality at any moment, and would inevitably become a reality at some point in the future, as the culture slid down the slippery slope on which it had been precariously placed by the Supreme Court in 1973.[2]

Faced with the prospect of legalized infanticide in the United States, Arkes urged the first President Bush to make what sounded like an extremely modest proposal. Congress should pass a law declaring that a child born alive after a botched late-term abortion—a child no longer present within his or her mother's body and thus no longer dependent upon her "choice"—is subject to the full protection of the laws, as is any other person. Not only would such a law prevent explicit acts of infanticide, but, far more importantly, it would also "plant a premise" in the law that would eventually lead in the opposite direction of *Roe v. Wade*, emphatically affirming the personhood of the newborn child and thus raising the morally troubling question of whether that dignity could really be denied to the same entity just seconds earlier, when it resided in the mother's womb. Arkes was convinced that, just as the logic of *Roe* led inexorably toward a right to infanticide, so a declaration of the personhood of the infant "born alive" would have the effect of persuading large numbers of Americans—and perhaps also a decisive number of Supreme Court justices—to reject abortion-on-demand and, ultimately, to favor outlawing it altogether.[3]

Unsurprisingly, the first President Bush decided against taking Arkes's advice to turn the presidential debates into multipart seminars on abortion ethics, and over the next twelve years the "born alive" proposal received little attention from politicians. Things began to change, however, in the wake of the *Stenberg* decision in 2000. Frustrated at their inability to make even the slightest legislative headway against abortion, a group of prolife House Republicans began to consider pushing Arkes's bill in Congress. Compared to a partial-birth-abortion bill, a law protecting a child "born alive" would accomplish very little, at least at first, but it would be nearly impossible for Democrats to oppose, and it would be certain to withstand judicial scrutiny. (The law would, in fact, merely restate what was already apparent at several places in the federal code—namely, that newborns, like all persons, are protected by federal law.)[4]

Titled the Born-Alive Infants Protection Act, the bill was introduced in the House by Representative Charles Canady of Florida in 2000. Arkes led the House testimony in July and was followed by Princeton's Robert P. George, who drew on arguments he had made in response to the *First Things* "End of Democracy?" symposium to proclaim that "if weak and vulnerable members of the human family . . . can be defined out of the community of [those] whose fundamental rights must be respected and protected by law, [then] the constitutional principle of equal protection becomes a sham."[5] Although the National Abortion Rights Action League (NARAL) and other prochoice groups recognized the threat posed by the bill and thus opposed its passage, most Democrats viewed it with a mix of perplexity and indifference. Representative Jerrold Nadler (D-NY) was an exception. Understanding perfectly well the pedagogical intent behind the bill, he nonetheless realized that there was no way to mount an effective opposition to it. The next best thing would be to deprive the Republicans of an opportunity to "educate" the public on the issue, and so Nadler advised his fellow Democrats to allow the bill to pass with overwhelming support and thus also with a minimum of publicity. And so it did, quietly passing the House by a lopsided vote of 380 to 15.[6]

With the 2000 presidential race entering its final months and the Bush campaign exceedingly nervous about raising any controversial issues, the Senate chose not to bring the bill to the floor for a vote. Plans to revive the bill in the next Congress were then delayed by the September 11 attacks, which forced all nonessential legislative business to the back burner for several months. But by March 2002 congressional Republicans were ready to try again. The bill quickly passed the House by a wide margin and then made its way to the Senate, where Senator Rick Santorum (R-PA) took on the task of ensuring the bill's passage. On July 18, 2002, the Born-Alive Infants Protection Act passed the Senate by voice vote with no dissent.

In a private conversation at the bill-signing ceremony in Pittsburgh on August 5, George W. Bush thanked Arkes for his tireless work and described the bill as "a first step in changing the culture" of the United States.[7] Echoing the sentiment in his public remarks, the president spoke about future battles on behalf of the "culture of life" and employed rhetoric derived directly from the writings of Neuhaus and the other theocons:

> The Born-Alive Infants Protection Act is a step toward the day when every child is welcomed in life and protected in law. It is a step toward the day when the promises of the Declaration of Independence will apply to everyone, not just those with the voice and

power to defend their rights. This law is a step toward the day when America fully becomes, in the words of Pope John Paul II, "a hospitable, a welcoming culture."[8]

From the president on down, the theocons considered the passage of the Born-Alive Infants Protection Act as the beginning of a long and difficult struggle to reverse abortion rights in the United States.

Building on the momentum generated by the passage of Arkes's bill, the theocons and their allies in Congress and the White House worked to enact two more prolife bills during President Bush's first term. On November 3, 2003, the president signed the Partial-Birth Abortion Ban Act, proclaiming that the new law called on all Americans to "build a culture of life" by living up to the standards "announced on the day of our founding in the Declaration of Independence." Less than six months later, on April 1, 2004, the president signed the Unborn Victims of Violence Act, which declared that any person who causes death or injury to a child in the womb while causing death or injury to the child's mother would be charged with a separate offense. Although President Bush, like the bill's congressional sponsors (Representative Melissa Hart [R-PA] and Senator Mike DeWine [R-OH]), claimed that the law was intended merely to affirm that violence against a pregnant woman often has "two victims," this very affirmation fundamentally challenged assumptions about the legal status of the fetus as it had been defined since *Roe v. Wade.*[9] After all, an assailant can only be prosecuted for inflicting violence on a fetus if the fetus is assumed to have rights. But once such rights had been legally recognized and established, it would become extremely difficult, if not impossible, to distinguish between an assailant and a doctor performing an abortion—both of whom presumably violate those rights.

Even more clearly than the Born-Alive Infants Protection Act, the Unborn Victims of Violence Act illustrated the strength and cunning of the theocon strategy of "planting premises" in the law. At some point in the future, the Supreme Court (most likely after President Bush had appointed several justices sympathetic to the theocon cause) would have to confront the contradiction between the view of the fetus articulated in the Unborn Victims Act and the one presupposed in the Court's abortion-related jurisprudence. It was hard to see how the justices could uphold the constitutionality of both. And the theocons were willing to bet that their own view of the personhood of the fetus would prevail, thereby leading to a reversal of *Roe*. They thus wholeheartedly agreed with President Bush when he declared upon signing the Unborn Victims Act that it demonstrated the commitment of the United States to "building a culture of life."

THEOCON BIOETHICS

When it came to the other "life" issues—embryonic stem-cell research, cloning, and euthanasia—the Bush administration was equally concerned with fulfilling the expectations of the theocons, though the president fell somewhat short of doing so when he announced his policy on federal funding for research on embryonic stem cells in his first nationwide television address on the evening of August 9, 2001. That policy—to fund research only on existing stem-cell lines (in which the embryo had already been destroyed) and not on new lines (whose derivation would require further embryo destruction)—has since come in for sharp criticism for its staunch conservatism. But the theocons criticized it from the opposite direction—for making a morally dubious compromise with absolute principle. The theocons were inclined to deny the moral distinction on which the policy was based—the distinction between destroying human embryos on the one hand and using stem cells derived from human embryos that had already been destroyed on the other. Moreover, they would have preferred that the president go a step further than he did—to issue an explicit moral condemnation of the research whose federal funding he had blocked.[10] Neuhaus thus spoke for his colleagues when he described the policy as "defensible" but "gravely imprudent."[11] Yet at the same time, he also considered the president's August address to the nation to have been "without doubt the most lucid and straightforward presidential statement on the beginnings of human life and our moral responsibility for such lives since the fateful turn of *Roe v. Wade* in 1973."[12] On the whole, the president had given a mixed performance.

For the theocons, the most positive thing to come out of the August address was Bush's announcement of the formation of a new President's Council on Bioethics to be headed by Leon Kass of the University of Chicago. Though too skeptical of rationalism and religious authority to be described as a full-fledged theocon, Kass was nonetheless an enormously gifted and influential ally of the movement—a man Neuhaus had described in 1998 as "simply one of the wisest and most morally serious people I have ever known."[13] Over the years Kass had signed on to several statements of the Ramsey Colloquium—the group of theocon theologians, philosophers, and scholars that considers questions of ethics, religion, and public life—including its 1995 declaration on embryo research, "The Inhuman Use of Human Beings." This statement had asserted that such research must be opposed in all cases in order to "maintain our sometimes fragile hold upon our own humanity."[14] It was a distinctively Kassian argument—attempting to inspire quasireligious anxiety about the existential consequences of biotechnology and medical research.

Kass took a similar approach in a widely discussed 1997 essay for *The New Republic*, in which he strenuously opposed all human cloning, whether for reproduction or for "therapeutic" purposes.[15] Appealing to our "intuitive recoil at the separation of sex from fertility," as well as to what he called the "wisdom of repugnance" at the thought of creating genetic copies of human beings, Kass likened a society that tolerates cloning to one that "permits (even small-scale) incest or cannibalism or slavery." Such a society has "forgotten how to shudder," "rationalize[d] away the abominable," and become less than fully human.[16]

The distinctive strengths and weaknesses of Kass's approach to discussing bioethical questions were vividly displayed in an essay he published in *First Things* just three months before the president appointed him to lead the administration's new advisory board. In "*L'Chaim* and Its Limits: Why Not Immortality," Kass (an observant but largely secular Jew) challenged the view, common in the Jewish community as well as in the American population as a whole, that modern medicine ought to pursue the eradication of disease and the extension of human life at all costs. "Is it really true that longer life for individuals is an unqualified good?" Kass posed this pointed question and answered it with a definitive no, setting out to show nothing less than that "the finitude of human life is a blessing for every human individual"—that, in other words, death is a good thing.[17]

In Kass's view, a world in which the "immortality project" of modern medicine and science had eradicated death would suffer from several serious spiritual debilities. It would, first of all, be plagued by an epidemic of boredom, as individuals struggled in vain to fill endless expanses of time with petty distractions. People would also live shallow and frivolous lives, no longer motivated by fear of death to accomplish great and honorable deeds that promise to grant us an immortal reputation. Moreover, once the distinction between what dies and what is eternal has ceased to have meaning, the desire to produce beautiful things ("objects whose order will be immune to decay") would vanish. The same would hold for the pursuit of virtue and moral excellence, which would wane in a world where individuals no longer sense their own vulnerability and thus strive to overcome it by grasping for "the noble and the good and the holy."[18] In all these ways, our humanity depends fundamentally upon our mortality.

Kass's essay presented a powerful account of human experience—one rooted as much in the worldviews of the ancient Greeks and the Hebrew Bible as in the scholarly writings of such modern authors as Leo Strauss and Hans Jonas. As an attempt to think through the deep connections between mortality and the moral texture of human life, it was a useful and enlightening exercise. But as an effort to persuade his readers to "resist the siren song of the conquest of aging and death," it had a serious flaw.[19] Kass persuasively argued that the achievement of immortality would radically alter the character of human life. Yet he failed to point to a single reputable scientist or doctor who seriously advocated the pursuit of "curing" death. Far from pursuing an "immortality project," defenders of biomedical innovations merely seek to extend life as much as possible within finite limits—by, say, ten or twenty or even fifty years—as well as to minimize suffering from illness and disease. To be sure, a world with an average life expectancy of 120 years would be very different than our own (it might be common in such a world to experience the birth of one's great-great grandchildren, for instance). But it would not be *fundamentally* different. People in such a world would still be born, they would still age, they would still be vulnerable to accidental (and sometimes fatal) injury, and they would still die; these life events would simply take place over a longer stretch of finite time than they do today. These biomedically "improved" men and women would thus also remain fully human—even according to Kass's exacting standards. It was therefore hard to say exactly what, in the end, Kass objected to in the efforts of scientists and doctors to extend human life.

Kass's essay for *First Things* was just the latest in a long line of similarly edifying and erudite warnings about equally mysterious biomedical threats to our humanity.[20] Such warnings typically concluded with moral injunctions to refrain from embracing new developments and technologies, along with defenses of traditional social norms and practices. At the end of his *First Things* essay, for example, Kass proposed that twenty-first-century Americans embrace "procreation" (or the vicarious enjoyment of immortality through the lives of one's children) as "life's—and wisdom's—answer to mortality." Instead of putting their faith in science and medicine, in other words, Americans should seek to satisfy their desire for longer life by having more babies.[21]

It was this deep conservativism that more than anything else persuaded the theocons that Bush had made an outstanding choice in asking Kass to lead the President's Council on Bioethics.[22] Theocon enthusiasm only increased when the list of additional appointments to the council was announced. Of the original eighteen members of the council, six were theocons or theocon fellow travelers: Robert P. George of Princeton, Mary Ann Glendon of Harvard Law School, Gilbert Meilaender of Valparaiso University, Alfonso Gómez-Lobo of Georgetown University, Paul McHugh of John Hopkins University, and Kass himself. Three additional members—Francis Fukuyama, James Q. Wilson, and Charles Krauthammer—would side with the theocons on several issues confronting the council. Then, when two of the more liberal and secularist members (biologist Elizabeth Blackburn and ethicist William May) resigned in March 2004, Kass chose to appoint three more theocon allies in their place: Diana Schaub, who had described embryonic stem-cell research as a morally insidious combination of slavery and abortion; Peter Lawler, who had written extensively on the threat posed to our humanity by antidepressants and other psychopharmaceuticals; and Benjamin Carson, a renowned pediatric surgeon and convert to Christianity who had lamented that "we live in a nation where we can't talk about God in public." Just over two years after its inaugural meeting, the President's Council on Bioethics was dominated by theoconservative ideology.[23]

In the council's deliberations and published reports—on topics ranging from stem-cell research and cloning to gene therapy, the use of steroids and psychotropic drugs, and the regulation of various forms of biotechnology—Kass and his colleagues did their best to frame the bioethical discussion in the terms favored by the theocons.[24] Conducted like a graduate philosophy seminar, the typical council meeting began with a close reading and discussion of a classic text— Ovid's *Metamorphoses*, the Book of Job, Nathaniel Hawthorne's *The Birthmark*, a selection from Leo Tolstoy's *War and Peace*—and then moved on to anguished reflections on the dire moral and existential consequences of bioethical developments for the timeless character of "humanity."²⁵ Some members of the council—such as George and Gómez-Lobo—remained focused on relatively narrow moral issues, insisting, for example, that embryonic stem-cell research should be prohibited by law in all cases, along with all forms of cloning. Others—such as Kass, Meilaender, and Lawler—sought to inspire a broader (and vaguer) sense of dread about contemporary biomedical trends. Would a person who lived much of his life on antidepressants—supposedly medicating himself into a state of happiness—still be fully human?²⁶ Would a woman given the opportunity to choose the sex of her child have cut herself off from the essence of motherhood, which ought to involve giving oneself over to chance? Would a society that allowed the cloning of a microscopic clump of cells for therapeutic purposes have given in to a monstrous temptation whose moral implications would irreversibly taint all medical breakthroughs to come from that research? These were the kinds of questions regularly pondered by the President's Council on Bioethics.

Despite the efforts of a handful of dissenters—including, prior to their 2004 resignations, Blackburn and May, as well as Michael S. Gazzaniga (professor of cognitive neuroscience at Dartmouth College)—the council consistently sought during President Bush's first term in office to act as a brake on medical research and technological development. Whether the summer 2005 resignation of Kass as chairman signaled a change of direction for the council was hard to say. As long as Kass's departure did not inspire a mass exodus of the theocons who made up such a large segment of the council's membership, a dramatic ideological shift seemed improbable. Under the leadership of its new chairman, the somewhat less intensely conservative Edmund Pellegrino of the Georgetown University Medical Center, the council would most likely continue to function as a powerful voice of moral traditionalism in debates related to biomedical and biotechnological trends in contemporary American society.

AGAINST GAY MARRIAGE

With the Bush administration fighting battles against abortion and medical research, Neuhaus and his colleagues felt free to focus on other perceived threats to Christian America. By far the greatest such threat was, they believed, the advent of same-sex marriage in the United States. While they felt assured that the American people would never vote to institute same-sex marriage, a new act of "judicial tyranny" remained a constant possibility. To be sure, the federal Defense of Marriage Act (DOMA)—overwhelmingly passed by Congress and signed into law by President Clinton in 1996—had explicitly defined marriage as an institution exclusively involving the union of one man and one woman, reinforcing similar laws in thirty-eight states. Yet the theocons sided emphatically with Supreme Court justice Antonin Scalia's blistering dissent in *Lawrence v. Texas,* the 2003 case that struck down Texas's antisodomy law. In his dissent (which had been joined by Chief Justice William Rehnquist and Justice Clarence Thomas), Scalia warned that the reasoning used by the majority in *Lawrence* not only invalidated antisodomy statutes but also implicitly rendered unconstitutional "state laws against bigamy, same-sex marriage, adult incest, prostitution, masturbation, adultery, fornication, bestiality, and obscenity." It was thus merely a matter of time before a liberal-secularist judge used *Lawrence* to overturn state and/or federal laws against same-sex marriage and insisted that the equal protection or due process clauses of the Constitution required the government to make marriage licenses available for all interested same-sex couples.

The theocons were convinced that the only thing that could stand in the way of judicially imposed same-sex marriage was the passage of a Federal Marriage Amendment (FMA) to the U.S. Constitution—an amendment that would place traditional marriage beyond the reach of judicial (or, for that matter, democratic) meddling. Mar-

riage needed to be constitutionally defined as a union between a man
and a woman, with homosexual relationships permanently relegated
to second-class status. Theocons Robert P. George and Gerard V.
Bradley had already authored the two-sentence text of an amendment
to accomplish both goals, and Neuhaus gave it his wholehearted endorsement in the October 2003 issue of *First Things*.[27] Yet the Bush
administration and several theocon allies in Congress remained cool
to the idea of backing the proposal.

Until, that is, November 18, 2003, when the Supreme Judicial
Court of Massachusetts (basing its argument in large part on the logic
of *Lawrence*) mandated that the state make marriage licenses available
to same-sex couples. As if the prospect of legalized same-sex marriage
in a single state were not horrifying enough, millions of conservative
Christians flew into a panic as they contemplated the possibility of
liberal judges around the country using the Full Faith and Credit
Clause of the U.S. Constitution to insist that same-sex marriages
contracted in Massachusetts had to be recognized in other states. All
that now stood in the way of nationwide same-sex marriage, it
seemed, was the legally vulnerable DOMA. Overnight Scalia's and
Neuhaus's apocalyptic warnings began to seem eerily prescient to
many orthodox Catholics and evangelicals. Including the president of
the United States.

In January 2004, President Bush invited several theocons to a private conversation at the White House to discuss the FMA. Neuhaus,
George Weigel, Mary Ann Glendon, and conservative columnist
Maggie Gallagher attended the meeting, but, as usual, the president
spent most of his time addressing "Father Richard."[28] Bush asked
Neuhaus to make the strongest possible case for supporting the
amendment and to suggest ways of framing that support. In fulfilling
his duty, Neuhaus drew on his recent *First Things* editorial as well as
a 1994 Ramsey Colloquium statement on "The Homosexual Movement."

In these and many other writings over the past decade and a half,

Neuhaus had argued that the dangers of same-sex marriage flowed from the pathologies of homosexuality as such.[29] The gay way of life, he claimed, is "chiefly marked by loneliness, promiscuity, self-pity, suicide, and deadly disease."[30] And this is precisely what one would expect from a form of sexual activity that everyone from "philosophers, psychologists, and theologians" to average American citizens recognized as an "objective disorder."[31] Following Kass's lead in appealing to the "wisdom of repugnance" inspired by cloning, Neuhaus pointed out that most Americans responded to homosexuality with an "intuitive recoil" and "pre-articulate anxiety."[32] This spontaneous expression of disgust was not only natural, it was also morally "salutary," since it is a good thing for people to "experience a reflexive recoil from what is wrong."[33] Indeed, "achieving such a recoil is precisely the point of moral education of the young."[34]

As far as the theocons were concerned, it would be enormously destructive to permit homosexuals to use the word "marriage" to describe their profoundly unnatural and disordered relationships. It would, in fact, represent the ultimate and final triumph of the sexual revolution, and especially radical feminism—which, like the homosexual movement it spawned, is based on the morally and socially pernicious "anthropological doctrine of the autonomous self," which "undercut[s] the common good" and "grotesquely exaggerates" the place of sex in human life.[35] As the Ramsey Colloquium put it in its influential 1994 statement, "Permissive abortion, widespread adultery, easy divorce, radical feminism, and the gay and lesbian movement have not by accident appeared at the same historical moment. They have in common a declared desire for liberation from constraint."[36]

To degrade marriage by allowing it be commandeered by the liberationist homosexual movement would subvert the utterly essential social institution of the traditional family from the inside, replacing it with a mere "simulacrum of marriage."[37] Children would be raised in a world where the word "marriage" described nothing more exalted than a contractual arrangement between two consenting adults for the purpose of friendship and mutual sexual gratification. The result would be a further and much more dramatic deterioration of the family structure than Western society had already witnessed in the years since the 1960s. This was the primary reason why the United States needed to take the unprecedented step of enshrining the special status of the traditional family in the text of the Constitution itself.[38]

Neuhaus's case against homosexuality and in favor of the FMA ultimately rested on his claim that acting on same-sex desires constituted an assault on the natural order of things. Yet his evidence for this claim was remarkably thin, consisting of little more than an appeal to the supposedly innate aversion that many people experience when they first encounter homosexuals. But is this aversion "natural"? Or is it, like a previous generation's visceral opposition to interracial marriage, a response rooted in socially and culturally conditioned ignorance and bigotry? The theocon fear that the advent of same-sex marriage would usher in an age of socially destructive tolerance for homosexuality—like their insistence on the need for "moral education" to reinforce antigay sentiments in children—seemed to indicate that not even Neuhaus and his colleagues were convinced that aversion to gays and lesbians is solidly rooted in human nature. Without a far more elaborate account of why homosexuality is wrong, readers of Neuhaus's writings on the subject were left with the distinct impression that the theocon position amounted to a defense of state-sponsored discrimination designed to perpetuate historically contingent antigay prejudice for its own sake.

Neuhaus's failure to provide a fuller justification of his views on homosexuality flowed primarily from political considerations. It was simply impossible to lay out his full position without making assumptions that were inextricably linked to the religious doctrine and moral teachings of orthodox Roman Catholicism.[39] And to make such assumptions explicit would be to concede that the theocons aimed to give "state sanction to one religious view of marriage while contravening other religious practices and beliefs," not to mention widespread secular practices and beliefs.[40] It would be to concede, in other words, that the theocons aimed to bring the Constitution of the United States into conformity with the moral and sexual worldview of the Vatican. Though remaining silent about the Catholic foundation of the theocon position risked intellectual incoherence, that was the price of political influence. Advancing the theocon agenda required making a populist appeal to widely shared antigay sentiments and leaving the root theological sources of his movement's support for the amendment in the dark.

Not all of the theocons possessed Neuhaus's political savvy and restraint, however. Provoked by the arguments of Andrew Sullivan, one of the country's most tireless and articulate advocates for gay marriage, Robert P. George penned an extremely important and revealing essay in which he exposed the theological underpinnings of the theocon position. In *Virtually Normal: An Argument About Homosexuality* (1995), Sullivan claimed that being gay is a fundamental component of a homosexual person's identity, just as being straight significantly determines what it means to be a heterosexual person. Homosexual sex is thus just as "natural" for a gay couple—it is just as wrapped up with meaning and value, and just as expressive of the human longing for love, affection, and wholeness with another person—as heterosexual sex is for a straight couple. Gays and lesbians are therefore "abnormal" only in the demographic sense that they constitute a small minority of the population. In their humanity they are "virtually normal"—in no significant sense different from heterosexuals. There is thus no legitimate basis—natural or otherwise—for excluding gays and lesbians from the financial and emotional benefits, as well as the civilizing influence, of marriage.

George's response to Sullivan was an exercise in icy consistency. His primary intent was to argue that those who define themselves as "gay"—those who, like Sullivan, place their homosexuality at the core of their identity—are indeed abnormal. To establish this crucial point, George made a single assertion—an assertion unlikely to be shared by any but the most conservative Catholics, and one from which each of his later claims followed with savage syllogistic rigor. George asserted that all forms of "nonmarital sex" are intrinsically immoral. By "nonmarital" George did not limit his prohibitions to sex acts undertaken by unmarried couples. On the contrary, he followed the Catholic Church in defining "marital sex" as "only acts of a reproductive type." Hence, "oral or anal sexual intercourse, whether engaged in by partners of the same sex or opposite sex, and, indeed, even if engaged in by marriage partners, cannot be marital."[41] And neither, of course, can sex in which artificial contraception of any kind is used. Moreover, "masturbatory and sodomitical acts" must be placed off limits as well, since they "instrumentalize the bodies of those choosing to engage in them in a way that cannot but damage their integrity as persons."[42]

With this panoply of Catholic prohibitions on human sexuality established with deductive exactitude, George went on to defend the church's stringent teaching on what homosexuals must do to live morally upstanding lives. Either, he claimed, they must repress their sexual desires by marrying a member of the opposite sex—or else they must embrace "sexual abstinence."[43] In *Virtually Normal,* Sullivan himself had explicitly warned that both alternatives condemned homosexuals to lives of "devastating loneliness." But George, thoroughly convinced of the righteousness of his church's commandments on the matter, simply dismissed such objections with a rhetorical wave of the hand.[44]

Luckily for Neuhaus and his colleagues, President Bush was not a moral philosopher and in his meeting with the theocons showed no sign of detecting the explicitly Catholic currents flowing just beneath the surface of their discussion of the FMA. The next day, Neuhaus cheerfully announced to his staff at the Institute on Religion and Public Life that the president had given his word that he would soon come out strongly in favor of the amendment. And sure enough, in a speech delivered in the Roosevelt Room of the White House on February 24, 2004—just days after the elected mayor of San Francisco (and not a tyrannical judge) began to distribute marriage licenses to same-sex couples in defiance of California state law—Bush fulfilled his promise by announcing his support for the FMA in terms derived directly from Neuhaus's conceptually muddled but rhetorically effective writings on the subject.

The union of a man and woman is, the president announced, "the most enduring human institution"—one that "cannot be severed from its cultural, religious, and natural roots" without collapsing. But now, "a few judges and local authorities are presuming to change [this] most fundamental institution of civilization," producing "confusion on an issue that requires clarity." On a matter of such importance, President Bush declared, "the voice of the people must be heard" in order to reign in "activist courts." Even the Defense of Marriage Act was in danger of being struck down, thereby forcing "every state . . . to recognize any relationship that judges in Boston or officials in San Francisco choose to call a marriage." Given the gravity of the situation—and above all the need to prevent "the meaning of marriage from being changed forever"—it was necessary to "enact a constitutional amendment to protect marriage in America."

Over the next few months, the president's support for the FMA became a centerpiece of his campaign for reelection. Although strong opposition from such moderate Republicans as Senator John McCain kept the amendment from passing Congress in 2004, the Bush administration's backing helped to motivate conservative Christians around the country to do their part to oppose same-sex marriage at the grass roots. Popular referenda on the ballots of twelve states (eleven in November and one—in Missouri—a few months earlier) sought to restrain the future actions of state courts relating to homosexual rights. In the end, all the antigay referenda passed by wide margins—from 56 percent in Oregon to 85 percent in Mississippi. Regardless of the FMA's ultimate fate, which would not be known for several years, Bush's decision to follow the advice of the theocons and come out in support of it motivated his electoral base and thus also contributed to his victory over John Kerry at the polls.

THE CATHOLIC INTERVENTION

The theocon contribution to Bush's triumph in November 2004 was not limited to advice on opposing gay rights. Long before Karl Rove and then-Governor Bush summoned Neuhaus to Texas in 1998 to discuss the prospect of building a theocon presidential coalition, Neuhaus understood that the religious right could only hope to reach and hold on to political power if American Catholics relinquished their historic support for the Democratic Party and began to identify much more closely with the Republicans. There were tentative signs of such a realignment in the presidential elections of 1980, 1984, and 1988, when a majority of Catholics voted for Ronald Reagan and George H. W. Bush. But the shift proved to be temporary, as Catholics reverted back to the Democrats through the following three elections, giving a plurality of their votes to Bill Clinton in 1992 and Al Gore in 2000, and a majority to Clinton in 1996.[45] President George W. Bush needed to reverse the recent trend in 2004 and hopefully lay the groundwork for an enduring majority for the Republicans in 2008 and beyond. Fear of terrorism would contribute in important ways toward tilting Catholics—as well as several other demographic groups—toward the president. But provoking such fear would likely be insufficient, for in 2004 President Bush faced the special challenge of running against a Catholic candidate—the first Catholic candidate to receive a major-party nomination since John F. Kennedy's 1960 presidential campaign.

In the months leading up to the 2004 election, Neuhaus became convinced that Catholics would be more likely to vote for the theoconservative candidate if they could be persuaded that the Methodist George W. Bush was, in effect, a better Catholic than the Catholic

John F. Kerry. In attempting to accomplish this challenging goal, Neuhaus participated in and decisively contributed to an intervention in American politics far bolder than anything envisioned at the time of JFK's historic 1960 pledge not to allow his Catholic faith to influence his political decisions. The intervention involved leading members of the American Catholic hierarchy as well as powerful forces in the Vatican—most prominently, Joseph Cardinal Ratzinger, the man who a mere five months after the American election of 2004 would ascend to the throne of St. Peter to become Pope Benedict XVI.

In the first of several lengthy essays on the election published in the months leading up to the November vote, Neuhaus made it very clear that his aim was to overthrow the "Catholic settlement" engineered by Kennedy in 1960. Neuhaus believed that his status as a priest, far from inspiring circumspection and restraint, empowered him to make public pronouncements on the quality of Catholic politicians' piety. He did not hesitate to proclaim, for example, that "Senator Kerry's education in Catholic teaching and practice is gravely deficient."[46] But Kerry was far from being the only one. In a remarkable passage, Neuhaus declared that it was for all intents and purposes impossible to be both a good Catholic and a member of the Democratic Party—and, likewise, that it was a duty of all Catholics who wished to participate in national politics to embrace the Republican Party. And the reason, as always, was abortion.

> Today, the official position and actual leadership of the Republican Party is in agreement with Catholic teaching on the moral imperative to protect unborn children. The Democratic Party, by way of sharpest contrast, permits, at least at the national level, not one hint, not one iota, of dissent from the lethal logic of *Roe*.[47]

In order to defuse the charge that he was encouraging the Catholic Church in America to engage in blatant partisanship, Neuhaus claimed that the current position of the two parties relative to abortion rights was a historical fluke that grew out of the "McGovern revolution" of 1972, after which the Democratic Party moved quickly to become the party of prochoice absolutism and the GOP adopted a prolife line as a way of exploiting the fact that the Democrats had alienated a large segment of their own voters. Neuhaus insisted that it could have been otherwise—that the Catholic bishops might have prevented the Democrats from driving over the electoral cliff if they had come out strongly in the weeks and months following *Roe* against the party becoming the defender of unlimited abortion-on-demand. But there had been no concerted Catholic effort to steer the direction of the party, and the result, three decades later, was the candidacy of John Kerry—a Catholic Democrat who regularly received perfect ratings from NARAL and other prochoice groups and who had voted in the Senate against both the Partial-Birth Abortion Ban Act and the Unborn Victims of Violence Act. In Neuhaus's view, the bishops needed to learn from their earlier mistake and realize the importance of intervening now, confronted as they were by "a presidential candidate who says he is Catholic and who publicly, persistently, and defiantly rejects the Church's teaching on the greatest moral-political question of our time." The stakes for the "polity of the nation" were very high, but they were "much higher for the polity of the Church."[48]

Citing canon law as well as the second-century Justin Martyr as authorities, Neuhaus reminded the bishops that Catholic tradition had historically held that no one who persists in "grave sin" can be admitted to Holy Communion. And it was a very grave sin "to knowingly, publicly, and persistently reject and encourage others to reject the moral law that it is intrinsically evil, always and everywhere wrong, to deliberately take innocent human life." Other issues— "capital punishment, the war in Iraq, and a host of other disputed questions"—simply did not rise to the same level of urgency, and it was "truly troubling . . . that some bishops [were] fudging the Church's teaching by suggesting . . . a moral equivalence." To deny the special status of abortion as a Catholic issue was, quite simply, "false."[49] Re-

verting to the kind of rhetoric he routinely employed as a radical ag-
itator during the 1960s, Neuhaus insisted that "the question for Kerry
and others similarly situated is inescapable: Whose side are you on?"
Would Kerry and like-minded Democrats side with Jesus Christ and
his church or with the abortionists who ran their political party? If, in
the end, Kerry and other prochoice Democrats refused to change
their ways and bring themselves into conformity with the church's
teaching on abortion, then the bishops would have no choice but to
exclude them from the sacrament of Communion and thereby deprive them of the ability to benefit from running for office as "good
Catholics." Would the bishops do their duty by standing up to wayward Democratic politicians? Uncertainty about the answer to that
question is what, according to Neuhaus, led the election of 2004 to
be "a historic moment of truth" for Catholicism in America.[50]

At a Denver meeting in June 2004, the Catholic bishops debated
what to do about the Kerry candidacy. Led by a core of over a dozen
conservative bishops—including Archbishop Charles Chaput of
Denver, Archbishop Timothy Dolan of Milwaukee, Francis Cardinal
George of Chicago, and Archbishop Raymond Burke of St. Louis—
the group endorsed a strongly worded statement, "Catholics in Political Life," by a vote of 183 to 6.[51] The document came very close to
adopting Neuhaus's uncompromising position, describing support for
the right to abortion as a grave sin and asserting that grave sin is a cause
for the withholding of Communion. Yet the bishops stopped just
short of theoconservative absolutism. Instead of explicitly mandating
that Communion be refused to all prochoice politicians, individual
bishops and priests were empowered to make the final determinations
for themselves.

On the whole, Neuhaus was pleased with the statement adopted
by the bishops, which went quite far in attempting to influence the
American political process. Yet Neuhaus had reason to suspect that
"Catholics in Political Life" might have turned out to be even more
radical. According to Neuhaus's account of deliberations at the Den-

ver meeting—based on information provided by several anonymous sources in the bishops' conference—the statement had been softened after testimony by Theodore Cardinal McCarrick of Washington, D.C., about a confidential communiqué he had received from Joseph Cardinal Ratzinger. Claiming to be articulating Cardinal Ratzinger's position on the matter, Cardinal McCarrick had defended a moderate view, arguing that although "life comes first," other issues must remain important for Catholics, including "faith and family, education and work, housing and health care." Most of all, McCarrick had claimed, the bishops must not allow themselves "to become used in partisan politics either by those who dispute" church teaching on life and dignity or by those who reduce that teaching "to a particular issue or partisan cause." Then, committing what Neuhaus considered to be the sin of moral equivalence, McCarrick had declared that although human life and dignity were threatened "preeminently by abortion," they were also imperiled by "widespread hunger and lack of health care, by war and violence, and by crime and the death penalty." Given these concerns and moral complexities, it was "counterproductive" to impose ecclesiastical penalties on Catholic politicians. McCarrick had urged—and had implied that in his confidential letter Cardinal Ratzinger had advocated—that the bishops engage in "dialogue and persuasion" with wayward politicians instead of acts of "discipline."[52]

Cardinal McCarrick's remarks had made a significant difference in the deliberations that led to the final draft of "Catholics in Political Life," ultimately convincing several wavering bishops to drop their support for a more extreme stance. Yet shortly after the conclusion of the Denver meeting, it became apparent that McCarrick had been somewhat less than forthright about the contents of the Ratzinger communiqué on whose authority he had built his case for moderation. To begin with, the Vatican let it be known that the letter was never intended to be secret; on the contrary, it was written for the

purpose of guiding the discussion in Denver. Moreover, in the letter
itself (which was soon leaked to an Italian newspaper), the future
Pope Benedict XVI had made it very clear that in the debate about a
"seamless garment" of Catholic concerns—including abortion, euthanasia, poverty, war, and the death penalty—he did not endorse the
position that McCarrick had attributed to him. Rather, he sided un-
equivocally with the theoconservative position. Abortion and euthanasia, Ratzinger claimed, exist in a moral class by themselves: "There
may be a legitimate diversity of opinion even among Catholics about
waging war and applying the death penalty, but not with regard to
abortion and euthanasia." Following the Neuhaus line nearly word
for word, Ratzinger asserted that when a Catholic politician cooper-
ates in the "grave sin" of "consistently campaigning and voting for
permissive abortion and euthanasia laws," his pastor must inform him
of his sin and tell him that he "is not to present himself for Holy
Communion until he brings to an end the objective situation of sin,
and warning him that he will otherwise be denied the Eucharist." If,
in the end, the politician refuses to follow the pastor's council and
continues to present himself for Communion, the priest "must refuse
to distribute it."[53]

The position staked out by the American bishops—the position
Cardinal McCarrick had encouraged them to adopt under what some
of the bishops were now prepared to describe (at least anonymously
to Neuhaus) as false pretenses—was thus considerably less stringent
than the stance that the second most powerful man in the Vatican hierarchy would have preferred them to adopt. What the American
bishops had treated as an option—the denial of Communion to prochoice Catholic politicians—Ratzinger considered to be mandatory.
And as Neuhaus put it, "There is every reason to believe that the
statement [of the bishops] would have been even more firm and coherent if, as Cardinal Ratzinger intended, the bishops had had the
benefit of his letter."[54] If Ratzinger had succeeded in his efforts—if the

Roman hierarchy (and its theoconservative apologists in the United States) had persuaded the American bishops as a whole to summarily deny the sacrament of Communion to nearly every Catholic Democrat in the nation—it would have been the most audacious act of religious interference in the political life of the country in American history.

As it was, Senator Kerry and other Catholic Democrats were able to delay a direct confrontation with the church by avoiding Mass attendance in the dioceses in which bishops had announced the intention to withhold Communion. Yet there is reason to believe that the watered-down statement of the bishops may nonetheless have contributed in an important way to Bush's victory in the 2004 election. Quite a lot of ink was spilled in the days and weeks following the election about the significance (or nonsignificance) of exit polls showing that 22 percent of voters made their electoral decisions on the basis of "moral values." Much less widely discussed were statistics with potentially far more long-term importance. These statistics showed that President Bush received 56 percent of the white Catholic vote compared to 43 percent for Kerry. And that Bush received 91 percent of the vote from those for whom religious faith was the most important factor in voting. And that 61 percent of those who attend church more than once a week voted for Bush, with an equal percentage of those comparatively few Americans who never attend church voting for Kerry. It seemed undeniable that in 2004 the Republicans managed to solidify the impression among large numbers of Americans that they are the country's party of religion—and, conversely, that the Democrats are the party of secularism.[55]

In remarks written days after the election, in a flush of excitement at the thought of four more years with unprecedented access to political power, Neuhaus went even further—to propose that Bush's victory confirmed nothing less than "the ascendancy of the religious-moral-cultural matrix of American politics."[56] It confirmed, in other words, the political triumph of the theoconservative movement in America. Neuhaus's assertion would be tested as never before in Bush's second term, as the theocons sought to consolidate their power and to use it in ever-bolder ways to inject orthodox Christianity into the political life of the nation.

6

AMERICA'S
THEOCONSERVATIVE FUTURE

RICHARD JOHN NEUHAUS gave no sign of doubting that George W. Bush would win reelection in 2004. Though he was momentarily shaken by the president's poor performance in his opening debate with Democratic challenger John Kerry, Neuhaus predicted that the theocon candidate would soon bounce back—and that on election day the American people would rally to his side, decisively rejecting Kerry's bid to turn back the advance of religious conservatism in the United States. All the theocons shared Neuhaus's confidence and optimism.

The outcome was thus hardly surprising. But the way it was interpreted by the press in the days following the election—in terms of a widespread vote for "moral values"—made the victory especially sweet. Everyone, even the incorrigibly secularist mainstream media, seemed to be "getting it" for the first time. The grandiose American exceptionalism of President Bush's second inaugural address—with its talk of the country moving the world in a "visible direction, set by liberty and the Author of liberty"—was very much an expression of the exultant mood on the religious right. For the president's most fervent supporters, anything and everything seemed to be possible. Bush had proclaimed throughout the campaign that freedom was "on the march" around the world because of his—and America's—leadership in the war on terror. The theocons were equally convinced that their ideology was on the march at home, transforming the nation, slowly bringing it into conformity with the theological vision Neuhaus and his colleagues had been proclaiming since the publication of *The Naked Public Square* in 1984.

But what, in concrete terms, was this vision? How would a theoconservative America differ from the one we live in today? What, in a word, would it be like to live in a country where the theocon project had been fulfilled?

On the surface, the triumph of theoconservatism in America would change very little. The United States would not become Afghanistan under the Taliban, forcing women to wear burkas and men to grow beards. As Michael Novak's numerous writings on capitalism have shown time and again, theocon ideology assumes that Catholic Christianity is perfectly compatible with modern American life, even those aspects of it that seem most secular. An America dominated by theoconservative ideology would thus be likely to *look* very much the same as it does today—with shopping malls and McDonald's, iPods and TiVo, SUVs and Home Depots—while also *feeling* very different. The residents of theoconservative America would make friends and go to school, date and learn to drive, find jobs and start families, buy homes and help their neighbors, get sick, grow old, retire, and die. But all of these events would be permeated by Christian piety and conviction. In the words of journalist Jonathan Mahler, Americans would strive to incorporate "Christian values into every aspect of their lives."[1] The result would be the thoroughgoing spiritualization of the American experience.

And the sanctification of American society would entail a host of dramatic political and cultural changes. To begin with the obvious, *Roe v. Wade* would either be reinterpreted to allow significant state regulation of abortion or else overturned altogether, thereby allowing abortion to be banned outright in states dominated by populist religiosity. The Constitution would likewise be amended to conform to theoconservative views of homosexuality.[2] When it came to elections, the Catholic Church would routinely exclude prochoice politicians from the sacrament of Communion, and perhaps even resort to automatic excommunication for all Catholic members of the Democratic Party.[3]

Other changes are less obvious—though several developments during the past decade give us important (and ominous) hints about where the theocons hope to take the country in the coming years. While some of these events and trends have received significant coverage in the media, the role of theoconservative ideas in fostering them has, as usual, been underreported—as has the extent to which each of these tendencies contributes to fulfilling a comprehensive theoconservative vision for the United States. The theocons inspired and strongly supported the highly irregular efforts of President Bush and the Republican Congress to intervene in the right-to-die case of Terri Schiavo. They have defended those who would sow skepticism about Darwinian evolution and teach the scientifically groundless theory of "intelligent design" in the public schools. They have explicitly advocated a return to patriarchy in the family. They have endorsed premodern notions of religious authority. And they have responded to Jewish dissent from their agenda with a mixture of irritation and contempt. Each of these examples provides us with a glimpse of a possible American future—a future in which American politics and culture have been systematically purged of secularism and the country reconstituted as an emphatically Catholic-Christian nation.

THE POLITICS OF LIFE AND DEATH

No recent event is more suggestive of where the theocons hope to take the country than the failed attempt of President Bush and the Republican Congress to save the life of forty-one-year-old Terri Schiavo—the severely brain-damaged woman whose fate became the focus of national attention for two weeks during March 2005. Schiavo's husband and legal guardian maintained that before his wife fell into a "persistent vegetative state" in 1990, she had conveyed her desire not to be kept alive indefinitely by artificial means—thus inspiring his efforts to have her feeding tube removed. Schiavo's parents, however, desperately wanted to keep their daughter alive at all costs and for years had pursued every available legal option to block her husband's drive to withdraw life-sustaining nourishment. But by late winter 2005 those options had been exhausted. Having finally and definitely been granted the right under Florida law to allow his wife to die, Schiavo's husband ordered her feeding tube removed on Friday, March 18.

The significance of the ensuing spectacle has been insufficiently appreciated by liberals, for whom the intervention (like all "cultural" politics pursued by the religious right) was a cynical ploy to distract the public from more pressing political (and especially economic) problems in the country.[4] However accurate this may be in the case of certain politicians (then–House Majority Leader Tom DeLay [R-TX] comes to mind as a likely example), these critics fail to appreciate the extent to which the theocons and their supporters genuinely believe that cultural and moral questions are the *core* of politics, rightly understood. As Neuhaus wrote in his introduction to the 1996 "End of Democracy?" symposium in *First Things*, "Politics . . . is free persons deliberating the question, How ought we to order our life together?"[5] And surely the issue of whether or not our political community would permit an incapacitated woman to have her feeding tube removed against the express wishes of her parents raised far more fun-

damental moral and existential questions than the mundane issues of
public policy and budgeting that usually dominate political discussion and debate in Washington. Would we as a nation watch passively
as a helpless woman was intentionally dehydrated to death? Or would
we, instead, follow the advice of President Bush and do everything in
our power to "err on the side of life"?[26] The answer to these questions,
Neuhaus believed, would determine the answer to the profoundest
question of all: Who are we as a people and as a country—in our own
eyes, in the eyes of the world, and, most of all, in the eyes of God?

Unlike much of the media and most members of the Democratic
Party, the religious right had known about the case of Terri Schiavo
long before the first few months of 2005. As her parents' appeals
worked their way through the Florida courts, leaders of the evangelical and conservative Catholic communities recognized that her case
could prove to be very useful for advancing the "culture of life." Not
since the quite similar death-by-dehydration of Nancy Cruzan in December 1990 had the antieuthanasia movement been presented with
a case that had such potential for changing hearts and minds.[7] And
Cruzan's death had taken place before the theocons had galvanized
and empowered the movement. Unlike in 1990, opponents of the
right to die now had talk radio and cable news—not to mention a
sympathetic president and Congress—on their side to counter the indifference of the mainstream media to their cause. They had every
reason to believe that their efforts would have a powerful impact on
public debate in the country.

Yet even the staunchest advocates of federal intervention in the
Schiavo case were heartened by the boldness displayed by the Republicans in Washington. It didn't matter to them that a total of nineteen
judges had ruled that Florida law permitted Schiavo's feeding tube to
be removed. It didn't matter that established legal procedures pre-
cluded further appeals to the federal courts. It didn't matter that the
U.S. Constitution left open no role for Congress or the president in
this wrenching family feud. The only thing that mattered to them was

that they act to turn back the "culture of death"—by any means possible.

Congress was in the midst of its Easter recess when Schiavo's feeding tube was removed. Two days later, the Senate approved legislation to allow Schiavo's parents one final appeal to a federal judge. House Republican leaders then summoned members back to Washington from across the country to vote on the measure. Meanwhile, taking the kind of drastic action usually reserved for dire national emergencies, President Bush cut short a vacation at his Texas ranch and returned to the White House so he could sign the Schiavo bill into law the moment it passed Congress. Just after nine o'clock on a rainy Sunday evening, Congress began an anguished debate on the measure, which stated that "any parent of Theresa Marie Schiavo" had legal standing to sue in federal court to keep her alive. Representative F. James Sensenbrenner Jr. (R-WI) spoke for many of his colleagues when he denounced the "merciless directive" handed down by the Florida courts and asserted that no constitutional right is "more sacred than the right to life."[8] Awoken after passage of the bill at 12:42 a.m., the president signed it while standing in the hallway of the White House residence. Moments later, Schiavo's parents began their frantic search for a judge who would order the reinsertion of their daughter's feeding tube—a quest that would prove to be futile.

Schiavo died on March 31, ten days after passage of the law designed to circumvent the nation's legal institutions. Many right-wing commentators reacted with populist fury as a series of federal and state judges (and the U.S. Supreme Court) refused to intervene in the case. Theocon popularizer William J. Bennett, for example, advised Florida Governor Jeb Bush to reject the principle of judicial review, disregard the Florida and federal courts, and send in the National Guard to reinsert Schiavo's feeding tube by force.[9] A handful of others were more circumspect, however, recognizing the irresponsiblity of Congress and the president in passing the Schiavo law. In the words of conservative lawyer Douglas Kmiec of Pepperdine University, it was "a benignly intended but tragically mistaken law" that "contravenes almost every principle known to constitutional jurisprudence."[10] Among those principles was the one enunciated in article 1, section 9, paragraph 3 of the U.S. Constitution, which precludes Congress from passing a "bill of attainer"—that is, legislation that singles out an individual or group for special treatment, which was the whole point of the Schiavo law.[11]

But the Schiavo affair was troubling on a more fundamental level. It showed that a significant number of American citizens and their representatives in Washington were unwilling to accept the injustices that occasionally arise under the rule of law. Instead, they demanded an extralegal means of bringing the nation into conformity with morality understood in the absolute, unambiguous terms defined by the Catholic Church under Pope John Paul II. For these moral perfectionists, the lawful course of action—accepting that Schiavo's parents had run out of legal options and then undertaking the slow, difficult, and possibly futile task of persuading Florida voters and their representatives to change the laws of their state so that a similar situation would not arise in the future—was an unacceptable compromise with the "culture of death." It was precisely the kind of radical religious populism—fired by contempt for institutional obstacles to the quest for divine justice—that the theocons had been advocating (and, on occasion, practicing) for years. Whether it was an anomalous event or the beginning of a long-term trend toward religious extremism in American political (and spiritual) life is one of the most troubling questions confronting our nation today.

PUTTING SCIENCE IN ITS PLACE

No less portentous is the country's ongoing debate about teaching evolution in the public schools. Such debates are, of course, nothing new in the United States. From the Scopes "monkey trail" of 1925 through arguments about "creation science" during the 1980s to today's fights about the theory of "intelligent design," Americans have a long history of contesting the findings of evolutionary biology. What has changed in recent years is the intellectual and political sophistication of the opponents of Darwinian evolution. Whereas critics of Darwin once advocated biblical literalism—arguing that the theory of evolution could not possibly be true because the Bible clearly states that God created the universe and all of life in a mere six days—they now portray themselves as defenders of skepticism and open-minded inquiry against dogmatic defenders of a fanatical atheistic ideology. This change has helped to convince the Catholic Church to revise its previous stance of relative openness to evolution and to adopt, instead, a far more critical position. Even President Bush has sided with those who would place limits on the teaching of science in American schools.

The theocons have played a significant role in promulgating the "intelligent design" (ID) theory that has been so successful in putting Darwinian evolution on the defensive. Less than a year after publishing its inaugural issue, *First Things* opened its pages to Phillip E. Johnson, the evangelical lawyer-turned-anti-Darwin-crusader who helped to develop and popularize the argumentative technique that eventually became ID. In a series of articles for Neuhaus's magazine during the early 1990s, Johnson portrayed Darwinism as the latest in a line of now-discredited ideologies (including Marxism and Freudianism) that have sought to dethrone the Christian God in the name of "science." To be truly open-minded, Johnson asserted, scientists would have to stop excluding evidence for divine creation from their work and realize how many problems in the standard evolutionary account would be solved by appeal to a cosmic designer of life.[12]

By the late 1990s, the case for ID had become more sophisticated. Starting in 1996 the Seattle-based Discovery Institute began to support the work of trained scientists who could make the argument against Darwinism with much greater authority.[13] Before long, two of the most formidable scholars associated with the think tank—

biochemist Michael Behe and mathematician William Dembski—became regular contributors to *First Things*, where they defended the "design inference" against Darwinian evolution. While both men granted the explanatory power of Darwinian assumptions, they also claimed that those assumptions left enormous gaps in the evolutionary account. Behe made his case by arguing that, although a process of environmental adaptation and random mutation could explain so-called "microevolution" (small changes in a preexisting organ or system in a species), it could not account for the origin of those organs or systems themselves, especially when they showed signs of "irreducible complexity." The human eye, for example, depends on the precise interaction of dozens of parts, the removal of any one of which makes vision impossible. The same holds for the process of blood clotting, which requires the presence and complicated interaction of multiple proteins.

According to Behe, it is simply inconceivable that such complex systems—which function only when each and every component is present and performing a particular and necessary role in the process—could have arisen out of adaptation and random mutation. Such complex systems, in other words, show signs of "intelligent design," just like any human invention (such as a wristwatch or a mousetrap) that requires the precise interaction of multiple parts. To hold otherwise is to maintain the far more fanciful view that one day millions of years ago a previously eyeless organism gave birth to a random mutation with precisely the right combination (and interaction) of parts to enable vision. Which explanation—the intervention of an intelligent designer or the random production of an irreducibly complex function out of thin air—sounds more sensible? That is the commonsense question posed by advocates of ID.[14]

For several years the theocons refrained from officially endorsing ID in the pages of *First Things*. And on one memorable occasion, they even allowed one of their most gifted writers (Edward T. Oakes, S.J.) to savage Phillip Johnson.[15] In his highly critical review of Johnson's

2000 book *The Wedge of Truth,* Oakes steered clear of ID's serious scientific deficiencies—never pointing out, for instance, that evolutionary biologists are perfectly capable of explaining the emergence of "irreducibly complex" systems by pointing to the ways that they evolved from earlier, somewhat less complex versions of the same systems.[16] And he took several swipes of his own at the supposed absurdities and dangers of Darwinian naturalism. Yet Oakes also showed that by pointing to the existence of a designer who normally allows evolution to proceed on its own but who also occasionally intervenes directly in the process in order to bring about significant changes— to attach "the flagellum to the first bacterium" or to toggle "a complex molecule to bring about the first act of self-replication"—ID produced a "grotesque" theology lacking any discernable connection to the God of the Bible or to the Christian theological tradition.[17]

The theocons thus recognized the significant intellectual limitations of ID. Yet they were also increasingly impressed by the Discovery Institute's ability to create a space for theistic assumptions in the nation's public schools. The strength of ID derived from its seeming modesty. Instead of claiming to possess a positive doctrine of divine creation, the Discovery Institute merely attempted to persuade school districts to "teach the controversy" over ID—to expose students to the skeptical objections of Behe, Dembski, and other critics of Darwinism as a way of suggesting that evolution is a "theory, not a fact." That ID had so far failed to propose a single empirically testable hypothesis of its own—and thus that it could not even properly be called a scientific theory—was irrelevant. An astonishing 51 percent of Americans already believed that God created human beings in their present form, with only 15 percent accepting the currently established scientific view (that human beings evolved through a process of random selection).[18] In such a country, ID promised to have a powerful effect, inoculating students against doubting the superstitions they brought with them to the classroom.

Newly convinced of ID's political and cultural potency, Neuhaus decided in the spring of 2005 to offer the antievolution movement his first unambiguous statement of support. The move was surprising, and not only because of his magazine's past acknowledgement of ID's intellectual shortcomings. Neuhaus's decision also appeared to diverge from the Catholic Church's deference to the findings of modern science, including evolutionary biology, since Vatican II. As recently as 1996, Pope John Paul II had endorsed evolution in a much-publicized address to the Pontifical Academy of Sciences, leading Catholics on the whole to be somewhat less concerned than literalistic evangelicals about the theological dangers of Darwinism.

Yet in his April 2005 column in *First Things*, Neuhaus showed that on this matter he believed it was Catholics who needed to follow the example of their evangelical brethren—to take up arms against the militant secularism of the scientific establishment. Following the lead of the Discovery Institute, Neuhaus asserted that evolution is a "theory," not a "fact." (He failed to say whether he supported instilling skepticism in students about other scientific theories, such as heliocentrism, general and special relativity, the Big Bang, or quantum mechanics.) According to Neuhaus, it was he and other evolutionary skeptics who were the true defenders of science; others (including, one imagines, the vast majority of scientists, for whom the overwhelming preponderance of the empirical evidence points to the truth of Darwinian evolution) are motivated by "a form of antireligious bigotry." Evidence for this bigotry is the demand by many of those scientists that "alternative ideas . . . not be discussed or even mentioned in the classroom." To defend the teaching of ID is thus to side with pluralism, reason, and science against their enemies. Hence his conclusion that "students, school boards, and thoughtful citizens" are in "fully justified rebellion against this attempted stifling of intellectual inquiry."[19]

It was a stunning example of sophistry—one in which the scientific method, peer review, standards of professionalism, and scholarly consensus counted for nothing against the objections of a handful of religious dissenters. Yet just three months later, Neuhaus was joined by the Vatican in his highly selective defense of doubt, demonstrating that the American theocons were not the only Catholics capable of taking advantage of an ideological opportunity. Shortly after Joseph Cardinal Ratzinger became Pope Benedict XVI, one of the new pontiff's closest deputies—Archbishop Christoph Cardinal Schoenborn of Vienna—crafted an op-ed essay for the *New York Times* in which he clarified the Catholic Church's position on Darwinian evolution.[20] Unhappy with the way Pope John Paul II's statements on evolution had been interpreted as a defense of "neo-Darwinism," Schoenborn dismissed the former Pope's famously latitudinarian lecture to the Pontifical Academy of Sciences as "rather vague and unimportant." The church's—and John Paul's—true teaching was that "any system of thought that denies or seeks to explain away the overwhelming evidence of design in biology is ideology, not science." Much as Neuhaus had recently done, the cardinal implied that the nearly unanimous consensus of the worldwide scientific community was irrelevant to determining truth—and that those who dissented from this consensus were the true defenders of free and open inquiry. Just as the church had once upheld the "reality of the Uncaused Cause, the First Mover, and the God of the philosophers" against skeptical critics, so it would now "defend human reason" by opposing those who dogmatically dismissed evidence of "purpose and design" in nature.

Less than a month after the appearance of Schoenborn's op-ed, President Bush joined his ideological allies in weighing in on the controversy. Replying to a reporter's question as if reading from Discovery Institute talking points, the president asserted that "both sides ought to be properly taught . . . so people can understand what the debate is about." This was, he offered, the only way to "expose people to different schools of thought."[21] With these remarks the new conservative consensus was complete: evangelicals, Catholics, and the president of the United States were now united in supporting "equal time" in public schools for science and its antithesis.[22] It was a significant triumph for anti-intellectualism in American life—one whose full political, cultural, and even economic ramifications will not be known for some time to come.[23] What is clear is that, with several dozen battles currently raging in thirty-one states over teaching evolution, those ramifications are liable to be significant.[24]

THE RIGHTLY ORDERED FAMILY

The theocons have always been staunch defenders of the traditional family. In this they are hardly alone. Family breakdown and its influence on perpetuating poverty in the nation's inner cities engaged the early neoconservatives as far back as Lyndon Johnson's Great Society.[25] Alarmed at astronomical and rapidly rising rates of divorce and out-of-wedlock births in urban ghettos, the neocons proposed the elimination of government programs that, in their view, had helped to produce these social pathologies. Neuhaus, Michael Novak, and Peter Berger contributed to this literature in the 1970s by treating the family as a crucial and highly fragile "mediating structure" in society— one that functioned best when unburdened by government.[26] By the early 2000s, there was some evidence that these proposals for reform (along with other social and cultural factors having little to do with public policy) had begun to have a positive effect.

But these encouraging developments did nothing to diminish theoconservative panic about the state of the American family. While the theocons welcomed (modestly) declining rates of black illegitimacy and poverty, they were far more troubled by broader trends in family structure—especially those involving changes in gender roles. Neuhaus and his colleagues agreed with the neocons that children were likely to thrive when there were two parents in the home, but they went on to insist that children benefit most when those parents take on the traditional roles of mother and father, with the woman devoting herself full time to raising the kids and with the man fulfilling his domestic duties by providing for the family's financial well-being through work outside the home. This traditional division of labor in the family—with the father standing at its head as a patriarch—conformed perfectly with the created natures of each sex, encouraging women to devote themselves to nurturing and men to competition with other men in the working world and to leadership at home. At the same time, it performed the important function of passing on this primordial wisdom to the next generation by example. Boys and girls reared in the traditional family learned what modes of behavior would fulfill their deepest natural needs and longings.[27]

The theocons lament the rise of the modern, egalitarian family because they feel that it denies this basic human wisdom. Women pursue careers instead of devoting themselves entirely to child-rearing, often relying on day care and other extrafamilial arrangements as a substitute for full-time mothering. As the theocons see it, such arrangements not only deprive children of essential nurturing (as well as the example of the natural vocation of women) but also produce profound (and justified) guilt on the part of mothers who betray their own instincts in order to pursue a false ideal foisted upon them by radical feminist ideology. It is a situation bound to produce anguish for mother and child alike.

But even more disturbing to the theocons is the phenomenon of the "new father," who (in the words of theocon Gilbert Meilaender) "is a deeply involved parent and companion, nurturing his children, freely expressing emotion, eager to move beyond gender stereotypes, more interested in being emotionally available than in being a good provider for his family." Whereas the "old father" viewed work outside of the home as a "way of being committed to his family," the new father sees things very differently, with "family and work as conflicting domains."[28] The result is a situation bound to make intolerable demands on men—demands that many men will refuse to fulfill, as they (regrettably but understandably) abandon their wives and children for the independence of a life without burdensome and unnatural expectations.

These, then, according to the theocons, are the true problems facing the American family. But what can be done about them? As Leon Kass acknowledged in an important essay he coauthored with his wife Amy in 1999, there is no easy answer. The breakdown of the patriarchal family is merely one aspect of a much broader modern trend toward the democratization and dissolution of traditional social roles.

> It is no accident that the meaning of being a man or a woman has been radically transformed in a society that celebrates freedom and equality, encourages individualism and autonomy, rejects tradition, practices contraception and abortion, sees marriage as a lifestyle, provides the same education and promotes the same careers for men and women, homogenizes fathers and mothers in the neutered work of "parenting," denies vulnerability and dependence, keeps morality out of sight, and raises its children without any sense of duty or obligation to future generations.[29]

A society permeated by so many pathologies will be hard pressed to find a solution to any one of them. They must be tackled all at once or not at all.

But how—especially when it is only in "strong religious communities" that men and women still learn "clearly defined positive mores and manners"? According to the Kasses, the answer, at least hypothetically, must involve the revival of courtship rituals. And the revival of courtship rituals—the return to "sound manners and mores regarding manhood and womanhood"—depends above all on the willingness of women, who "control and teach" proper sexual habits, to practice "modesty" and "sexual self-restraint." Once women begin to withhold sex from men, men will be forced to revert to their traditional "active role" in courtship, which is to "woo" the woman, who allows herself to be "wooed" only when she has been convinced that the man will treat her with due respect and fulfill his role as a devoted and faithful provider.[30] As far as the theocons are concerned, the revival of the traditional family depends above all else upon women returning to the traditional feminine ideal of "chastity."[31]

No doubt most Americans—men and women alike—would look upon these reactionary proposals with a mixture of dread and amazement. Nowhere in their writings on the subject do the theocons acknowledge that a great many Americans consider themselves to be well rid of traditions that frequently bred ignorance, superstition, and shame about sexual desire and pleasure. Or that the exclusion of women from activities outside the home was often unjust and at least partially based on false assumptions about the activities to which they are naturally suited. Or that the structure of premodern social life, which provided substantial familial and community support to stay-at-home mothers, has largely broken down during the past few decades, leaving many such mothers feeling isolated and overwhelmed. Or that these changes have come about for complex social, economic, and cultural reasons, and not just because of the influence of an insidious feminist ideology. Or that some men genuinely wish to take part—and that children may actually benefit from their fathers' taking part—in the domestic goods (and sacrifices) from which they had been (to some extent arbitrarily) excluded in the traditional family. Or that under modern conditions equality in love and respect may ultimately prove to be a firmer foundation for the family than patriarchy. For the theocons, such objections are merely an expression of the very decadence that their writings are meant to overturn.[32]

Yet for all of their longing to return to a premodern family structure, the theocons are realistic enough to recognize that there is little they can do to bring about such a reversion. At least directly. As for indirect influence, their goals can be furthered (or at least not set back) by standing with the Republican Party in its opposition to government support for day care and paid maternity and paternity leave. The GOP opposes such policies—which have been adopted in some form by 120 nations and by all but two of the member states in the Organization for Economic Cooperation and Development

(OECD)—largely because of the economic burdens they place on business.[33] But the theocons reject them for different reasons—primarily because they provide social and economic support for modern, egalitarian families, thereby increasing the likelihood that they will thrive and ultimately replace the traditional family for good. As far as the theocons are concerned, the wiser course is to stand back and allow the modern family to collapse under the weight of its stresses, tensions, and contradictions. Perhaps from the wreckage of the modern family the traditional family will be reborn, stronger and more vital than ever. That, at least, is the theocon hope. In twenty-first-century America, the probusiness emphasis of the Republican Party harmonizes perfectly with the "profamily" agenda of the religious right.

TO BELIEVE AND OBEY

Growing numbers of Americans—most of them Protestants—worship in megachurches. What these massive congregations lack in liturgical formality they more than make up for in spiritual comprehensiveness. Resembling shopping malls and sports arenas more than chapels or cathedrals, these churches seek to supply their parishioners with something that early twenty-first-century America otherwise fails to provide them—a community, a network of social support, a place to congregate with neighbors, an accessible public sphere in which to interact with fellow citizens. And all in the name of Christ—understood as an emphatically personal, welcoming, forgiving, affirming God. In such churches, there is no distinction between sacred and secular. They provide everything from Christ-based child care, career counseling, and financial planning to more traditional options for prayer and Bible study. No wonder that the megachurches are especially popular in the "exurbs," those sprawling, rapidly expanding, prefabricated clusters of homes in "towns" far from any city or other centralized public space. No wonder, too, that ninety-seven out of the one hundred fastest growing counties in the United States voted in 2004 for the ever-more-explicitly religious Republican Party.[34] Going to church is the only civic experience many Americans will ever know.

The theocons are ambivalent about these trends. On the one hand, they are encouraged by the resilience and adaptability of American piety, as well as by the synthesis of sacred and secular that prevails in these massive congregations. On the other hand, the subjectivism, informality, and insipid sentimentalism of megachurch Protestantism offend their Catholic sensibilities, as does the schismatic character of American religion, which leads every disagreement, no matter how seemingly insignificant, to be treated as an occasion to break off and start a new congregation or church—and sometimes even an entirely new religion.[35] For all their success at educating evangelical elites in the history and theology of the orthodox Christian tradition, the Catholic theocons have thus far had only modest success in elevating the mainstream of American Christianity.[36]

To judge from Neuhaus's writings, the fundamental problem with American religion—and indeed, with much of post-Reformation Christianity—is its troubled relationship with authority.[37] For Neuhaus and the theocons more generally, to be a Christian is to be a member of a church to which one must fully submit oneself. Authentic piety requires the critical intellect to be tamed and placed under absolute ecclesiastical rule. Following the nineteenth-century John Henry Newman, one of Catholicism's greatest modern apologists and a convert from an Anglican Church he thought to be infested with a pernicious theological liberalism, Neuhaus has claimed that a genuine Christian has to train himself to "think with the Church." For such a believer, "ten thousand difficulties" with the church's teachings on faith, morals, or doctrine "do not make one doubt" about their ultimate truth.[38] Neuhaus parses this remarkable statement as follows:

> Given a decision between what I think the Church should teach and what the Church in fact does teach, I decide for the Church. I

decide freely and rationally—because God has promised the apos-
tolic leadership of the Church guidance and charisms that He has
not promised me; because I think the Magisterium [the teaching
authority of the Church] just may understand some things that I
don't; because I know for sure that, in the larger picture of history,
the witness of the Catholic Church is immeasurably more important than anything I might think or say. In short, I obey.[39]

Believe and obey. Period. That is the core of Neuhaus's message to
American Christians.

The Wages of Obedience I: A Higher Education

Outside of the megachurches, and especially among selected groups
of fervent Catholics, this ultraorthodox, authoritarian version of
Christianity is already being developed and practiced. European-
based lay organizations such as Opus Dei and the Legionaries of
Christ have had considerable success in spreading their highly secre-
tive, far-right version of Catholicism in the United States, thanks in
large part to the efforts of Pope John Paul II, Pope Benedict XVI, and
the theocons—all of whom strongly support their work.[40] Then there
is the circle of small Catholic colleges that teach a cramped, deeply
conservative form of the faith. At such schools as the Franciscan
University of Steubenville (Ohio), Christendom College, Magdalene
College, Thomas Aquinas College, and Thomas More College, strict
Catholic orthodoxy is mandatory, permeating nearly every course in
every subject and thoroughly shaping the social lives of the students,
many of whom have been homeschooled by equally conservative
parents. Lacking any sustained contact with secular culture, these
students tend to be paranoid about modern America and defensive
about their faith. While some of them harbor political ambitions, most embrace a longer-term, demographic strategy for routing
contraceptionist culture—by starting huge families with a dozen or

more children who will grow up to become a God-fearing Catholic majority in a future United States.[41]

Over the coming years, the leader of this Catholic insurgency in higher education is likely to become Ave Maria University—a school founded by Thomas Monaghan, the ultraorthodox Catholic entrepreneur who decided in the early 1990s to use the vast fortunes he acquired from founding and then selling Domino's Pizza to advance a right-wing religious agenda. Despite the enormous difficulty of starting a university from scratch, Monaghan has thus far been remarkably successful. Not only has he recruited a first-class faculty of conservative legal scholars for Ave Maria School of Law (currently located in Ann Arbor, Michigan), but he has also used a $250 million grant to acquire large tracts of land in the swamps east of Naples, Florida, where a fully functional university campus along with an orthodox Catholic "Ave Maria Town," including housing, shopping, and a golf course, will be built, with an expected date of completion for the project's "first phase" in mid-2007.

On the academic side, Monaghan has appointed a close friend and ally of Pope Benedict XVI, Joseph Fessio, S.J., as the incipient university's provost—a decision that helped to persuade Neuhaus, Michael Novak, Robert P. George, and Mary Ann Glendon to serve on the school's Board of Regents.[42] Fessio has also managed to convince several dozen intensely pious Catholic academics to join Ave Maria at its interim campus in Naples. The school opened its doors in August 2003 with 100 students; a year later, the number was 310. By the time construction on the university and the town has finished in 2016, planners expect a total population of approximately 30,000 people.

Assuming the project succeeds, life in Ave Maria will be a peculiar combination of Disneyworld and Torquemada's Spain—as it might have been imagined by George Orwell. Monaghan himself has declared that he anticipates that the town and university will be uniformly and comprehensively Catholic. "We're going to control all the commercial real estate," so residents can be assured that there will be "no pornography sold." Censors will likewise "control the cable system" and Internet access to ensure the exclusion of "televised smut," just as pharmacies will be forbidden from "sell[ing] condoms or dispens[ing] contraceptives." Private chapels will be located within walking distance of every home, while a sixty-thousand-square-foot church in the center of town, complete with a sixty-foot-tall bleeding Jesus (the nation's largest crucifix) and room for up to 3,500 worshipers, will offer Mass hourly, seven days a week, beginning promptly at six o'clock in the morning.[43]

From their homes and offices in "blue-state" New York City and Washington, D.C., the leaders of the theoconservative movement have long sought to empower the piety and parochialism of "red-state" America, while also Catholicizing it. There is thus every reason to believe that Monaghan's blood-red American Catholicism is a perfect expression of their religious ideal—and his university and town the distillation of their vision of America's future. The students and residents of Ave Maria will be true-believing theoconservatives, thoroughly committed to banishing secularism from American life, firmly in favor of enforcing absolute, Newmanian obedience to Catholic orthodoxy, including (and especially) its uncompromising moral and sexual teachings. What more—or what else—could a theocon want?

The Wages of Obedience II: Fidelity and the Catholic Sex-Abuse Scandal

Readers of *First Things* were given a very different example of Newmanian obedience in action during the 2002 pedophilia scandal in the Catholic Church. For over a year, Neuhaus wrote thousands of words in nearly every issue of the magazine, tying himself in verbal knots trying to defend the church and its institutions and traditions. For those not bound by Newman's strictures on free thinking, the scandal raised serious questions about what it was in the institutional practices of the church that made this particular kind of scandal possible. The fact that priests were accused of sexually abusing (usually male) children and teenagers—as opposed to, say, embezzling from church coffers—seemed to point directly to a problem in the church's teachings and practices regarding sex. But readers would never know that from Neuhaus's voluminous writings on the subject, which seemed designed to obfuscate the matter.

Neuhaus's initial response to the outbreak of the scandal in January 2002 was appropriately tough-minded. Directing justified outrage at the grotesque crimes committed by priests and covered up by bishops, he surveyed the sordid scene: "Children have been hurt, solemn vows have been betrayed, and a false sense of compassion—joined to a protective clericalism—has apparently permitted some priests to do terrible things again and again."[44] Yet two months later, in his next essay on the subject, Neuhaus shifted his attention from the victims of sexual abuse to its perpetrators. And in doing so, he began to fashion a distinctive theocon response to the scandal. First, the entirety of the blame belonged to the individual priests who committed the unspeakable abuse and to the individual bishops who covered it up—and none to the church and its practices and traditions.[45] Second, the scandal was caused by a widespread lack of "fidelity" among clergy to the moral and sexual teachings of the church: "If bishops and priests had been faithful to the teaching of the Church and their sacred vows, there would be no scandal." Acknowledging that some would find the argument to be facile, Neuhaus responded with preemptive defensiveness: "Those who would confuse the subject reflexively reach for complexity. No, I am sorry, it is as simple as that. We are reaping the whirlwind of widespread infidelity." Above all, Neuhaus insisted that the scandal had nothing whatsoever to do with the practice of mandatory clerical celibacy—and everything to do with priests who had been sworn to celibacy failing to live up to it.[46]

It was, to say the least, an odd interpretation of the scandal—one that was about as enlightening as saying that theft would never occur if people obeyed laws against stealing. It was true but tautological. Yet Neuhaus repeated the claim with perfect consistency, in his magazine column and in dozens of radio, television, and print interviews, over the following year.[47] What changed was his level of anger—and its focus. In the early days of the scandal, the tone of his writing varied from weary disappointment to stern condemnation, as he reprimanded wayward priests and absent-minded bishops for failing to uphold Catholic ideals. But by the time of his third essay on the topic, the bishops had transgressed once again—and this time against ostensibly innocent priests. In a June 2002 meeting in Dallas, the bishops adopted a "zero tolerance" policy against priestly sexual abuse—a policy under which even a single charge of alleged abuse, even if it involved an alleged act several decades in the past, could lead to the immediate dismissal of a priest.

It was clearly an overreaction, inspired by incessantly negative media coverage since the scandal broke and the desire of the bishops to be seen as acting decisively against clerical abuse. But to judge from the ferocity of Neuhaus's response to what he labeled a "draconian, no mercy, zero tolerance rule," it was something more than a mere mistake or misjudgment. It was an outrage greater than the sex-abuse scandal itself. The bishops were guilty of "scapegoating" harmless hypothetical priests "who did one bad thing thirty years ago and have since had an impeccable record and are clearly no threat to anybody."[48] And that was a fundamental betrayal of the bishops' ecclesiastical office.

Neuhaus's rage would build further over the next few months, leading him to write some of the most remarkable columns of his career. In October 2002, he raised the possibility that the sexual abuse of children might not be quite so bad after all. Quoting at length from a statement by Michael Bailey, a professor of psychology at Northwestern University whose work purports to show that many sexual abuse victims are often severely troubled prior to being molested, Neuhaus indicated that it might be sensible to question the "universal and extreme harmfulness of childhood sexual abuse." Such questioning was useful, according to Neuhaus, because it could help to "counter widespread, and sometimes self-serving, hysteria with a modicum of calm deliberation and simple honesty."[49]

Equally useful was the work of Joseph Davis, a sociologist at the University of Virginia, which showed that "ideas about the sexual abuse of children have a social history." Relying on Davis's work, Neuhaus pointed out that several psychology and psychiatry textbooks from the 1960s and 1970s "scarcely mentioned pedophilia." "But now," Neuhaus sardonically intoned, " 'everybody knows' that pedophilia is an incurable disease, that the diseased are incorrigible predators, and that there is no such thing as a 'one-time' offense."[50] Right before his readers' eyes, Neuhaus the moral absolutist had transformed himself into a historical relativist.

At least until December 2002, when his capacity for moral indignation returned. In that month's column, Neuhaus devoted several paragraphs to the memory of Father Maurice Grammond, a Portland, Oregon, priest who had recently died at the age of eighty-two. Eleven years before his death, Grammond had been suspended from the priesthood for "having had a habit of groping boys during a period from the 1950s into the early 1980s." Apparently this pedophile priest had "made a will asking for a funeral Mass in Portland's Church of St. Ignatius Loyola, where he had said his first Mass, and for burial in the section for priests in Mount Calvary Cemetery." Neuhaus informed his readers that Grammond "received neither." And that was unacceptable. Writing at greater length, and with greater fury, than he ever had about any victim of clerical sexual abuse, Neuhaus unleashed a venomous tirade:

> Forty-one years of priesthood, however marred by sins grave and venial, and there is nothing. . . . In those rural parishes where he undoubtedly presided at hundreds of baptisms and marriages,

where he counseled the anguished and comforted the grieving, where he thousands of times brought heaven to earth in the Real Presence, was there no one to say a good word on behalf of Fr. Grammond? . . . No, he is beyond the pale. He is an embarrassment. He is not one of ours. He is a sinner.[51]

Neuhaus had now come around to the view that obedience to the church demanded that the parishioners of Portland owed an expression of gratitude to the unjailed child molester in their midst.

George Weigel took a somewhat different, though no less curious approach to elaborating on the requirements of Catholic "fidelity." In a book-length account of the scandal published in September 2002, Weigel traced the immoral actions of priests and bishops to a general "culture of dissent" in the church that had begun with what he called the "Truce of 1968."[52] That was the year that Pope Paul VI issued the encyclical *Humanae Vitae*, which reaffirmed the church's prohibition on the use of artificial contraception, even among married couples. Upon the encyclical's release, nineteen priests in Washington, D.C., publicly denounced it. Their archbishop (Patrick Cardinal O'Boyle) threatened them with punishment for their dissent, but the Pope failed to back him up. In Weigel's words, "Pope Paul VI wanted the 'Washington Case' settled without a public retraction from the dissidents, because the Pope feared that insisting on such a retraction would lead to schism."[53] And the result was a devastating loss of authority for the church hierarchy. Now that dissidents knew that they could publicly break with impunity from official church teaching on faith, morals, and doctrine, they began to subvert Catholicism from the inside, refusing to defend the Vatican's ban on contraception, and even convincing the clergy that they need not respect their own celibacy vows. The 2002 scandal of abuse by priests was merely the latest and most disturbing example of the destruction wrought by the triumph of the culture of dissent back in 1968.[54]

As Garry Wills pointed out in a scathing review of Weigel's book, those nineteen Washington priests were hardly alone in dissenting from *Humanae Vitae*. Indeed, refusal to accept the truth of the document was "worldwide and instantaneous."[55] Over thirty-five years later, the church's teaching on contraception is ignored among a vast majority of the Catholic laity in the United States. Polls show that between 70 and 80 percent of American Catholics reject the ban on contraception—and that so few Catholics in their twenties and thirties accept the church's teaching on the subject that the percentage of those who do falls within the margin of error (less than 3 percent).[56] The "culture of dissent" thus goes far beyond the Catholic clergy. It is, in fact, the Catholic norm in modern America. And yet the sexual molestation of children is not widespread among the Catholic laity. It would seem, then, that "dissent" is far from being a sufficient explanation of why significant numbers of Catholic priests (and not only in the incorrigibly dissenting United States) have ended up as sexual predators.[57]

But such complications are irrelevant to Neuhaus and Weigel, for whom dissent from authority is always, somehow, the culprit.[58] As Wills concisely put it, the theocon answer to every problem seems to involve insisting that "everyone must believe everything, even the unbelievable."[59] Perhaps Newman would have approved of this refusal to allow so many difficulties from devolving into even a single doubt—about the sometimes monstrous psychological consequences of mandatory celibacy, about the secrecy and self-interestedness bred by the church's hierarchical, clericalist culture, about the wisdom of the Vatican's devoting so much time and energy to enforcing a sexual teaching rejected by the vast majority of modern Catholics. Others, however, were likely to be less impressed by the sight of intelligent men using their considerable talents to defend the indefensible. Yet this was what it meant to "think with the church"—to submit to the authority of the institution empowered by God to lead humanity to salvation. In their response to the sexual abuse scandal in the church, Neuhaus and Weigel showed their fellow American Christians where their political and religious movement ultimately hoped to lead them—into the arms of absolute ecclesiastical authority.

THE "JEWISH PROBLEM"

If America's Christian identity continues to assert itself in future years, the Christian majority will have to confront the problem of how to relate to the country's non-Christians—and especially to its highest profile non-Christians, the Jews. Over the past two thousand years, wherever and whenever Jews have lived among Christians, those relations have been marked by tension and, not infrequently, violence directed at the Jewish minority. The United States has, for the most part, been a happy exception. And several recent developments—including Pope John Paul II's numerous gestures of contrition for past acts of Catholic anti-Semitism, as well as staunch evangelical support for Israel—indicate that the trend may well continue into the future, no matter how prominent conservative religiosity becomes in the nation's public life.

Or perhaps not. Neuhaus's history of engagement with Judaism reflects the complexity of the question. On the one hand, Neuhaus has worked tirelessly to foster theological discussion and debate between religiously observant Christians and Jews. In his youth his primary interlocutor was Abraham Joshua Heschel, a prestigious ally in the antiwar movement. More recently, he has cultivated intellectual friendship and strenuous interreligious discussion with a group of Orthodox Jewish scholars, most notably Rabbi David Novak of the University of Toronto. These conversations have led Neuhaus to stake out a theological position that can only be described as philo-Semitic. In his view, which echoes several statements by Pope John Paul II, Christians must come to understand the absolutely essential role of the Jews in the Christian story of salvation—as the people through whom

God revealed himself to humanity. Recognition of this primordial tie between the two religions can and should serve as a foundation for mutual respect and solidarity.[60]

But things are not so simple. While Neuhaus has attempted to find religious common ground with Judaism, he has also become embroiled in rancorous arguments with less theologically minded Jews on a number of occasions. There was, first of all, the clash between Christian theocons and Jewish neocons that grew out of the 1996 "End of Democracy?" symposium in *First Things*. While political expediency eventually caused that rift to be healed, other conflicts followed. Throughout much of 2002, Neuhaus engaged in a heated debate with Gabriel Schoenfeld of *Commentary* magazine about anti-Semitism and support for Israel.[61] Neuhaus became even more incensed at the Jewish publisher (Martin Peretz) and literary editor (Leon Wieseltier) of *The New Republic* for running a twenty-seven-thousand-word essay by Daniel Jonah Goldhagen attacking Pope Pius XII (and the Catholic Church more generally) for not doing more to save Jews from the Holocaust during World War II.[62] Neuhaus responded to the essay by commissioning and publishing a twenty-thousand-word point-for-point rebuttal by Pius defender Ronald Rychlak.[63]

But the most intense moment of conflict took place with the release of Mel Gibson's scaldingly violent film *The Passion of the Christ*, in 2004. Neuhaus's initial reaction to the movie (which he viewed at an advance screening several weeks before its official release on Ash Wednesday 2004) was overwhelmingly positive; he declared it "an extraordinary film" and "certainly the best cinematic treatment of the passion or, indeed, of any biblical subject that I have ever seen."[64] On the question of anti-Semitism, he was equally unambiguous, quoting Father Augustine Di Noia of the Congregation for the Doctrine of the Faith to the effect that "there is absolutely nothing anti-Semitic or anti-Jewish about Mel Gibson's film." Yes, the Sanhedrin who condemn Jesus to gruesome torture, suffering, and death are Jews, but "so are members of the Sanhedrin who protest the proceedings, so are a large number in the crowd who are depicted as sympathizing with Jesus, so are Mary and the disciples, and, above all, so is Jesus. Jews one and all." While "untutored viewers" may come away from the film with the "distinct impression that 'the Jews' killed Jesus," Gibson clearly intended his movie to conform to the orthodox Christian message that all of humanity is equally guilty of killing Christ.[65]

Neuhaus was thus astonished and infuriated by the way the film was treated by critics—and especially by secular Jewish critics. His old antagonist at *The New Republic*, Leon Wieseltier, declared *The Passion* "a repulsive masochistic fantasy, a sacred snuff film."[66] *The New Yorker*'s David Denby likewise described it as "a sickening death trip, a grimly unilluminating procession of treachery, beatings, blood, and agony."[67] Even such neoconservative allies as Charles Krauthammer and Gertrude Himmelfarb denounced the film, failing to find anything redemptive in its relentless portrayal of boundless violence.[68] As the negative reviews piled up, Neuhaus's mood darkened. When the subject of the Jewish reaction to *The Passion* was raised in the *First Things* offices, he responded by muttering ominously and elliptically, "It can't continue."

Attentive readers of his column would have understood Neuhaus's meaning. Back in 2002, during the height of his disputes with *Commentary* and *The New Republic*, Neuhaus had penned a subtle essay in which he attempted to think through what he called the "Jewish problem" in America. It was an indisputable fact, he claimed, that at "2 percent of the population," Jews exercise "an influence far out of proportion to their numbers." Indeed, in certain sectors of American life—above all in "media, entertainment, prestige research universities, and to a lesser extent in finance"—Jews hold "20, 40, or even more than 50 percent of the positions of greatest influence."[69] While noting that anti-Semites invoke conspiracy theories to explain this influence, and "others" trace it to the habits of "an achievement-oriented subculture," "genetic superiority," and even the status of Jews as "God's chosen people," Neuhaus himself offered no explanation.[70] He wished merely to point out that the prominence of Jews in Christian America was nothing short of remarkable.

And not just remarkable. Over the next few paragraphs Neuhaus delicately raised the possibility that Jewish prominence in America— or at least a certain kind of Jewish prominence—might, in fact, be dangerous to the Jews. Neuhaus began by noting that, beginning with the rise of the Old Left, Jews have been "conspicuously prominent in attacking . . . the American way of life." Then there was the "notable" role of "Jewish activists and ideologues in defining the newer leftisms of the sixties and onward." Moreover, in the "culture war, and especially in the central dispute over abortion, Jews are overwhelmingly on one side." And of course, Jews also "tend to be Democrats, and on the left of the party."[71]

But perhaps most troubling of all, "Jews have in the last fifty years been at odds with most Americans" on "church-state relations." Deeply implicating the Jews in the secularization of American life and law during the past several decades, Neuhaus claimed that "generally speaking, [Jews] have thought the naked public square a very good thing." This was certainly the view of Leo Pfeffer of the American Jewish Congress, who beginning in the 1940s almost single-handedly "persuaded the Supreme Court to rule again and again against religious expressions and symbols—inevitably Christian in nature—in our public life." Despite his own tendency to describe the enemies of Christian America as "liberals" and "secularists," Neuhaus here made it very clear that these enemies could much more accurately be described as liberal and secular Jews.[72]

Although Neuhaus conceded that it was "understandable" for Jews to think that the "secularization of our public life has been good for [them]," he also maintained that this assumption was profoundly wrong—that "a devotion to secularism is no longer, if it ever was, a source of Jewish security and flourishing." As far as Neuhaus was concerned, the future of Christian-Jewish relations in the United States depends primarily on greater numbers of secular Jews accepting that their opposition to public Christianity has become "a liability that unnecessarily places American Jewry in an adversarial relationship to the culture." Given that Jews make up only 2 percent of the population, staking out such an adversarial relationship is foolish— something more than likely to "provoke the perception that Jews . . . are . . . strangers in their own country."[73] For all of his rhetorical cautiousness, Neuhaus's message was clear: it was in the interest of America's secular Jews to stop antagonizing their Christian hosts by making unreasonable secularist demands.[74]

After May 2002, Neuhaus refrained from raising the issue again— until, that is, the string of secular-Jewish condemnations of *The Passion* convinced him that the point needed to be reiterated. Strangely, he chose to do so in reaction to a relatively moderate essay on the film by David Berger in *Commentary*.[75] In his essay, Berger made a series of criticisms of Gibson's movie—among them that "no one who actually cared about avoiding anti-Semitism could have produced anything resembling it." He also chided the Catholic bishops for praising the film despite its failure to conform to the bishops' own guidelines for presenting the Passion. Yet Berger concluded with a call to mutual understanding and even affection between religiously conservative Christians and Jews:

> If amity is to prevail, traditionalist Christians will have to force themselves to understand that reasonable people have grounds for genuine concern about this movie, that its critics do not necessarily hate them, and that some [of those critics] like them very much indeed.[76]

Neuhaus accurately described this conclusion as "judicious," but he also found it to be more than a little disingenuous. While Berger was right that some "critics of the film do not . . . necessarily hate Christianity and Christians," it was "also true that many of them apparently do." After rehearsing a series of attacks on *The Passion* by Wieseltier and other secular Jews, Neuhaus went on to assert that the "amity" for which Berger called would "likely" survive the Jewish assault—though he also pointed out that it was a "shock" to many Christians to learn "that many Jews have nothing but fear and loathing for their religion and, by extension, for them."[77] Above all, the behavior of certain "prominent Jews"—particularly their decision to teach "contempt for Christianity and Christians"—bore witness to "the Jewish sense of security in this overwhelmingly Christian society." Then, with more than a touch of sarcasm, Neuhaus dismissed Jewish fears of anti-Semitism by asserting that "hysterical allegations to the contrary," the anti-Christian animus expressed by secular Jews showed that they "obviously do not believe that Christians want to harm them."[78] Seen in light of Neuhaus's earlier writings on the subject, it was difficult not to read the statement as another warning to secular Jews: Watch yourselves—Christian America is not now anti-Semitic, but it may one day grow (justifiably) impatient with your provocations.[79]

He had a point. An America in which Neuhaus's ideological movement had triumphed—in which politics had been suffused with Catholic moral absolutism, in which scientific knowledge and superstition were granted equal time in schools, in which the modern family was widely viewed as an abomination, in which large numbers of citizens freely surrendered their critical faculties to unchecked ecclesiastical authorities—such a country might very well be inclined to respond to a handful of dissenting non-Christians with annoyance or, perhaps, worse. In that case, the anti-Judaism that has always marked Christian civilization would be reborn in America, albeit in slightly different form—with a handful of Orthodox Jewish allies exempt from the hostility (at least in theory).[80] Call it the darkest of many possibilities in America's theoconservative future.

7

AGAINST THE THEOCONS

If there were only one religion in England there would be
danger of despotism, if there were two they would cut
each other's throats, but there are thirty, and they live in
peace and happiness.

—Voltaire

BY LATE 2005, the dizzy enthusiasm that followed the 2004
election had largely vanished. During the first year of President
Bush's second term in office, the theocons experienced a series of
unanticipated setbacks in their effort to enact their agenda. The Federal Marriage Amendment appeared to be permanently stalled in the
Senate. Polls showed that a large majority of Americans opposed the
intervention of the president and the Republican Congress in the Terri
Schiavo case. The theocons' lead candidate for the presidency in
2008—Senate majority leader Bill Frist (R-TN)—seemed to go out
of his way to alienate the religious right by coming out in favor of
some forms of embryonic stem-cell research.[1] The president's decision
to nominate White House counsel Harriet Miers to succeed the retir-

ing Sandra Day O'Connor on the Supreme Court temporarily fractured the conservative movement, with some members of the religious right strongly opposing and others moderately favoring Bush's choice.[2] And then there was the dramatic slide in the president's popularity—brought about by continuing violence in Iraq, the administration's bungled response to Hurricane Katrina, and an ongoing scandal surrounding the leak of an undercover CIA officer's identity to the press. All these developments significantly weakened the president politically, making it much less likely that he would push to enact controversial new theocon policies. All told, 2005 was a surprisingly bad year for the theoconservative movement.

Yet opponents of theocon ideology would be foolish to take these recent stumbles as an indication that the religious right will simply self-destruct, vanishing from the American political scene. Liberals made that mistake in 1992, when Bill Clinton's victory convinced them that the influence of conservative Christians on the nation's public life during the 1980s had finally come to an end. A mere eight years later the conservative Christians were back, better organized and far stronger (politically as well as intellectually) than ever before. Regardless of what happens to theoconservatism during the closing years of the Bush presidency, we have every reason to believe that the movement will be a fixture in American political life for the foreseeable future, pushing its policy agenda, politicizing religious faith, defending conservative trends in the churches, influencing the nation's self-understanding, and working to transform the terms of discussion and debate in Washington and throughout the country. All these efforts are likely to keep would-be champions of secular politics on the defensive.

In formulating a response to this challenge, defenders of secularism have two options. The first is to take on discrete elements of the theocon agenda, one at a time—defending a woman's "right to choose" when the president nominates a theoconservative judge to the federal bench, denouncing in terms of freedom and fairness theocon efforts to pass an antigay constitutional amendment, decrying the extremism of congressional Republicans when they subvert the rule of law in order to build a "culture of life," and so forth. Such efforts are in most cases sensible and necessary, and in the short run they might prove to be quite effective politically, but they are also gravely insufficient. Piecemeal attacks on theocon policy must be coupled with a much broader response—one that seeks to push back, at the level of ideas, against the ongoing theoconservative assault on secular politics in America. Those who wish to reverse the theocon offensive must directly confront and respond to the manifestly false—and profoundly dangerous—historical, political, sociological, moral, and religious claims of theoconservative ideology.

A HISTORICAL FANTASY

Theoconservative ideology was devised as a response to what Richard John Neuhaus and Michael Novak considered to be a potentially fatal crisis of meaning in modern American life—a crisis brought about by the secular drift of the United States since the 1960s. In order to turn back the advance of secularism in America, the theocons proposed that the nation adopt a unifying religious ideology. This ideology would transform American culture and religion while also inspiring a populist insurgency that would come to political power through the nation's democratic institutions. Later on, Neuhaus and George Weigel decided to ground their movement in concepts derived from Roman Catholicism—and to claim that what they advocated was not the imposition of an alien religious ideology onto an otherwise secular nation but rather the recognition that American ideals and institutions ultimately derive from and depend on Catholic-Christian principles and assumptions. The theoconservative revolution in American life would be a recovery operation, not an act of innovation.

This is a historical fantasy—one that simply ignores or grossly distorts the complicated religious views of the American founders as well as their justified fears of religiously inspired tyranny and sectarian violence. Benjamin Franklin, Thomas Jefferson, John Adams, George Washington, James Madison—all of them were either deists or liberal Christians inclined to doubt the divinity of Jesus Christ and the possibility of revelation. Madison believed, for example, that "more or less in all places" Christianity had produced "pride and indolence in the clergy, ignorance and servility in the laity, [and] in both, superstition, bigotry, and persecution."[3] Jefferson dismissed the Book of Revelation as "the ravings of a maniac" and predicted that "the day will come when the mystical generation of Jesus, by the supreme being as his father in the womb of a virgin, will be classed with the fable of the generation of Minerva in the brain of Jupiter."[4] Franklin went even further, flatly declaring that Revelation carried "no weight with me."[5] Not even Alexander Hamilton—who appears to have been something of an orthodox Christian in his personal life—allowed his religious faith to influence his contribution to writing the U.S. Constitution and ensuring its ratification; the document itself is, after all, famously silent about God, as are (aside from two passing references by Madison) the eighty-five essays that comprise the *Federalist Papers*.[6] As if to underscore the secular implications of these silences, the 1797 Treaty of Tripoli—signed by Washington, endorsed by Adams, unanimously ratified by the Senate—forthrightly declared that "the Government of the United States of America is not in any sense founded on the Christian religion."

Not that this handful of quotes can settle the controverted question of whether and to what extent the founders thought that the new American republic needed to depend on some form of religion to support popular morality. There is, in fact, quite a lot of evidence that many of them thought a liberalized form of Christianity (most likely in the form of an interdenominational civil religion) should play just such a social role in the nation.[7] What these quotes do show, however, is that the founders were not theocons *avant la lettre,* encouraging a wide public role for robust Catholic-Christian orthodoxy and insist-

ing on the explicit religious foundations of the country and its underlying principles.

The founders' concerns about the public role of religion flowed
from their knowledge of recent European history. The theologically
motivated violence and oppression that convulsed early modern Europe convinced them that religious passions and certainties are inim-
ical to good government. When a single religion dominates a nation,
it will incline toward despotism; when two religions (or two sects of
the same religion) vie for power, it will be prone to civil war. In this,
the American founders agreed with Voltaire, whose exile in England
during the 1720s convinced him that the theological-political problem could best be mitigated not by attempting to suppress religion
but rather, paradoxically, by allowing it to flourish in freedom. When
religious sects are permitted and even encouraged to proliferate, each
acts as a check on the political power of the others, thereby diminish-
ing the overall threat of tyranny and creating a powerful incentive for
each faith to embrace toleration as a guarantee of civil peace and its
own freedom to worship. This is how England's "thirty" religions
managed to "live in peace and happiness."[8]

Madison expanded on the point in his discussion in the *Federalist Papers* of factions (including religious factions).[9] There he famously
argued that the continental republic of the United States would solve
the perennial political problems of despotism and violent factional-
ism by encouraging "society itself" to be "broken into so many parts,
interests, and classes of citizens" that no single sect or pair of sects
would be capable of attaining enough power to undermine the common good or infringe the rights of minorities. The key to eliminating
the political threat of religion, in other words, was religious pluralism.

In this sense, then, Neuhaus has been right to argue that the First
Amendment's Establishment and Free Exercise Clauses were intended
to complement one another—though he partially misconstrues their
combined purpose. The amendment certainly does guarantee religious liberty, but not simply for its own sake. While the ban on an es-

tablished church makes free exercise of religion possible, free exercise guarantees the proliferation of religious sects—and the proliferation of sects, in turn, helps to ensure that none of them will be strong enough to seek the (formal or informal) establishment of religion in the United States. In this way, the guarantee of religious liberty institutionalizes the perpetual political impotence of religion.

Nothing could be further from the pluralizing intent of the founders than theocon efforts to form an interdenominational coalition of religious groups united by common political interests and ambitions. That the theocons place Catholicism at the core of this coalition would be, from the standpoint of the founders, especially troubling, though also unsurprising. All the early modern liberals viewed the Catholic Church as the greatest obstacle to establishing free government in the Western world. Its transnational scope, its doctrinal homogeneity, its hierarchical and authoritarian structure, its historic hostility to religious "error," its record of political ambitions on the Italian peninsula and beyond—in all these ways, Catholicism seemed to be the religious "faction" least likely to play by the rules of a pluralistic liberal order. These fears were confirmed in Europe during the nineteenth and early twentieth centuries, when the church became the most powerful reactionary force on the continent, strenuously opposing democracy, liberalism, and religious toleration with every resource at its disposal, including open support for antiliberal political parties and governments in several countries (including fascism in Italy and Spain).[10]

A somewhat more democratic (in Catholic terms, "conciliar") form of Catholicism grew up in the United States, showing that it was possible under certain circumstances for the church to reconcile itself to modern, liberal politics. And in the Second Vatican Council, the hierarchy explicitly abandoned its temporal ambitions and went a long way toward reconciling itself to the more tolerant and democratic form of the faith that had until then flourished only in the New World. Yet the church remains (and under Pope Benedict XVI is likely to remain) a profoundly authoritarian institution—one that claims with perfect certainty to possess the absolute, unchanging truth about God and his relation to humanity, as well as the right to insist that its members affirm and proclaim that truth, in both their public and private lives. Whether this conservative retrenchment in the church will continue or instead prove to be a temporary pause on the path to greater liberalization and modernization remains an open question. What is clear is that, either way, Madison and the other founders would have considered theocon efforts to Catholicize American democracy an ominous innovation in the country's political life—and a profoundly foolish one.

A SOCIOLOGICAL FANTASY

Historical criticism is unlikely to convince theocons. Like so much in their ideology, their insistence on the religious character of the American founding is a matter of faith. But even if they could be convinced that their ambitions are discontinuous with those of the founders, it is doubtful that it would have any effect on the potency of their project. Though it would complicate their attempt to portray themselves as conservatives, Neuhaus and his colleagues could always maintain that the American founders, like their more explicitly anti-clericalist European counterparts in the eighteenth century (and liberal secularists today), had a superficial understanding of religion and the necessarily religious foundations of a free society.[11] Rather than portraying itself as a movement to recover the (imaginary) Catholicity of the founding, then, theoconservatism could simply recast itself as an ideology that seeks to *refound* the country on a much more explicitly Catholic-Christian basis.[12] Shorn of its unconvincing historical assertions, this streamlined version of theocon ideology would be based entirely on the claim that Catholicism can serve as a much needed unifying force in the contemporary United States.

Yet this, too, is a fantasy—this time a sociological one. Short of universal conversion to orthodox Catholicism on the part of the American people, Catholic-Christian belief will fail to unify the country. In fact, the more the church and its ideological champions seek to impose such belief on the nation's public life, the more they will generate division and heighten sectarian tensions. Neuhaus himself once understood this social dynamic very well. Indeed, it formed the core of his critique of evangelical Protestantism in *The Naked Public Square*. The Moral Majority was incapable of providing the nation with a unifying religious ideology, he argued, because nonevangelical Americans would inevitably view the attempt as one group's illegitimate effort to impose its private theological convictions on the nation as a whole. Conservative Protestants thus negated their claim to speak for the whole of society in the very act of presuming to do so.[13]

The legitimacy of theocon ideology—its potential to unify, rather than polarize, the nation—stands or falls on its ability, somehow, to avoid this problem. Over the years, Neuhaus and his colleagues have gone out of their way to show that their ideological version of Catholicism is capable of performing precisely such a trick—of speaking with equal moral force to all Americans, regardless of their religious attachments (or lack of attachments). Unlike evangelicalism, which is based on subjective born-again experiences, Catholicism, the theocons claim, makes publicly verifiable truth claims and principled moral arguments that are equally accessible to all citizens. In the church's natural law tradition and its series of social encyclicals can be found the rudiments of a spiritual and moral outlook that is perfectly compatible with democracy and pluralism in the United States. Whether or not individual American citizens are conservative Catholics—or even liberal Catholics, or even Christians, or even Judeo-Christians, or even believers in a personal God, or even believers in any spiritual reality at all—they can and should accept the universal validity of orthodox Catholic moral arguments and employ them as an ideological framework through which to understand the nation and its role in the world.

It is a lovely story, but it is a fairy tale. On issue after issue—from same-sex marriage and euthanasia to the role of men and women in the family—the theocons endorse policies that are indefensible outside a universe of Catholic assumptions that are shared (and will likely continue to be shared) by only one segment of the nation's citizenry—namely, its most conservative Christians. Even on abortion, the theocons are driven by their Catholic-Christian assumptions to an absolutist position far outside the mainstream of American opinion. While numerous polls show that a majority of Americans supports greater restrictions on abortion than are permitted under the prevailing interpretation of *Roe v. Wade*, a majority does not follow the theocons in supporting the outright repeal of *Roe* along with the widespread criminalization of the procedure. Yet that is and will remain the theocons' unwavering, uncompromising view: abortion must be outlawed in the United States, either by individual state legislatures or, preferably, by a Supreme Court that is persuaded by Robert P. George's creative reading of the Fourteenth Amendment to declare that the Constitution already protects the unborn from lethal violence.

Theoconservatism might not be based on "private" born-again experiences, but its rationalistic moral absolutism renders it as least as ill-suited as evangelical piety to serve as the unifying ideology for a liberal democratic nation. In such a nation, public officials have to govern in the knowledge that in every election, even in a "landslide," large numbers of citizens cast their votes for someone other than the front-runner. This obvious fact is easily obscured by America's winner-take-all electoral system, in which receiving just over 50 percent of the vote (and in a three-way race, where a plurality is a sufficient threshold, even less) entitles the victor to 100 percent of the political power at stake in the contest. But a moment's reflection reminds us that this is an illusion—that nearly every "mandate" proclaimed by a victorious politician is, at most, an expression of the will of somewhat more than half of the people who participated in the election. As for the not-quite-half of the voters who preferred another person, another party, another set of policies—they must resign themselves to their defeat and hope that the winner will govern with humility, aware that his or her power rests on a foundation more partial and more partisan than it might seem.

Theocon ideology encourages its political allies to take a far less humble—and much more divisive—approach to governing. Unwaveringly convinced that the nation as a whole (or at least the overwhelming majority of its citizens) shares their Catholic-Christian outlook, the theocons urge sympathetic politicians to treat their often narrow victories as confirmation that the American people broadly support the theocon agenda. Yet so far this agenda is supported only by, at most, a well-organized minority of Americans—and a great many other Americans strongly and passionately reject it. The theocons thus seek to inspire a narrow and extreme part of America to govern as if it spoke for and represented the views of the whole of America. Even if they manage with some future candidate to cobble together enough votes to replicate or slightly surpass Bush's bare majority victory in 2004, treating that victory as a mandate to impose their divisive theological vision on the nation would be a monumental act of hubris—one that Garry Wills has aptly dubbed "government from the fringes."[14] For all of its emphasis on national unity, the theoconservative movement contributes in an important, even decisive, way to the rancorous polarization of American politics in our time.

POLITICS WITHOUT RELIGION

But let us suppose otherwise. If theoconservatism were capable of galvanizing the nation under God, would that make the ideology more appealing? Would Neuhaus and his colleagues then deserve our nation's gratitude for providing it with the comprehensive Catholic-Christian foundation that it sorely lacks and desperately needs in

order to flourish? We have considerable reason to doubt it. The theocon insistence that American democracy requires a religious foundation ties the ideology very closely to the reactionary tradition of
modern political thought. Like the other members of this tradition—
including such luminaries of the European (and Catholic) far-right as
Joseph de Maistre, Juan Donoso Cortés, and Carl Schmitt—the theocons fundamentally fail to understand the distinctive character of
modern political life, above all the fact that liberal democratic government works perfectly well (and perhaps best) without any religious or
metaphysical foundation at all.

The possibility that nations could thrive without religion is so
terrifying—and so thoroughly vexing—to the theocons that they
have come to adopt a deeply defensive and highly tendentious atti-
tude toward contemporary Europe—a continent filled with nations
that falsify the central assertion of theocon ideology. From public
opinion polls on religious beliefs to rates of church attendance, the
empirical evidence confirms that Europe has become a largely godless
civilization. And yet it gets along quite well.[15] Indeed, Europe's break
with religion has taken place during a period in which it has enjoyed
unprecedented peace, stability, and prosperity. When it comes to
overall quality of life, in fact, some have even argued that Europe has
managed in recent years to surpass the United States, despite the significant (but by no means insurmountable) economic and demographic challenges confronting the continent.[16]

But one need not go to European secularist extremes to find na-
tions that put the lie to theoconservative assertions about the indis-
pensability of mixing politics and religion. Throughout much of
Latin America, for example, rates of church attendance and private
piety match or surpass those typically found in the United States.
When it comes to *public* expressions of religiosity, however, Latin
America resembles Europe far more than it does the United States.[17]
The United States is the only nation in the Americas in which polit-

ical leaders regularly invoke God in their public pronouncements—just as it is the only place to have given birth to an ideological movement designed to ensure that the public presence of religion will expand still further over time.

In all of the Western world, only one nation besides the United States conforms to theoconservative assumptions: Poland. Only in Poland do majorities strongly support public expressions of piety—and only in Poland do citizens commonly believe that the health of their society depends on the vitality of the country's religious (meaning Catholic) beliefs.[18] The theocons would have us believe that the prominence of (two very different forms of) Catholic-Christian spirituality in Poland and the United States demonstrates that politics as such requires a religious foundation. It makes far more sense to draw a more modest and more skeptical conclusion—namely, that for complicated historical and cultural reasons America and Poland are developing at this moment in history on a parallel course toward increased public religiosity. And that in neither case is it obvious that this trend is necessary or good for the country concerned. In America's case, for example, the rise of public religion may very well lead to international isolation, as the community of nations increasingly responds to the world's God-intoxicated hegemon with understandable apprehension. And then there is the possibility of domestic economic stagnation, as the theologically inspired denigration of science in American classrooms begins to undermine the country's educational standing and technological edge in the global marketplace.

AMERICAN DEMOCRACY AND THE
AUTHORITARIAN SENSIBILITY

There is thus little to no evidence that the United States requires the kind of religious foundation advocated by the theocons. But even if it did, we have reason to conclude that the version of public religiosity advocated by Neuhaus and his colleagues is particularly unsuitable for the nation. From the time of his earliest political activity (if not before), Neuhaus has combined a longing to obey absolute divine authority with often violent hostility to those temporal authorities who fail (in his judgment) to live up to the metaphysical ideal. He has also come to combine this desire to uphold absolute Christian truth with a populist defense of American democracy, while refusing to accept the enormous tension between the two views or the practical implications of this tension. Orthodox Christianity holds, for example, that authority comes from God and is exercised by and through his church and its appointed spokesmen. American democracy, by contrast, maintains that authority comes from the people and is exercised by and through their elected representatives. Because the United States happens to be a democracy in which a majority of citizens profess some kind of Christian faith, the theocons are able to deny the need to choose between these two sources of authority, claiming that in America politics is based on the consent of the governed, the governed spontaneously affirm divine authority, and everyone lives happily ever after, under God. Aside, of course, from a handful of troublemaking secularists who dissent from the nation's theological-political consensus and thereby exclude themselves from full participation in the American experiment.

But in reality the relation between divine and democratic authority in America is far more complicated than the theocons are willing to concede. And this unacknowledged complexity produces extreme volatility in their judgments about the country. When the American people seem to be fulfilling theocon hopes—during Jimmy Carter's 1976 campaign, for example, or throughout George W. Bush's presidency—Neuhaus and his colleagues are inclined to sanctify the country, its leaders, and its people, and to counsel extreme deference to political authorities, who are assumed to be doing God's work in the world. But when the people fail to conform to theoconservative expectations—throughout the 1960s, for instance, or dur-

ing Bill Clinton's presidency—the theocons lurch to the opposite position, demonizing the country, and its leaders, its people, and even
going so far as to declare that the nation is on the verge of totalitarianism, civil war, justified revolution, or perhaps all three at once. This
is the permanent theocon dynamic—hurtling wildly from theological
affirmation of the country to theocratic denunciation and back again,
as they respond to the (supposed) oscillation of the American people
between upholding divine authority and flouting it.[19] Such volatility
is precisely what one would expect from those who choose to attrib-
ute cosmological significance to the vagaries of democratic public
opinion.[20]

Not that theoconservative ideology would be any more respectable if it settled on one of these two extremes. The profound political irresponsibility of the radical, even apocalyptic, position staked
out in the 1996 "End of Democracy?" symposium is clear enough.
But the more affirmative view the theocons have adopted since the
resolution of the 2000 presidential election is no better. Regardless of
whether an authoritarian outlook is harmful in religion, it can be
downright destructive in politics. A nation in which such an outlook
is explicitly cultivated and esteemed will be tempted to support political leaders who promise to redeem us from our uncertainties, our
skepticism, and our doubts—from, in short, the inherent complexity
and difficulty of truth itself. This temptation is especially dangerous
in liberal democratic nations, which depend on citizens informing
themselves about exceedingly complicated issues, making use of alternative sources of information, doubting the assertions of public
authorities, and thrashing out an inevitably tentative truth in open-
ended argument and debate. This is the unavoidable price of citizenship in a free society. We should be suspicious—and we should
cultivate suspicion—of any and all who promise to save us from the
exigencies of freedom.

SUCCUMBING TO THE
INCARNATIONAL TEMPTATION

Theoconservatism is thus bad for American politics on several counts. But its influence on American religion is no less pernicious. Theocon ideology was devised in large part to fill the vacuum left after the implosion of the liberal Protestant mainline, which according to Neuhaus and Weigel had once supplied the nation with precisely the kind of unifying religious ideology it now lacks and desperately needs. In response, the theocons have encouraged the creation of a kind of super-mainline—one that would be composed of devout Catholics, conservative Protestants, and perhaps even a handful of Orthodox Jews. This religion of Judeo-Christian "mere orthodoxy" would then serve as a new unofficial national faith for the United States.

It is a perpetual Christian temptation—one growing out of that most distinctively Christian doctrine, the bodily incarnation of God—to sanctify (and to see God embodied in) the political order that prevails at a given moment in history. In one of the earliest examples of the tendency, the fourth-century Eusebius of Caesarea wrote an influential history of the church in which the Roman Empire served as a providential conduit for spreading Christianity throughout the world. The interpretation was perfectly persuasive—at least while Rome maintained its preeminence. When the empire was invaded and the city sacked by the Visigoths in 410 CE, however, the Eusebian equation of the fate of Rome with the fate of the church seemed to imply that Christianity, too, was under assault. Had God abandoned the faithful, withdrawing his guidance and protection?

This terrifying thought eventually inspired St. Augustine to write an elaborate and sustained refutation of Eusebian history. In *The City of God*, Augustine insisted that divine providence is and must remain a mystery to human beings, arising as it does from outside of history and ultimately pointing beyond history, toward transcendent ends known only to God. We must have faith and we must hope that God plays a role in guiding the course of human events, but we can never know how he does so. To suppose otherwise is to fall prey to a basic historical fallacy—the fallacy of mistaking one's own passing moment in the flow of time for a privileged vantage point, for the eternal vantage point of God. Not only does this fallacy gravely distort one's judgment and unjustly exaggerate the importance of one's time and place in the order of creation, but it also ties the church too closely to the fallen and sinful world of politics, tempting Christians to find their salvation in the city of man—with its partisan pursuits and lust for power—instead of in the city of God that lies beyond this life.

Over the centuries, Christians have failed to follow Augustine's example and have succumbed to the incarnational temptation time and time again. Christians upheld the "divine right of kings"—and popes claimed the right to rule temporal affairs—throughout medieval Europe. The Catholic clergy and laity deferred to monarchical absolutism in early modern France. Liberal Protestants sanctified the Rechtsstaat in nineteenth-century Prussia. Right-wing clerics threw their support behind Nazi Germany in the 1930s.[21] The American Protestant mainline endorsed New Deal liberalism in the middle decades of the twentieth century. And now the theocons propose to consecrate the twenty-first-century United States—provided, of course, that a conservative Republican remains at the helm.[22]

Thoughtful Christians should be very cautious about following the theocons in their foray into the public square. Such political interventions nearly always end in disgrace for the church, as its moral witness gets corrupted by political ambition and its claim to speak for something higher and more timeless than temporal affairs gets discredited by proximity to power. Then there is the ever-present possibility that political authorities will manipulate Christians—telling them what they want to hear in return for valuable support—in order to further less noble ends. The members of the theoconservative electoral coalition could use a refresher course in these and other equally valuable Augustinian lessons.

Neuhaus is fond of describing himself as a disciple of St. Augustine, but the gesture is unconvincing.[23] The fact is that the theoconservative movement—with its impatient, eschatological longing for the radical transformation of the nation, along with its willingness to bestow theological legitimacy on one particular ideological configuration of one particular political system—is profoundly un-Augustinian.[24] In seeking to elide the distinctions on which all responsible religious and political thinking is based—distinctions between reason and revelation, the secular and the sacred, the city of man and the city of God—the theocons produce a volatile and muddled conceptual cocktail that threatens to degrade American religion no less than its politics.

THE LIBERAL BARGAIN AND ITS ENEMIES

Which brings us back to the problem of religion in a free society— and to the political and social arrangements the American founders proposed to mitigate and manage it. Under our system of government, religious believers are required to leave their theological passions and certainties out of public life, but *pace* the theocons, this requirement does not amount to an assault on religious freedom. On the contrary, it is the *precondition* of religious freedom in a pluralistic society. The privatization of piety creates social space for every American to worship God as he or she wishes, without state interference. In return for this freedom, believers are expected *only* to give up the ambition to political rule *in the name of their faith*—that is, the ambition to bring the whole of social life into conformity with their own inevitably partial and sectarian theological convictions. This is *the liberal bargain* that secures social peace and freedom for all Americans.

This bargain—novel when it was first proposed by the American founders in the late eighteenth century, now accepted, with minor variations, by free and democratic nations throughout the world— has produced an extraordinary degree of political stability in the

United States. But it also established the preconditions for a thriving religious life. The latter point is especially significant in light of theocon claims about secular liberalism's tyrannical assault on religion during the past half-century of American history. Back in 1992, Neuhaus summarized the theoconservative position on the matter by declaring that "the great problem today is not the threat that religion poses to public life, but the threat that the state, presuming to embody public life, poses to religion."[25] To which informed readers cannot help but respond with dismay. Religion under siege in America? Hardly. While such an assertion might be useful for rallying a political movement and crafting effective fund-raising letters, as an empirical claim it is impossible to take seriously. As any visitor to the United States from Canada or Europe will attest, twenty-first-century America is awash in Christian piety—which strongly suggests that the liberal bargain has been very good indeed for the life of religion in America.

Why, then, has theoconservatism been so successful in persuading certain religious groups to flirt with rejecting the liberal bargain that has manifestly benefited them and the country so profoundly for over two hundred years? As the American founders would have predicted, the answer follows from the character of the country's various religious sects. Some religious groups—ultra-Orthodox and Hassidic Jews, the Amish and Mennonites—support the liberal bargain because they are nonproselytizing, highly sectarian communities that have no desire to impose their piety on the nation as a whole, and as small minorities they gain security through the political disestablishment of the country's larger faiths. A similar dynamic applies to secular and less fervently religious Jews, liberal and nonpracticing Christians, agnostics, and atheists—all of whom benefit greatly and lose nothing from the bargain, since they have little interest in using the power of the state to impose their private religious (or antireligious) views on the whole of society.

Those most likely to refuse the bargain are orthodox Christians—

especially conservative Catholics and evangelical Protestants—both because of their relatively large numbers and because they are called by their faith to remake the world and spread the word of God (as they understand it) with missionary zeal. As long as these two religious groups view each other as rivals, they will support the bargain in order to check each other's power, just as James Madison predicted they would. But to the extent that they come to consider each other allies and to recognize their potential combined political clout, they will be tempted to view the separation of church and state as something less than a bargain—as an unacceptable sacrifice of their freedom to do everything they can to bring the country's public life into conformity with what they believe to be the truth proclaimed by Jesus Christ.

Detecting the first rumblings of such theological-political restlessness and ambition among pious Christians during the final third of the twentieth century, the theocons might have acted responsibly. They might have reminded their fellow believers of the preciousness of the liberal bargain, and of its fragility. They might have invoked the great Augustinian Reinhold Niebuhr on the sin of pride and the virtue of humility. They might have used their considerable rhetorical talents to tame the incendiary passions driving the nascent populist insurrection against secular politics in the United States. Instead they chose to do everything in their power to encourage, justify, and intensify those passions—and to become the leaders of the rebellion. And they did so without showing even the slightest concern that their efforts threatened to lead the country back to a world of religiously inspired social and political strife—to the world from which the American founders worked so hard to liberate us two centuries ago.

Defenders of the liberal bargain in America have been slow to recognize the threat posed by the revival of theologically inspired politics in our time. For the past three decades, enemies of the bargain have been working tirelessly to transform the United States in their image, and secularists have responded by ignoring or dismissing their efforts. Hopefully such intellectual and political insouciance is now a thing of the past. The theocons speak of and to very real human longings—the longing for meaning and morality, purpose and providence, order and truth—and they respond with great passion and eloquence to widespread and, in some cases, understandable moral revulsion at certain aspects of modern American life. Yet the basic point remains: in a modern, liberal, democratic society, social peace and individual freedom depend on these longings and revulsions being deflected out of public life. They certainly should not be deliberately channeled into it. We have reason to suspect that a majority of our citizens can be persuaded that a tolerantly secular liberalism is the only viable governing philosophy for an America worth living in. But only if we begin to take up the task of persuasion.

ACKNOWLEDGMENTS

I T GIVES ME great pleasure to thank publicly those individuals who contributed to the writing of this book. Tina Bennett, my spectacular agent, expressed enthusiasm for the project from the start and has acted as a tireless advocate ever since. I have benefited immeasurably from her shrewd judgment, sound advice, and keen editorial eye. At Doubleday, Phyllis Grann and William Thomas convinced me early on that we shared a common vision of the project. Their excitement has been contagious and their expertise greatly and humbly appreciated.

It is especially gratifying to single out Eric Alterman for special thanks. It is not an exaggeration to say that, through an act of gratuitous generosity for which I am and will remain deeply grateful, Eric made it possible for me to write this book. Be assured: I won't forget it.

A number of friends have contributed to my thinking about the issues I treat in *The Theocons*, including William Ruger, Russell Arben Fox, and the members of the "Fox & Friends" e-mail discussion group, especially Matthew Stannard, J. Scott Craig, James Meloche, and Nick Zukin.

Without realizing it, Jerrold Seigel played a very large role in preparing me for this project—by teaching me to appreciate the manifold complexities of modern life as well as the importance of honoring complication in my writing and thinking. Which is just another way of saying that he provided me with that rarest and most precious of gifts, a liberal education.

My greatest debt as a writer and intellectual I owe to Mark Lilla—once an esteemed teacher, now a treasured friend and colleague. Balancing passion, eloquence, rigor, and responsibility in a life devoted to ideas is a surprisingly difficult trick, but Mark makes it look easy. I am profoundly grateful for his incisive comments on every chapter in this book—as well as for all the comments he has provided on nearly everything I've written since I first poked my head into his office as a first-year graduate student at New York University back in the fall of 1991. He has also been an extraordinarily loyal supporter, doing his best to keep up with me as I've plunged along on my somewhat circuitous political, spiritual, and intellectual journey.

To my father, Irwin Linker, I owe more than I can say. Among many other gifts, he managed to instill in me from a very young age a deep appreciation of doubt—skepticism that served me very well in thinking my way through and out of some recent confusions. Both he and my brother, Mitchell Linker, have also been ideal conversation partners through good times and bad, proving that it is possible to be closest of friends with the closest of family.

My greatest personal debt is to my wife, Beth Linker, to whom this book is warmly dedicated. Above all else I owe her thanks for sticking by me—and us—through an awful period in our lives that at times seemed interminable. I have also benefited enormously from her formidable intelligence, her pitch-perfect ear for historical narrative, and her exacting standards of clarity and synthesis. She has been an inspiration and a constant source of insight through the marathon of writing this book. She also read, criticized, and commented on every word—including many words that (thankfully) never made it into the final draft.

To our beautiful children, Mark Daniel and Kaitlyn Rose—the first barely old enough to understand what Daddy meant when he said he was writing a book, the second conceived as I began to write and born as I finished the final revisions—I sincerely hope you'll both one day read this book for yourselves, if not to learn something about what was happening in the country when you were very young, then at least as a way of coming to understand your father. In any event, it was with your futures in mind that I first set out to tell this story.

Finally, a word about my former colleagues in the theoconservative movement. For all the severity of my criticism of theocon ideology in this book, I harbor no ill will toward the individual theocons, least of all my former boss, Richard John Neuhaus, who was always unfailingly generous to me. My break from the theocons had nothing to do with personal animus. It was about ideas and their practical effects. Once I became convinced that the ideology promulgated by the magazine for which I worked was having a significant negative influence on the country, I reluctantly concluded that I had to do what I could to counteract that influence. Loyalty to the truth and devotion to the good of the nation demanded nothing less.

NOTES

PREFACE

1. Kennedy's only mention of God in his speech was in the common phrase "God will-ing": "Our goal is not the victory of might, but the victory of right—not peace at the expense of freedom, but both peace and freedom, here in this hemisphere, and, we hope, around the world. God willing, that goal will be achieved."

INTRODUCTION: THE END OF SECULAR POLITICS

1. "Bush Calls for 'Culture Change,'" edited transcript of May 26, 2004, White House meeting, at www.christianitytoday.com/ct/2004/121/51.0.html.
2. Joseph Bottum, "Just the Right Amount of God," *Weekly Standard,* January 31, 2005, 24–26.
3. The term was first employed by Jacob Heilbrunn in "Neocon vs. Theocon," *New Republic,* December 30, 1996, 20–24.
4. See, for example, Franklin Foer, "Spin Doctrine: The Catholic Teachings of George W.," *New Republic,* June 5, 2000, 18–20.
5. "The End of Democracy? The Judicial Usurpation of Democracy," Introduction, *First Things,* November 1996, 10.

1: THE ORIGINS OF AN IDEOLOGY

1. Richard John Neuhaus, "The 'Lessons' of Vietnam," The Public Square, *First Things,* March 1996, 67; see also Neuhaus, *America Against Itself: Moral Vision and the Public Order* (Notre Dame, IN: University of Notre Dame Press, 1992), 69.
2. Quoted in Philip Weiss, "Going to Extremes," *Harper's,* November 1983, 14–15. See also Richard John Neuhaus, "Like Father Like Son, Almost," The Public Square, *First Things,* August/September 1994, 70.
3. "Again, God's Country," *Time,* October 20, 1975, 60.
4. Ibid.; see also Neuhaus, *America Against Itself,* 56.
5. John Sibley, "Clergymen Defend Right to Protest Vietnam Policy," *New York Times,* October 26, 1965.
6. "3 Clergymen Here Begin Protest Fast," *New York Times,* July 4, 1966.
7. Weiss, "Going to Extremes," 16.
8. "Again, God's Country," 60; and Richard John Neuhaus, *Time Toward Home: The American Experiment as Revelation* (New York: Seabury Press, 1975), 14.
9. Neuhaus quoted in Weiss, "Going to Extremes," 16.
10. Neuhaus quoted in Mitchell K. Hall, *Because of Their Faith: CALCAV and Religious Opposition to the Vietnam War* (New York: Columbia University Press, 1990), 81.
11. J. Anthony Lukas, "Thousands March," *New York Times,* August 30, 1968; and Neuhaus, *America Against Itself,* 58.
12. Peter L. Berger and Richard J. Neuhaus, *Movement and Revolution: Peter L. Berger and Richard J. Neuhaus on American Radicalism* (New York: Anchor Books, 1970), 239–40.
13. Ibid., 234, 145.
14. Ibid., 154, 166–68.
15. Ibid., 220.
16. Ibid., 94–95: "The test of manhood is still to be, in the words of Che Guevara, 'one of those who risks his skin to prove his truths.'" But see also p. 233: "Advocating revolution is not a matter of balls but of vision."
17. Ibid., 227, 240.
18. Ibid., 178.
19. Michael Novak, *A Theology for Radical Politics* (New York: Herder & Herder, 1969), 15.
20. A novel, *The Tiber Was Silver,* had appeared in 1961.
21. Novak, *Theology for Radical Politics,* 117–18.
22. Ibid., 100.
23. Ibid., 117.
24. Hall, *Because of Their Faith,* 37.
25. Novak, *Theology for Radical Politics,* 17.
26. Ibid., 28, 60.
27. Ibid., 29, 10–11.
28. Ibid., 92–93, 15.

29. Ibid., 72.

30. Ibid., 103–04.

31. Ibid., 79–80.

32. Ibid., 81.

33. See, for example, Richard John Neuhaus, "Notes on the Culture Wars," The Public Square, *First Things,* January 1991, 59–63.

34. For Neuhaus's early opposition to abortion, see "The Dangerous Assumptions," *Commonweal,* June 30, 1967, 408–13. For his post-*Roe* views, see the brief, nuanced, and tentative discussions of abortion in *Time Toward Home,* 215; and Richard John Neuhaus, *Christian Faith and Public Policy: Thinking and Acting in the Courage of Uncertainty* (Minneapolis: Augsburg Publishing, 1978), 114–17.

35. Richard John Neuhaus, "The Loneliness of the Long-Distance Radical," *Christian Century,* April 26, 1972, 481. See also the dismissive comments about the "new faddishness" of the cultural revolution in *Movement and Revolution,* 136, 207; "Pope's Aid Sought on Birth Control," *New York Times,* November 26, 1966; and Neuhaus, "Dangerous Assumptions," 412–13.

36. Neuhaus, "Dangerous Assumptions," 412–13.

37. Neuhaus, *Christian Faith and Public Policy,* 112ff.

38. Hall, *Because of Their Faith,* 123.

39. See Neuhaus, *America Against Itself,* 61; and Weiss, "Going to Extremes," 16.

40. Neuhaus, "Long-Distance Radical," 477.

41. Ibid., 479.

42. Ibid., 480.

43. In 1976 Neuhaus still believed that the radical injustice of the previous decade was obvious: "There are historical times when evil is so clearly defined that all Christians are called to come to witness. The '60s were one of those times." Quoted in Hall, *Because of Their Faith,* 170.

44. Richard John Neuhaus, "The Democratic Prospect," *Worldview,* July/August 1976, 13.

45. Neuhaus, *Time Toward Home,* 154.

46. "Again, God's Country," 60.

47. Neuhaus, "Democratic Prospect," 20.

48. Ibid., 20.

49. Ibid., 20.

50. Neuhaus, *Time Toward Home,* 11.

51. Neuhaus, "Democratic Prospect," 20.

52. Neuhaus, *Time Toward Home,* vii.

53. See Neuhaus, *Time Toward Home,* vii; and "Democratic Prospect," 19. See also the editorial statement in the inaugural issue of Neuhaus's influential magazine, *First Things,* "First Things First," March 1990, 7.

54. Neuhaus, *Time Toward Home,* 46–47.

55. Neuhaus, "Democratic Prospect," 20.

56. Neuhaus, *Time Toward Home,* 46–47.

57. See Neuhaus, *Time Toward Home,* 66.

58. Neuhaus, *Time Toward Home,* 64. See also "Again, God's Country," 60. And for a recent and explicit restatement of this view, see Neuhaus, "Our American Babylon," *First Things,* December 2005, 23–28.

59. Neuhaus, "Democratic Prospect," 20.

60. Neuhaus, *Time Toward Home,* 66, 177.

61. Ibid., 154–55.

62. Quoted in Michael Novak, "Controversial Engagements," in *Three in One: Essays on Democratic Capitalism, 1976–2000,* ed. Edward W. Younkins (Lanham, MD: Rowman & Littlefield, 2001), 322.

63. Michael Novak, "Engagement but No Security," *Commonweal,* January 30, 1981, 44.

64. Michael Novak, *The Rise of the Unmeltable Ethnics* (New York: Macmillan, 1972).

65. See Gary Dorrien, *The Neoconservative Mind: Politics, Culture, and the War of Ideology* (Philadelphia: Temple University Press, 1993), 216–18.

66. See, for example, Michael Novak, "A Closet Capitalist Confesses," *Washington Post,* March 14, 1976; and "The Closet Socialists," *Christian Century,* February 23, 1977, 171–74.

67. Michael Novak, "An Underpraised and Undervalued System," *Worldview,* July/August 1977, 11.

68. Michael Novak, "Rethinking Social Policy," *Worldview,* July/August, 1979, 40.

69. Ibid.

70. Novak, "Controversial Engagements," 317.

71. Michael Novak, *The Spirit of Democratic Capitalism* (New York: Simon & Schuster, 1982), 14–15.

72. Michael Novak, "Class, Culture, and Society," review of *The Winding Passage: Essays and Sociological Journeys, 1960–1980,* by Daniel Bell, *Commentary,* July 1981, 72.

73. For an early statement on the Trinitarian system of democratic capitalism, see Novak, "Rethinking Social Policy," 43.

74. Michael Novak, *Toward a Theology of the Corporation* (Washington, DC: American Enterprise Institute, 1981), 41–43.

75. See, for example, Novak, *Spirit of Democratic Capitalism,* 89; Michael Novak, *Confessions of a Catholic* (New York: Harper & Row, 1983), 115–18; Michael Novak, "Errand into the Wilderness," in *Political Passages: Journeys of Change Through Two Decades, 1968–1988,* ed. John H. Bunzel (New York: Free Press, 1988), 254–55, 269–72; and Michael Novak, "The Return of the Catholic Whig," *First Things,* March 1990, 38. See also the potent criticism of Novak by Peter Steinfels in "Michael Novak and his Ultrasuper Democraticapitalism," *Commonweal,* January 14, 1983, 11–16.

76. On this distinctly American mix of ideals, see Garry Wills, *Reagan's America: Innocents at Home* (New York: Doubleday, 1987).

77. Neuhaus, *Time Toward Home,* 215.

78. Neuhaus, *Christian Faith and Public Policy,* 97–101, 117–20, 144–45.

79. Neuhaus, "A Carter Presidency and the Real Watershed," *Worldview,* September 1976, 28–29.

80. Ibid., 29–30.

81. Ibid., 29.

82. Ibid., 30.

83. See the account in Richard John Neuhaus, *The Naked Public Square: Religion and Democracy in America* (Grand Rapids, MI: Eerdmans, 1984), 96–97.

84. Patrick Allitt, *Religion in America Since 1945: A History* (New York: Columbia University Press, 2003), 150–52.

85. Through the first year of the Reagan administration, Neuhaus limited himself to reproving liberals for overreacting to the new president. See Weiss, "Going to Extremes," 17.

86. Laurie Goodstein, "How the Evangelicals and Catholics Joined Forces," The Week in Review, *New York Times,* May 30, 2004.

87. See, for example, Harvey Cox, "Putting God Back in Politics," *New York Times Book Review,* August 26, 1984; J. M. Cameron, "Meeting the Lord in the Air," *New York Review of Books,* October 11, 1984; Michael Scully, "Finding a Place for Religion in Public Life," *Wall Street Journal,* July 30, 1984; John Herbers, "Political and Religious Shifts Rekindle Church-State Issue," *New York Times,* September 2, 1984.

88. Neuhaus, *Naked Public Square,* x.

89. Ibid., 79, 7.

90. Ibid., 37.

91. Ibid., 87.

92. Hall, *Because of Their Faith,* 170.

93. Neuhaus, *Naked Public Square,* 225.

94. Ibid., 81–82, 204. For sociological evidence of secularism's incompatibility with human social life, Neuhaus pointed to the work of Émile Durkheim on the religious foundations of society and the writings of his old friend Peter Berger on the "sacred canopy" under which all human communities supposedly live and thrive.

95. Ibid., 78–80, 85–87.

96. Ibid., 259.

97. Ibid., 87.

98. Neuhaus quoted this arresting phrase of MacIntyre's at several points in *Naked Public Square.* See 21, 99, 111, and 163.

99. Ibid., 101–02. See also "Contending for the Future: Overcoming the Pferrian Inversion," *Journal of Law and Religion* 8, no. 1 (1990).

100. Neuhaus, *Naked Public Square,* 197.

101. See the tentative discussion of Catholicism's potentially "culture-forming influence" in ibid., 262.

2: THE PATH TO POWER

1. Irving Kristol, "Business and the 'New Class,' " in *Neo-Conservatism: The Autobiography of an Idea* (New York: Free Press, 1995), 207.

2. Lionel Trilling, "Preface to *Beyond Culture,*" in *The Moral Obligation to be Intelligent,* ed. Leon Wieseltier (New York: Farrar, Straus and Giroux, 2000), 552.

3. Kristol, "Business and the 'New Class,' " 207.

4. Kristol's shift toward more active political engagement seems to have begun around 1976, when he spent a year as a visiting fellow at the American Enterprise Institute in Washington. See Irving Kristol, "An Autobiographical Memoir," in *Neo-Conservatism,* 34.

5. On the idea of the neoconservative "counterintellectual," see Mark Lilla, "Zionism and the Counterintellectuals," in *Israeli Historical Revisionism: From Left to Right,* ed. Anita Shapira and Derek J. Penslar (London: Frank Cass, 2002), 77–83; and James Nuechterlein, "Life at the Intellectual Barricades," *First Things,* October 1994, 12–13.

6. Irving Kristol, "The New Populism: Not to Worry," in *Neo-Conservatism,* 360–63.

7. Quoted in Mark Gerson, *The Neoconservative Vision: From the Cold War to the Culture Wars* (Lanham, MD: Madison Books, 1997), 258.

8. Irving Kristol, "The Coming 'Conservative Century,' " in *Neo-Conservatism,* 365; Irving Kristol, "The New Face of American Politics," in *Neo-Conservatism,* 372; and Irving Kristol, "My Cold War," in *Neo-Conservatism,* 485–86.

9. For further evidence of the theocon-neocon convergence, see Richard John Neuhaus, "Pop Goes the Culture," The Public Square, *First Things,* June/July 1991, 57: "A few months ago, the Brad[le]y Foundation brought together a passel of mainly neoconservative types in Chicago to ponder the shape of struggles ahead. There was a ready, and perhaps remarkable, consensus that the cultural questions—as distinct, albeit not separate, from the economic and political questions—are now center stage. It was further agreed that at the heart of culture is religion."

10. Gerson, *Neoconservative Vision,* 312ff.

11. Ibid., 309–12.

12. Richard Bernstein, "Magazine Dispute Reflects Rift on U.S. Right," *New York Times,* May 16, 1989.

13. Richard John Neuhaus, "Democratic Conservatism," The Public Square, *First Things,* March 1990, 66.

14. Robert Wuthnow, *The Restructuring of American Religion: Society and Faith Since World War II* (Princeton: Princeton University Press, 1988). The trend was perhaps first noticed in Dean Kelly's prescient book *Why Conservative Churches Are Growing* (New York: Harper & Row, 1972).

15. A similar pattern can also be seen in the growing polarization of the nation's Protestant denominations—with liberal mainline churches squared off against much more conservative evangelicals, fundamentalists, Pentecostals, Reformed Calvinists, and Mormons. Other recent developments—from the rancorous split within the

Episcopal Church over the ordination of an openly gay bishop to analogous battles within the United Methodist Church and the Evangelical Lutheran Church in America—indicate that the trend is likely to continue for the foreseeable future.

16. As Patrick Allitt points out in *Catholic Intellectuals and Conservative Politics in America, 1950–1985* (Ithaca: Cornell University Press, 1993), 196–97, Phyllis Schlafly's alliance of Protestant and Catholic religious women to fight the Equal Rights Amendment during the 1970s (StopERA) was an important precursor of the trend toward "mere orthodoxy."

17. Neuhaus, *Naked Public Square,* 262. There were approximately fifty million Catholics in the United States in 1984. By 2001 there were approximately sixty million.

18. Richard John Neuhaus, *The Catholic Moment: The Paradox of the Church in the Postmodern World* (New York: Harper & Row, 1987), 284.

19. Kennedy quoted in Neuhaus, *Catholic Moment,* 250.

20. See George Weigel, *Tranquillitas Ordinis: The Present Failure and Future Promise of American Catholic Thought on War and Peace* (New York: Oxford University Press, 1987). See also the discussion in chapter 4 of this volume.

21. Quoted in George Weigel, *Catholicism and the Renewal of American Democracy* (New York: Paulist Press, 1989), 1.

22. Weigel, *Catholicism and Renewal of Democracy,* 5.

23. Neuhaus, *Catholic Moment,* 242, 253, 286.

24. Ibid., 248–50.

25. Allitt, *Catholic Intellectuals and Conservative Politics,* 35.

26. Ibid., 34.

27. For Neuhaus's most ambitious attempt to make this argument in his own name, see "The Liberalism of John Paul II," *First Things,* May 1997, 16–21.

28. Richard John Neuhaus, "A New Order of Religious Freedom," *First Things,* February 1992, 14–15. See also "Our American Babylon," *First Things,* December 2005, 27, where Neuhaus writes that there is a line that runs "from the errand in the wilderness to Martin Luther King, Jr.'s 'beloved community' to Ronald Reagan's 'city on a hill' and George W. Bush's second inaugural on America's appointed task in advancing freedom and democracy in the world."

29. Weigel, *Catholicism and the Renewal of Democracy,* 90.

30. Ibid., 93–94.

31. Ibid.

32. Neuhaus, *Catholic Moment,* 168ff.

33. Weigel quoted in Richard John Neuhaus, *Doing Well and Doing Good: The Challenge to the Christian Capitalist* (New York: Doubleday, 1992), 62.

34. Ibid.

35. See Pat Windsor, "Neoconservatives Capitalize on Papal Encyclical," *National Catholic Reporter,* May 17, 1991, 3; Charlotte Allen, "What Did He Say?" *Insight,* July 8, 1991, 24–25; William McGurn, "Is the Pope Capitalist?" *American Spectator,* August 1991, 12–14; and "That Encyclical," Editorial, *First Things,* August/September 1991, 11–12.

36. *Centesimus Annus,* 1991, paragraph 41.

37. See Neuhaus, *Doing Well and Doing Good,* 49; and "The Novak Achievement," The Public Square, *First Things,* November 1993, 67, where Neuhaus writes, "It is no secret that John Paul has read Novak's work. Those who worked closely with the Pope on [*Centesimus Annus*] can testify to the influence of Novak's thought on crucial passages." See also the critical review of *Doing Well and Doing Good* by Milwaukee's Archbishop Rembert G. Weakland, "Abridging Pontifex Maximus," *Commonweal,* November 6, 1992, 30–31, and the resulting exchange between Neuhaus and Weakland in *Commonweal,* December 18, 1992, 2, 30.

38. Compare Neuhaus, *Christian Faith and Public Policy,* 114–17, to the editorial from the inaugural issue of *First Things,* "Redefining Abortion Politics," March 1990, 9–11.

39. Richard John Neuhaus, "Nihilism Without the Abyss: Law, Rights, and the Transcendent Good," *Journal of Law and Religion,* 1987, 55, 58.

40. The most fully developed statement of this view can be found in the 1995 encyclical *Evangelium Vitae.*

41. *Evangelium Vitae,* paragraph 58.

42. Ibid.

43. See *Centesmus Annus,* paragraph 46, on how a "democracy without values easily turns into open or thinly disguised totalitarianism."

44. Whereas the Catholic bishops had come out in immediate opposition to *Roe v. Wade,* evangelicals were slow to adopt the prolife line. Even the ultraconservative Southern Baptist Convention approved of the 1973 decision at first—as did the Episcopalians, Lutherans, United Methodists, Disciples of Christ, Presbyterians, and Mormons. See Patrick Allitt, *Religion in America Since 1945: A History* (New York: Columbia University Press, 2003), 159ff.

45. Richard John Neuhaus, "The Longest War," The Public Square, *First Things,* November 1994, 66.

46. On contraception and the culture of death, see *Evangelium Vitae,* paragraph 13. The most lengthy public discussion of contraception among the theocons took place in a symposium in the December 1998 issue of *First Things,* to which several Catholics and Protestants contributed, thereby distancing the magazine itself from either side of the divisive issue.

47. Richard John Neuhaus, "Can Atheists Be Good Citizens?" *First Things,* August/September 1991, 21.

48. Ibid.

49. Charles W. Colson and Richard John Neuhaus, "Introduction," *Evangelicals and Catholics Together: Toward a Common Mission* (Dallas: Word Publishing, 1995), x.

50. Neuhaus, *Catholic Moment,* 284.

51. Richard John Neuhaus, "How I Became the Catholic I Was," *First Things,* April 2002, 18.

52. Peter Steinfels, "Citing Luther, a Noted Theologian Leaves Lutheran Church for Catholicism," *New York Times,* September 9, 1990.

53. According to a press release from the Catholic News Service (CNS) on September

9, 1991, Neuhaus's ordination was attended by Cardinal Anthony J. Bevilacqua of Philadelphia, Archbishop J. Francis Stafford of Denver, and Bishop Rene H. Gracida of Corpus Christi, Texas, as well as by New York auxiliary bishops Patrick J. Sheridan, Patrick V. Ahern, and William J. McCormack.

54. See Peter Steinfels, "Catholics and Evangelicals: Seeking a Middle Ground," *New York Times,* March 30, 1994.

55. "Evangelicals and Catholics Together," *First Things,* May 1994, 18.

56. Ibid., 19.

57. Ibid., 19–20.

58. Quoted in Richard John Neuhaus, "A Sense of Change Both Ominous and Promising," The Public Square, *First Things,* August/September 1995, 67.

59. See Laurie Goodstein, "How the Evangelicals and Catholics Joined Forces," The Week in Review, *New York Times,* May 30, 2004.

60. Richard John Neuhaus, "The Catholic Difference," in *Evangelicals and Catholics Together,* 176.

61. Charles W. Colson, "The Common Cultural Task: The Culture War from a Protestant Perspective," *Evangelicals and Catholics Together,* 30ff.

62. Ibid., 4.

63. Ibid., 31.

3: FROM DESPAIR TO REDEMPTION

1. Stanley Fish, "Why We Can't All Just Get Along," *First Things,* February 1996, 18–26 and 35–40; and Richard John Neuhaus, "Why We Can Get Along," *First Things,* February 1996, 27–34.

2. Charles W. Colson, cofounder and coorganizer of Evangelicals and Catholics Together, won the same prize the previous year (1993) for his work with Prison Fellowship Ministries.

3. Quoted in Andrew Sullivan, "Going Down Screaming," *New York Times Magazine,* October 11, 1998, 50.

4. Hadley Arkes, recounting a conversation with Neuhaus in "The New Pro-Life Hope?" *Crisis,* July/August 1998, 10.

5. See the numerous hopeful quotations from Neuhaus's January 1993 appearance on the *MacNeil/Lehrer Newshour* in "Bill Clinton and the American Character," The Public Square, *First Things,* June/July 1999, 63–64.

6. Ibid., 64.

7. Neuhaus quoted in Robin Toner, "Anti-Abortion Group Maps Strategy," *New York Times,* June 27, 1993.

8. Richard John Neuhaus, "A Time Bomb, Ticking, Ticking," The Public Square, *First Things,* February 1995, 63.

9. Richard John Neuhaus, "The Dred Scott of Our Time," *Wall Street Journal,* July 2, 1992. See also "Abortion and a Nation at War," Editorial, *First Things,* October 1992, 9–13.

10. George Weigel, "The Neo-Conservative Difference: A Proposal for the Renewal of Church and Society," *Pro Ecclesia* IV, no. 2 (1996): 208–09.

11. For the theocon position on euthanasia, see the statement of the Ramsey Colloquium, "Always to Care, Never to Kill," *First Things*, February 1992, 45–47.

12. In fact, the Supreme Court overruled the Ninth Circuit in *Washington v. Glucksberg* (1997), which denied any "right to die" in the Constitution. But this would provide little solace for the theocons, since they believed that the Ninth Circuit had decided the case correctly: under *Casey* there *was* no ground for denying a person's right to die. The Supreme Court had thus merely put off the inevitable. A similar dynamic would play itself out on the issue of sodomy, the banning of which was held first to be constitutional in *Bowers v. Hardwick* (1986) and then unconstitutional in *Lawrence v. Texas* (2003)—the latter of which relied in large part on *Casey.*

13. "The Ninth Circuit's Fatal Overreach," Editorial, *First Things*, May 1996, 13.

14. For the distinctively rationalistic character of the theocon position on abortion, see the revealing debate between Arkes and neocon James Q. Wilson in Arkes, "Abortion Facts and Feelings," *First Things*, April 1994, 34–38; and Wilson and Arkes, "Abortion Facts and Feelings II: An Exchange," *First Things*, May 1994, 39–42.

15. James Nuechterlein, interview by author, May 15, 2005.

16. "The End of Democracy? The Judicial Usurpation of Politics," Introduction, *First Things*, November 1996, 18.

17. Ibid., 19.

18. Ibid.

19. Ibid., 20.

20. Ibid., 19.

21. Robert H. Bork, "Our Judicial Oligarchy," *First Things*, November 1996, 21.

22. Ibid., 23.

23. Russell Hittinger, "A Crisis of Legitimacy," *First Things*, November 1996, 25, 26.

24. Ibid., 29.

25. Charles W. Colson, "Kingdoms in Conflict," *First Things*, November 1996, 35.

26. Ibid., 37.

27. Ibid., 38.

28. Robert P. George, "The Tyrant State," *First Things*, November 1996, 42.

29. Ibid., 41.

30. Ibid., 42.

31. Bork, "Judicial Oligarchy," 23–24.

32. Hadley Arkes, "A Culture Corrupted," *First Things*, November 1996, 33.

33. "End of Democracy?" 19–20.

34. Colson, "Kingdoms in Conflict," 37, 38.

35. George, "Tyrant State," 40.

36. Midge Decter, "The End of Democracy? A Discussion Continued," *First Things*, January 1997, 21.

37. Nuechterlein, interview.

38. Frank Rich, "The War in the Wings," *New York Times*, October 9, 1996; Garry

Wills, "A Mandate to Get Along," *New York Times,* November 7, 1996; Peter Steinfels, "Religious Nuances in Debate on 'Government by Judges,' " *New York Times,*
December 14, 1996.

39. See, for example, Steven Calabresi, "Out of Order," *Policy Review,* September/
October 1996; "First Things First," Editorial, *National Review,* November 11, 1996,
16, 18; "It's Time to Take on the Judges," Editorial, *Weekly Standard,* December 16,
1996, 9–10; "Who's Boss?" Editorial, *Wall Street Journal,* December 20, 1996.

40. Samuel Francis, *The End of Democracy? The Judicial Usurpation of Politics,* ed.
Mitchell S. Muncy (Dallas: Spence Publishing, 1997), 134, 138.

41. Walter Berns, Correspondence, *First Things,* January 1997, 2–3: "You do not speak for
me . . . when you say that the government of the United States is morally illegitimate
and come close to advocating not only civil disobedience but armed revolution."

42. Gertrude Himmelfarb, Correspondence, *First Things,* January 1997, 2.

43. David Brooks, "The Right's Anti-American Temptation," *Weekly Standard,* November 11, 1996, 23–26.

44. William Kristol, *End of Democracy?* 94.

45. Norman Podhoretz, letter to Neuhaus, quoted in Podhoretz's contribution to
Commentary magazine's own special issue on the *First Things* symposium: "On the
Future of Conservatism: A Symposium," February 1997, reprinted in *End of
Democracy?* 101–02.

46. Jacob Heilbrunn, "Neocons vs. Theocons?" *End of Democracy?* 143–55; see also
Decter, "End of Democracy? A Discussion Continued," 21.

47. Himmelfarb, correspondence.

48. Quoted in Heilbrunn, "Neocons vs. Theocons," 153.

49. Quoted in ibid.

50. James C. Dobson, "End of Democracy? A Discussion Continued," 21–22.

51. Peter Berger, *End of Democracy?,* 72.

52. Although polls sometimes purport to show that a majority of Americans support a
prochoice position, Neuhaus's line since the late 1980s (based on his own reading
of the polling data) has been that 70 percent of Americans support laws that would
prohibit 90 percent of the abortions currently performed in the United States. In
other words, while most Americans believe abortion should be legal in cases of rape,
incest, life of the mother, and other "extreme" circumstances, that support collapses
when they are asked about cases in which abortion is used as a form of birth control or as a way of maintaining a childless lifestyle.

53. Robert P. George, *The Clash of Orthodoxies: Law, Religion, and Morality in Crisis*
(Wilmington, DE: ISI Books, 2001), 144–45. Neuhaus's response to Berger was, by
comparison, much less substantial and forthcoming, amounting to little more than
the claim that if "Congress had done what the Court did in *Roe v. Wade,* we would
obviously be living in a very different America, so radically disordered in its morals
and laws that government would likely be unsustainable." See Richard John
Neuhaus, "The Anatomy of a Controversy," *End of Democracy?* 180.

54. George, *Clash of Orthodoxies,* 146–47.

55. Hadley Arkes, "Crossing the Threshold," *End of Democracy?* 171. The quote is from a letter Lincoln wrote to his friend Joshua Speed: "You ought . . . to appreciate how much the great body of the Northern people do crucify their feelings in order to maintain their loyalty to the Constitution and the Union."

56. Weigel, *End of Democracy?* 109.

57. Richard John Neuhaus, "The Anatomy of a Controversy," 263–64.

58. Ibid., 265–66.

59. Released on July 4, 1997, the document was later published in the November 1997 issue of *First Things,* 51–54, exactly one year after the original symposium. See also Richard John Neuhaus, " 'We Hold These Truths'—An Argument to Be Engaged," The Public Square, *First Things,* November 1997, 66–73.

60. "We Hold These Truths," Documentation, *First Things,* October 1997, 51–52.

61. Ibid., 53–54.

62. Quoted in "A Mirror of the National Soul," The Public Square, *First Things,* March 1997, 56.

63. Ibid.

64. See Robert Bork, "Hard Truths About the Culture War," *First Things,* June/July 1995, 18–23; and *Slouching Toward Gomorrah: Modern Liberalism and American Decline* (New York: Regan Books, 1996).

65. William J. Bennett, *The Death of Outrage: Bill Clinton and the Assault on American Ideals* (New York: The Free Press, 1998).

66. Quoted in Neuhaus, "Bill Clinton and the American Character," 78.

67. See Alan Wolfe, "Look Who's Turning Off and Tuning Out This Time," *New York Times,* February 22, 1999.

68. *First Things* editor James Nuechterlein was the only member of the theocon inner circle to oppose removing Clinton from office. See Nuechterlein, "Punishment Yes, Impeachment, No," *First Things,* January 1999, 7–8.

69. Neuhaus, "Bill Clinton and the American Character," 79.

70. Richard John Neuhaus, "Clinton and Character Revisited," The Public Square, *First Things,* October 1999, 85.

71. Quoted in Arkes, "New Pro-Life Hope?" 10–11.

72. Ibid.

73. Franklin Foer, "Spin Doctrine: The Catholic Teachings of George W," *New Republic,* June 5, 2000, 19; Laurie Goodstein, "Personal and Political, Bush's Faith Blurs Lines," *New York Times,* October 26, 2004.

74. Richard John Neuhaus, "While We're At It," The Public Square, *First Things,* October 1998, 91.

75. Goodstein, "Personal and Political."

76. Foer, "Spin Doctrine," 19.

77. See ibid., 18: "Intellectual genealogies of the Bush campaign usually trace back to Marvin Olasky, the evangelical University of Texas academic who wrote the 1992 book *The Tragedy of American Compassion.* But Olasky's big idea—junking the welfare state in favor of moralistic charities—didn't come out of nowhere. It has strong

roots in . . . the work of two intellectuals, Richard John Neuhaus and Michael No-vak." See also Neuhaus's response to the Foer article, "While We're At It," The Pub-lic Square, *First Things,* August/September 2000, 99: "There is considerable truth in the claim that Governor Bush has embraced, at least in part, the concept of 'sub-sidiarity' and the role of 'mediating institutions' in society, as is evident in, for exam-ple, his proposals for parental choice in education, the importance of faith-based institutions in meeting social needs, and the devolution of decision making to those most affected by the decisions made."

78. Richard John Neuhaus, "The Two Politics of Election 2000," The Public Square, *First Things,* February 2001, 57.

79. Ibid., 60. See also Gary Rosen's critical essay on the ease with which Neuhaus and other conservatives abandoned their principles in order to embrace the ruling that ended the Florida recount: "Reconsidering *Bush v. Gore,*" *Commentary,* November 2001, 35–41.

CHAPTER 4: THEOCONS AT WAR

1. These weekly conversations would come to an abrupt end in the summer of 2004, when Hudson was forced to resign from *Crisis* amid accusations of sexual miscon-duct.

2. Gerson would be succeeded in Bush's second term by Catholic theocon William McGurn, a former chief editorial writer for the *Wall Street Journal.*

3. See David Kirkpatrick, "Aide Is Bush's Eyes and Ears on the Right," *New York Times,* June 28, 2004. Shortly after September 11, 2001, Goeglein would tell the evangel-ical *World* magazine: "I think President Bush is God's man at this hour, and I say this with a great sense of humility." See Joel C. Rosenberg, "Flash Traffic: Political Buzz From Washington," *World,* October 6, 2001, at www.worldmag.com/display-article.cfm?id=5425.

4. Richard John Neuhaus, "September 11—Before and After," The Public Square, *First Things,* November 2001, 65.

5. William Kristol and Robert Kagan, "Toward a Neo-Reaganite Foreign Policy," *For-eign Affairs,* July/August 1996, 31–32. Kristol would push this synthesis of foreign and domestic moralism in the pages of his new magazine, the *Weekly Standard.* One of the journal's senior editors, David Brooks, picked up the theme in "A Return to National Greatness," *Weekly Standard,* March 3, 1997, 16–21, where he advocated a foreign policy of "global purpose" in order to fight the tide of "nihilistic medioc-rity" at home. Brooks would also write in a striking statement that "it almost doesn't matter what great task government sets for himself, as long as it does some tangible thing with energy and effectiveness." The neocons appealed to Theodore Roosevelt as an early advocate of this "national greatness" conservatism, claiming that he too viewed "foreign policy activism and patriotism as remedies for cultural threats he perceived at home"—threats such as "the soft and easy enjoyment of material com-fort." See Brooks, "Politics and Patriotism: From Teddy Roosevelt to John Mc-

Cain," *Weekly Standard,* April 26, 1999, 16–23; see also Max Boot, "The Unrealistic Realism of Henry Kissinger," *Weekly Standard,* June 18, 2001, 31–34.

6. Robert Kagan and William Kristol, "A National Humiliation," *Weekly Standard,* April 16, 2001, 11–16.

7. Andrew Sullivan, "Why Did It Have to Be a Perfect Morning?" *Sunday Times of London,* September 16, 2001.

8. Samuel Huntington, *The Clash of Civilizations and the Remaking of World Order* (New York: Simon & Schuster, 1996).

9. "In a Time of War," Editorial, *First Things,* December 2001, 12.

10. See historian James Turner Johnson's "Just War, As It Was and Is," *First Things,* January 2005, 14–24; and also Johnson's "The Right Wrongs," *First Things,* March 2005, 45: "When used justly—and in the American system this means at its basis to protect the essential goods of life, liberty, and the pursuit of happiness at which American democracy aims—coercive force is not an evil at all but an instrument of good."

11. "In a Time of War," 13.

12. Ibid., 12.

13. Ibid., 14–15.

14. Ibid., 16. See also Richard John Neuhaus, "Religious Freedom in a Time of War," The Public Square, *First Things,* January 2002, 75: "The war against terrorism is . . . a war of religion."

15. Andrew Sullivan, "This Is a Religious War: September 11 Was Only the Beginning," *New York Times Magazine,* October 7, 2001, 44–47, 52–53.

16. "In a Time of War," 16.

17. See, for example, the Founding Document that Neuhaus penned for the Institute on Religion and Democracy in 1981, at www.ird-renew.org.

18. Later changed simply to *Crisis.*

19. Michael Novak, *Moral Clarity in the Nuclear Age* (Nashville: Thomas Nelson Publishers, 1983).

20. See Patrick Allitt, *Catholic Intellectuals and Conservative Politics in America, 1950–1985* (Ithaca: Cornell University Press, 1993), 81–82.

21. Ibid., 291–93.

22. Despite Weigel's attempts to link the "just war" tradition to Catholicism—as well as his efforts to portray that tradition as requiring retrieval from obscurity and neglect—"just war" thinking had already been influentially revived by Jewish scholar Michael Walzer in his 1977 book *Just and Unjust Wars,* which discussed "just war" thinking in less sectarian terms, and which Weigel barely mentioned in his own book.

23. As Peter Steinfels wrote in an incisive review of the book in *Commonweal* magazine, Weigel's argument was deeply disingenuous: "The reader who approaches *Tranquillitatis Ordinis* suspecting a strong political spin on its theological argument will not be mistaken. Weigel is doing precisely what he accuses, with some justification, many peace activists of doing: using Catholic teaching to support specific pruden-

tial judgments that rest not on the teaching alone but on 'political' readings of fact and history." See "The Heritage Abandoned?" *Commonweal,* September 11, 1987, 487–92.

24. See, for example, Richard John Neuhaus, "Just War and This War," *Wall Street Journal,* January 29, 1991.

25. George Weigel, "The Churches and the War in the Gulf," *First Things,* March 1991, 37.

26. Ibid., 42.

27. Ibid., 43.

28. See *Washington Post* columnist Charles Krauthammer's "The False Promise of Deterrence," *Weekly Standard,* December 9, 2002, 22–24.

29. See *Los Angeles Times* columnist Max Boot's "American Imperialism? No Need to Run Away from Label," *USA Today,* May 5, 2003.

30. Norman Podhoretz, "How to Win World War IV," *Commentary,* February 2002, 19–29; Michael Ledeen, "The War Won't End in Baghdad," *Wall Street Journal,* September 4, 2002.

31. See George Weigel's disclaimer in his debate with the Anglican Archbishop of Canterbury Rowan Williams in "War and Statecraft: An Exchange," *First Things,* March 2004, 18: "In writing 'Moral Clarity in a Time of War,' my first intention was not to promote a reading of the just war tradition that would provide a secure moral rationale for preemptive U.S.-led military action against the regime of Saddam Hussein, similar outlaw states, or international terrorism; it was to propose a revitalization of the just war way of thinking as the basis of morally serious statecraft in the Western democracies in the circumstances of a post-September 11 world. To be sure, Iraq was an urgent test case for the just war tradition in this new and dangerous situation; and it is no secret that, in my judgment, a just war case for military action against the Saddam Hussein regime could be mounted. Still, I trust that my essay did not put the policy cart before the theological horse."

32. The following summary is based on the argument of George Weigel's "Moral Clarity in a Time of War," *First Things,* January 2003.

33. Ibid., 27.

34. Richard John Neuhaus, "Sounds of Religion in a Time of War," The Public Square, *First Things,* May 2003, 77, 80. See also Richard John Neuhaus, "The Vatican vs. 'Americanism,' " The Public Square, *First Things,* December 2004, 72: "It would be an exquisite irony of history if, when war is declared on the Christian West by those inspired by a possibly perverse but undeniably Islamic ideology, the Vatican refused to take sides; thus, willy-nilly, taking the other side. . . . An enemy has declared war and sides must be taken," and "the United States is . . . on the Christian side."

35. Neuhaus, "Sounds of Religion," 79. This passage inspired one critic of the theocons to reply tartly, "Cheerleading is not an alternative to badgering." See Peter Dula, "The War In Iraq: How Catholic Conservatives Got It Wrong," *Commonweal,* December 3, 2004, 17.

36. See Neuhaus, "Sounds of Religion," 77, where he wrote that in order for a war to

be just, "the cause must be just, and the just cause in this case is the disarmament of Iraq."

37. Tony Judt, "America and the World," *New York Review of Books,* April 10, 2003, 31.

38. Richard John Neuhaus, "War in a New Era," The Public Square, *First Things,* August/September 2003, 64–65.

39. For a transcript of the meeting, during which the president twice singled out Neuhaus (whom he called "Father Richard") for praise, see "Bush Calls for 'Culture Change' " at the *Christianity Today* website, www.christianitytoday.com/ct/2004/121/51.0.html.

40. Richard John Neuhaus, "Drawing the Line Against Torture," The Public Square, *First Things,* October 2004, 82.

41. Richard John Neuhaus, "Speaking About the Unspeakable," The Public Square, *First Things,* March 2005, 62.

42. On the *First Things* weblog (www.firstthings.com) on November 28, 2005, Neuhaus seemed to revert to his original statement of absolute condemnation of torture, endorsing Senator John McCain's proposed ban on torture against the pro-torture arguments of neocon Charles Krauthammer.

43. Dula, "War in Iraq," 21.

44. Richard John Neuhaus, "Internationalisms," The Public Square, *First Things,* December 2004, 67.

45. Ibid., 66.

46. One need not assume—as some critics of the war have done—that the Bush administration deliberately lied about Saddam's arsenal of weapons in order to persuade the country to go to war with Iraq. Given the broad consensus that weapons would be found in the country, it is highly implausible that the administration claimed that such weapons existed while knowing that in fact they did not, which is what the charge of lying assumes. It is far more likely that the administration unintentionally deceived itself along with everyone else. On the administration's strenuous efforts to ensure that the intelligence confirmed its a priori assumptions about the Iraqi threat, see John B. Judis and Spencer Ackerman, "The First Casualty: The Selling of the Iraq War," *New Republic,* June 30, 2003, 14–18, 23–25; and Franklin Foer, "Intelligence Design," *New Republic,* November 21, 2005, 6.

47. See, for example, Michael Massing, "Now They Tell Us," *New York Review of Books,* February 26, 2004, 43–49; and "The Times and Iraq," *New York Times,* May 26, 2004.

48. Rowan Williams, "War and Statecraft: An Exchange," 17. See also Weigel's weak response on page 20, where he asserts that "from my own experience with the present U.S. administration, I can say with some assurance that this point is well understood in the White House, the National Security Council, and the Department of Defense."

49. Ron Suskind, "Without a Doubt," *New York Times Magazine,* October 17, 2004, 51.

50. Neuhaus, "Internationalisms," 67.

51. Ibid., 66.

52. Ibid., 66–67.

53. The most extreme theocon endorsement of the president's ambition to democratize the Middle East came in Michael Novak's 2004 book *The Universal Hunger for Liberty: Why the Clash of Civilizations Is Not Inevitable* (New York: Basic Books). Neuhaus commissioned a surprisingly negative review of the book for *First Things,* marking one of the few times when a theocon publicly criticized a member of the "family" in the pages of the movement's flagship journal. See Lawrence A. Uzzell's "Muffling the Clash," *First Things,* February 2005, 48–52.

54. In fall 2005, Neuhaus would restate his position on Iraq once again, this time in an even less triumphalist tone than he had adopted the previous year. Yet the fundamentals of his position remained unchanged. At every point—when discussing the continued absence of weapons of mass destruction, when reflecting on the mounting Iraqi and American casualties, when responding to the Downing Street Memo showing that the administration had decided to go to war nine months before the invasion and that it had deliberately "sexed up" evidence of Iraqi weapons of mass destruction in order to justify an invasion—Neuhaus refused to criticize the war and its aftermath, claiming to possess insufficient information to make an informed moral judgment. Yet Neuhaus's seeming modesty served only to insulate the Bush administration from criticism and thus to make it easier for him to continue to place his faith in the president. It was yet another example of theocon eagerness to defer to authority—provided it was the "right" authority. See "Iraq and Moral Judgment," The Public Square, *First Things,* October 2005, 71–75.

55. George Weigel, "Europe's Problem—and Ours," *First Things,* February 2004, 18. Weigel went on to expand the argument of this essay in a book, *The Cube and the Cathedral: Europe, America, and Politics Without God* (New York: Basic Books, 2005). See also Weigel, "War and Statecraft: An Exchange," 20: "In my view, the recent debacle in the Security Council with respect to Iraq demonstrates that, in dealing with international security issues, today's UN is entirely the tool of states, many of the most important of which—again, France, Germany, and Russia—are certainly not making their policy calculations . . . on grounds of moral reason rightly understood." Unlike, naturally, the United States.

56. Weigel, "Europe's Problem," 20; *Cube and the Cathedral,* 18, 20.

57. On the all-important theocon issue of declining birthrates, the statistics simply do not correlate with theocon assumptions. While Catholic Ireland and France have some of the highest fertility rates in Europe (1.87 and 1.85 children born per woman, respectively, as of 2005), Catholic Italy, Spain, and Poland have some of its lowest (1.28, 1.28, and 1.24 respectively). Meanwhile, fertility rates in historically Protestant (and today thoroughly secular) Scandinavia are much higher (1.78 in Norway, 1.74 in Denmark, 1.73 in Finland, and 1.66 in Sweden). See "The World Factbook" from the Central Intelligence Agency, www.cia.gov/cia/publications/factbook/rankorder/2127rank.html.

58. Weigel, "Europe's Problem," 20.

59. Quoted in Weigel, "Europe's Problem," 23.

60. See also Richard John Neuhaus, "While We're At It," The Public Square, *First*

Things, October 2003, 90: "Europe itself is dying—spiritually, culturally, demo-graphically, politically, and, it seems, economically. Every indicator of the vibrancy of America only feeds the furious fires of *ressentiment,* one of the least pleasant ex-pressions of the deadly sin of envy." And see Richard John Neuhaus, "The New Eu-ropes," *First Things,* October 2005, 12–15.

61. Weigel, "Europe's Problem," 24. In its opinion in *Lawrence v. Texas,* the Supreme Court majority relied in part on the rulings of European courts.

62. Ibid., 25.

63. For an account of Western Europe's struggles with the disestablishment of religion since the seventeenth century, see Mark Lilla, *The Stillborn God* (New York: Knopf, 2006). And for a view of contemporary European societies and cultures very differ-ent (and far more optimistic) than Weigel's, see Tony Judt, "Europe vs. America," *New York Review of Books,* February 10, 2005, 37–41.

5: THEOCON NATION

1. See Elisabeth Bumiller, "Bush Says $2 Billion Went to Religious Charities in '04," *New York Times,* March 2, 2005.

2. See Hadley Arkes, "Bush Second Chance," *First Things,* April 2005, 14–15; and Hadley Arkes, *Natural Rights and the Right to Choose* (Cambridge: Cambridge Uni-versity Press, 2002), 234. See also pp. 248 and 251–52, where Arkes discusses con-gressional testimony by two nurses from Christ Hospital in Oak Lawn, Illinois, about the practice of "live-birth" abortion (or infanticide) in which they were ex-pected to participate at the hospital.

3. Arkes, *Natural Rights,* 245. On the importance of "planting premises," see pp. 247, 261, and 284.

4. Ibid., 245.

5. Quoted in ibid., 255.

6. Ibid., 268–69.

7. Arkes, "Bush's Second Chance," 15.

8. "President Signs Born-Alive Infants Protection Act," August 5, 2002. Available at www.whitehouse.gov/news/releases/2002/08/20020805-6.html.

9. See Richard John Neuhaus, "While We're At It," The Public Square, *First Things,* November 2001, 76: "The pro-abortionists are right in thinking that [the Unborn Victims of Violence Act] is . . . intended as a step toward legal recognition of the humanity of the unborn child."

10. The theocon view on embryonic stem-cell research is nicely captured in the title of the epilogue to Robert P. George's *The Clash of Orthodoxies* (Wilmington, DE: ISI Books, 2001): "We Should Not Kill Human Embryos—For Any Reason."

11. Richard John Neuhaus, "While We're At It," The Public Square, *First Things,* March 2002, 80.

12. See Richard John Neuhaus, "While We're At It," The Public Square, *First Things,* October 2001, 98.

13. Richard John Neuhaus, "A World of Our Own Making," The Public Square, *First Things,* November 1998, 71.

14. "The Inhuman Use of Human Beings: A Statement on Embryo Research by the Ramsey Colloquium," *First Things,* January 1995, 17.

15. Leon Kass, "The Wisdom of Repugnance," *New Republic,* June 2, 1997, 17–26.

16. Quoted in Neuhaus, "World of Our Own Making," 71, 72.

17. Leon Kass, *"L'Chaim* and Its Limits: Why Not Immortality," *First Things,* May 2001, 19–20.

18. Ibid., 21–22.

19. Ibid., 24.

20. For a representative selection of Leon Kass's essays, see his *Life, Liberty, and the Defense of Dignity* (New York: Encounter Books, 2002).

21. Kass, *"L'Chaim,"* 23–24.

22. For further evidence of just how conservative Kass really is, see the essay, cowritten with his wife Amy A. Kass, "Proposing Courtship," *First Things,* October 1999, in which the authors defend traditional courtship rituals, based on the "chastity and modesty" of women (41). For more on this article, see the discussion in chapter 6, this volume.

23. Eight present or former members of the council have published essays or reviews in *First Things:* Kass, Robert P. George, Mary Ann Glendon, Gilbert Meilaender, Peter Lawler, Diana Schaub, Paul McHugh, and James Q. Wilson.

24. See *Human Cloning and Human Dignity: An Ethical Inquiry,* President's Council on Bioethics, Washington, DC, July 2002; *Beyond Therapy: Biotechnology and the Pursuit of Happiness,* President's Council on Bioethics, Washington, DC, October 2003; *Reproduction and Responsibility: The Regulation of New Biotechnologies,* President's Council on Bioethics, Washington, DC, March 2004; and *White Paper: Alternative Sources of Pluripotent Stem Cells,* President's Council on Bioethics, Washington, DC, May 2005. All are available free of charge through the council's website: www.bioethics.gov.

25. The council even published a six-hundred-page anthology of excerpts from these (widely available) texts: *Being Human: Readings from the President's Council on Bioethics* (Washington, D.C.: Government Printing Office, 2004).

26. See, for example, Leon Kass, "The Pursuit of Biohappiness," *Washington Post,* October 16, 2003.

27. The text of the proposed amendment reads as follows: "Marriage in the United States shall consist only of the union of a man and a woman. Neither this Constitution or the constitution of any state, nor state or federal law, shall be construed to require that marital status or the legal incidents thereof be conferred on unmarried couples or groups." Quoted in "The Marriage Amendment," Editorial, *First Things,* October 2003, 14.

28. For President Bush's use of this appellation, see "Bush Calls for 'Culture Change,' " at the *Christianity Today* website, www.christianitytoday.com/ct/2004/121/51.0.html.

29. For Neuhaus's earlier and much more moderate views on homosexuality, see *Christian Faith and Public Policy* (Minneapolis: Augsburg Publishing, 1977), 112ff.

30. Richard John Neuhaus, "Recruiting for the Revolution," The Public Square, *First Things,* October 1993, 63. Four years later he added "compulsion" and "depression" to the list of maladies related to homosexuality. See Richard John Neuhaus, "Love, No Matter What," The Public Square, *First Things,* October 1997, 82.

31. "The Uses of Homophobia," Editorial, *First Things,* November 1990, 7.

32. "The Homosexual Movement: A Response by the Ramsey Colloquium," *First Things,* March 1994, 16. And see also Neuhaus, "Love, No Matter What," 84, where he claims that the "largely intuitive and pre-articulate" response to learning about gay sex acts is to exclaim, "But that's disgusting!"

33. "Homosexual Movement," 16; Neuhaus, "Recruiting for the Revolution," 63.

34. "Homosexual Movement," 19.

35. Ibid., 16–17.

36. Ibid., 17.

37. "Marriage Amendment," 15.

38. Identical fears have been inspired by many proposals for legal reform over the past century. As historian George Chauncey points out, the Catholic Welfare Committee (CWC) strenuously opposed the liberalization of marriage law in 1934 to allow divorce on the grounds of desertion, a reform that permitted women to remarry after having been abandoned by their husbands. Allowing such a change in marriage law would, the CWC argued, "weaken the law concerning . . . marital status" and thus "strike at the foundation of society," since "marriage is the basis of the family—and the family is the cornerstone of society." See Chauncey, *Why Marriage? The History Shaping Today's Debate Over Gay Equality* (New York: Basic Books, 2004), 83–84.

39. Exactly what constituted orthodox Catholic teaching on the matter would change in late November 2005, when the Vatican released new guidelines on admitting homosexual men into the priesthood ("Instruction Concerning the Criteria of Vocational Discernment Regarding Persons with Homosexual Tendencies in View of Their Admission to Seminaries and Holy Orders"). Whereas the church once claimed that it was perfectly acceptable for a homosexual man to be ordained, provided that he adhered to the priestly vow of chaste celibacy, Pope Benedict XVI now seemed to be saying that homosexual desires are so disordered that gay men are uniquely incapable of remaining true to their vows and thus on principle should be denied ordination.

40. Chauncey, *Why Marriage?* 78.

41. George, *Clash of Orthodoxies,* 267–68.

42. Ibid., 269.

43. Ibid., 270–271.

44. Ibid., 271.

45. See Marjorie Connelly, "How Americans Voted: A Political Portrait," The Week in Review, *New York Times,* November 7, 2004.

46. Richard John Neuhaus, "Communion & *Communio,*" The Public Square, *First Things,* August/September 2004, 86.

47. Ibid., 87.

48. Ibid., 88.

49. Ibid.

50. Ibid., 89. At the time of Neuhaus's essay, a handful of bishops (the most prominent being Archbishop Raymond Burke of St. Louis) had already begun to refuse Communion to prochoice politicians, and some even began to ask if Communion should also be withheld from Catholics who vote for prochoice politicians. Neuhaus opposed such strictures, since politics often requires trade-offs between lesser and greater evils. Neuhaus gave the example of President Bush and Pennsylvania's senator Rick Santorum supporting the reelection of prochoice Republican senator Arlen Specter so that the Senate would remain in GOP hands, thus allowing the party to advance the prolife cause. In such cases, voting for a prochoice politician might be required—and the church could not begin to judge the complexity of such cases.

51. In addition to the four listed above, Neuhaus's honor roll of allies in the bishops' conference included: Bishop William Lori of Bridgeport, Connecticut; Bishop Allen Vigneron of Oakland; Bishop Thomas Olmstead of Phoenix; Bishop Samuel Aquila of Fargo, North Dakota; Bishop Peter Sartain of Little Rock; Auxiliary Bishop José Gomez of Denver; Archbishop Sean O'Malley of Boston; Bishop Leonard Blair of Toledo, Ohio; Archbishop John Myers of Newark; Bishop Robert J. McManus of Worcester, Massachusetts; and Archbishop Joseph Naumann of Kansas City, Kansas. See "Bishops at a Turning Point," The Public Square, *First Things*, October 2004, 78.

52. Quoted in ibid., 79.

53. Quoted in ibid., 80. The cardinal's last statement ("must refuse to distribute it") is itself a citation from an earlier statement of the Holy See.

54. Ibid., 81.

55. For an insightful analysis of this trend prior to the 2004 election, see Louis Bolce and Gerald De Maio, "Our Secularist Democratic Party," *Public Interest,* Fall 2002, 3–20.

56. Richard John Neuhaus, "While We're At It," The Public Square, *First Things,* January 2005, 63.

6: AMERICA'S THEOCONSERVATIVE FUTURE

1. Jonathan Mahler, "The Soul of the New Exurb," *New York Times Magazine,* March 27, 2005, 34.

2. An act that Hendrik Hertzberg has memorably described as "defac[ing] the Constitution with anti-gay graffiti." See "Unsteady State," Talk of the Town, *New Yorker,* February 2, 2004, 25–26.

3. In the months leading up to the 2004 election, there was a groundswell of support among right-wing Catholics in the United States for the Vatican to pronounce that a politician's support for abortion rights produces a "latae sententiae"—or automatic—excommunication from the Catholic Church. Under Pope Benedict XVI, such populist appeals to ultraorthodoxy are likely to be taken very seriously.

4. The most influential recent statement of this view is in Thomas Frank's *What's the Matter with Kansas?* (New York: Metropolitan Books, 2004).

5. "The End of Democracy?" Introduction, *First Things,* November 1996, 18.

6. Quoted in Anne E. Kornblut, "After Signing Schiavo Law, Bush Says 'It Is Wisest to Always Err on the Side of Life," *New York Times,* March 22, 2005.

7. See Richard John Neuhaus, "The Death Watch," The Public Square, *First Things,* March 1991, 52–55; "Euthanasia: Final Exit, Final Excuse," Editorial, *First Things,* December 1991, 4–8; and "Always to Care, Never to Kill: A Statement of the Ramsey Colloquium," *First Things,* February 1992, 45–47.

8. Quoted in Carl Hulse and David D. Kirkpatrick, "Moving Quickly, Senate Approves Schiavo Measure," *New York Times,* March 21, 2005.

9. William J. Bennett and Brian T. Kennedy, "The Right to Life: Protecting One Woman," *National Review Online,* March 24, 2005, www.nationalreview.com/comment/bennet_kennedy200503240814.asp.

10. Quoted in Adam Liptak, "Small Law, Big Implications," *New York Times,* March 22, 2005.

11. Bills of attainder usually seek to inflict punishment on a select individual or group, but the principle holds for any form of special treatment. Under the Constitution, laws are supposed to apply equally to all citizens.

12. See, for example, Phillip E. Johnson, "Evolution as Dogma: The Establishment of Naturalism," *First Things,* October 1990, 15–22; Johnson, "Creator or Blind Watchmaker?" *First Things,* January 1993, 8–14; and Howard J. Van Till and Johnson, "God and Evolution: An Exchange," *First Things,* June/July 1993, 32–41.

13. See the discussion in Jodi Wilgoren, "Politicized Scholars Put Evolution on the Defensive," *New York Times,* August 21, 2005.

14. Behe makes his case in *Darwin's Black Box: The Biochemical Challenge to Evolution* (New York: Free Press, 1998). Dembski reaches similar conclusions using probability theory, which provides him with "complexity-specification criteria." See William Dembski, *The Design Inference: Eliminating Chance Through Small Probabilities* (Cambridge: Cambridge University Press, 1998), as well as Dembski, "Science and Design," *First Things,* October 1998, 21–27; and Dembski, "Are We Spiritual Machines?" *First Things,* October 1999, 25–31.

15. See Edward T. Oakes, "Newman, Yes; Paley, No," *First Things,* January 2001, 48–52; and "Edward T. Oakes and His Critics: An Exchange," Correspondence, *First Things,* April 2001, 5–13.

16. See, for example, the exhaustive (and devastating) discussion of ID by Jerry Coyne, "The Faith That Dare Not Speak Its Name," *New Republic,* August 22 & 29, 2005, 21–33.

17. "Oakes and His Critics," 8.

18. Data from the CBS News poll of October 23, 2005. Available at www.cbsnews.com/stories/2005/10/22/opinion/polls/main965223.shtml. According to the same poll, 77 percent of white evangelicals, 74 percent of weekly churchgoers, and 64 percent of self-described conservatives say that God created humans in their present form.

19. Richard John Neuhaus, "Stifling Intellectual Inquiry," The Public Square, *First Things,* April 2005, 59–60.

20. The *Times* op-ed was published on July 7, 2005. On the role of the Discovery Institute in helping Cardinal Schoenborn to place his essay in the *Times,* see Wilgoren, "Politicized Scholars."

21. Peter Baker and Peter Slevin, "Bush Remarks on 'Intelligent Design' Theory Fuel
Debate," *Washington Post,* August 3, 2005.

22. Not that the consensus on the right is unanimous. In the fall of 2005, conservative
columnists George F. Will and Charles Krauthammer came out in strong opposition to ID. See Will, "Grand Old Spenders," *Washington Post,* November 17, 2005;
and Krauthammer, "Phony Theory, False Conflict," *Washington Post,* November 18,
2005. Neuhaus replied to this dissent in conservative ranks by writing on the *First
Things* weblog (www.firstthings.com, on November 23, 2005): "We are still in the
early phases of the ID movement. The arguments are still in the process of being
sorted out. That is being done with great care in a number of venues, and not least
in the pages of *First Things.* It is not helpful for mandarins of the conservative cause
to declare the questions raised to be beyond the pale, lest the respectability of the
cause be tainted by association with the great unwashed whose motivations they do
not share." In subsequent issues of *First Things,* Neuhaus ran an essay critical of Cardinal Schoenborn's op-ed (Stephen M. Barr, "The Design of Evolution," *First
Things,* October 2005, 9–12), as well as a restatement by Cardinal Schoenborn
himself (Christoph Cardinal Schoenborn, "The Designs of Science," *First Things,*
January 2006, 34–38) and a rejoinder to this restatement (Stephen M. Barr, "The
Miracle of Evolution," *First Things,* February 2006, 30–33), showing that the theocon position on ID remained quite complicated.

23. It is unlikely that a nation that actively denigrates the authority of science in its
classrooms can remain a worldwide leader of technological innovation.

24. As of the summer of 2005, the National Center for Science Education was tracking
seventy-eight such battles. (Cited in Wilgoren, "Politicized Scholars.") At the same
time, the anti-ID ruling of U.S. district judge John E. Jones in the high-profile
Dover, Pennsylvania, case demonstrates the significant legal obstacles that remain in
the way of the ID movement.

25. The seminal document is Daniel Patrick Moynihan's 1965 report, "The Negro
Family: The Case for National Action," Office of Policy Planning and Research,
United States Department of Labor, March 1965. Available at www.dol.gov/asp/
programs/history/webid_moynihan.html. The topic was also treated frequently in
the early issues of *The Public Interest,* the influential quarterly journal founded by
Irving Kristol and Daniel Bell in the same year.

26. See the discussion in chapter 1, this volume.

27. For more on the virtues of patriarchy, see Leon Kass's 650-page commentary on the
Book of Genesis, *The Beginning of Wisdom: Rereading Genesis* (New York: Free Press,
2003), 247–303.

28. Gilbert Meilaender, "The Eclipse of Fatherhood," *First Things,* June/July 1995, 39.

29. Amy A. Kass and Leon R. Kass, "Proposing Courtship," *First Things,* October 1999, 32.

30. Ibid., 33, 39–40.

31. Ibid., 40. Of course this also implied that the collapse of the traditional family could be traced to the sexual liberation of women.

32. For an elaboration of these objections—as well as theocon responses to them—see Damon Linker, "Fatherhood 2002," *First Things,* November 2002, 7–8; and "The New Fatherhood?" Correspondence, *First Things,* February 2003, 2–8.

33. As of fall 2005, Australia and the United States were the only two OECD countries (out of thirty) to provide no paid maternity leave.

34. See Mahler, "Soul of New Exurb," 33. See also Malcolm Gladwell, "The Cellular Church," *New Yorker,* September 12, 2005, 60–67.

35. See Neuhaus's condescending discussion of Mormonism, which he definitively declares to be non-Christian: "Are Mormons Christians?" The Public Square, *First Things,* March 2000, 97–104.

36. See Mark Noll, "The Evangelical Mind Today," *First Things,* October 2004, 34–39, in which the author updates his doleful 1994 book *The Scandal of the Evangelical Mind* (Grand Rapids, MI: Eerdmans, 1994). In Noll's view, nearly all the intellectual progress made by evangelicals in the past decade is the result of Catholics providing them with tutorials in historic Christianity.

37. This is a very old theme in the Catholic reactionary tradition. For two very different accounts of this tradition, see Darrin McMahon, *Enemies of the Enlightenment: The French Counter-Enlightenment and the Making of Modernity* (New York: Oxford University Press, 2001); and Paul Gottfried, *Conservative Millenarians: The Romantic Experience in Bavaria* (New York: Fordham University Press, 1979).

38. John Henry Newman, *Apologia Pro Vita Sua* (London: Fontana Books, 1959) (originally published 1864), 276.

39. Richard John Neuhaus, "The Persistence of the Catholic Moment," *First Things,* February 2003, 29. See also Neuhaus, *Confusion, Controversy, and the Splendor of Truth* (New York: Basic Books, 2006) and Damon Linker, "Without a Doubt," *New Republic,* April 3, 2006, 25–33.

40. Opus Dei has recently received wide attention due to the unflattering fictionalized treatment in Dan Brown's runaway bestseller *The Da Vinci Code.* For an account of the numerous scandals (many of them sexual) swirling around the Legionaries, see Garry Wills, "God in the Hands of Angry Sinners," *New York Review of Books,* April 8, 2004, 68–74.

41. See the brief discussion of these colleges in Naomi Schaefer, *God on the Quad* (New York: St. Martin's Press, 2004), 244ff. For an account of Patrick Henry College, which plays a similar (though much more explicitly political) role in the evangelical world, see Hanna Rosin, "God and Country," *New Yorker,* June 27, 2005, 44–49.

42. For links between Fessio and the new pope, see Garry Wills, "Fringe Government," *New York Review of Books,* October 6, 2005, 46–49.

43. See Adam Reilly, "City of God: Tom Monaghan's Coming Catholic Utopia," *Boston Phoenix,* June 17–23, 2005. See also Bill Berkowitz, "Mr. Monaghan Builds His Dream Town," *Working for Change,* August 25, 2005, at www.workingforchange.com/article.cfm?itemid=19522.

44. Richard John Neuhaus, "Scandal Time," The Public Square, *First Things,* April 2002, 61.
45. Richard John Neuhaus, "Scandal Time (Continued)," The Public Square, *First Things,* June/July 2002, 75.
46. Ibid., 77.
47. See, for example, Richard John Neuhaus, "Seeking a Better Way," The Public Square, *First Things,* October 2002, 89–90; and Neuhaus, "Boston and Other Bishops," The Public Square, *First Things,* February 2003, 70.
48. Richard John Neuhaus, "Scandal Time III," The Public Square, *First Things,* August/September 2002, 86–87.
49. Neuhaus, "Seeking a Better Way," 86.
50. Ibid., 87.
51. Richard John Neuhaus, "The Embarrassment of Sin and Grace," The Public Square, *First Things,* December 2002, 68–69.
52. George Weigel, *The Courage to Be Catholic* (New York: Basic Books, 2002).
53. Quoted in Garry Wills, "High Fidelity," *New York Review of Books,* December 5, 2002, 40.
54. For Neuhaus's view of the pernicious influence of opposition to the church's stance on birth control, see "A World of Our Own Making," The Public Square, *First Things,* November 1998, 73–74, where he describes *Humanae Vitae* as "prophetic" and claims that "the separation of the sexual act from its unitive and procreative end" has led to "easy divorce to abortion to same-sex marriage to cloning human beings. And all in only thirty years."
55. Wills, "High Fidelity," 40.
56. Ibid., 40–41. These statistics can be found in Dean R. Hogue, William D. Dinges, Mary Johnson, and Juan L. Gonzales Jr., *Young Adult Catholics: Religion in the Culture of Choice* (Notre Dame, IN: University of Notre Dame Press, 2001).
57. In Ireland, for example, the causality runs in the opposite direction. As late as the early 1990s, contraception was illegal in the country, aside from condoms, which were only dispensed by doctors to married couples. Homosexuality and divorce were also banned. But a mere decade and a half later, after a series of brutal sexual abuse cases and cover-ups by clergy, the church's standing in the country has collapsed. Contraception is now legal, and Mass attendance (though still high in comparison to other Catholic countries) has plummeted. A similar dynamic has played itself out in Canada, where a once deeply Catholic Quebec has embraced secularism in the wake of a series of sexual abuse scandals.
58. In the wake of the Vatican's 2005 prohibition against ordaining men plagued by "disordered" homosexual desires, Neuhaus updated Weigel's analysis of the consequences of the "Truce of 1968"—warning Pope Benedict XVI not to permit a new "Truce of 2005." In other words, the new pope needed to enforce his edict or face even greater acts of disobedience in the ranks of the Church. See Richard John Neuhaus, "The Truce of 2005?" The Public Square, *First Things,* February 2006, 55–61.
59. Wills, "High Fidelity," 41. Wills also reports on the same page that "I recently heard

two priests, [Ave Maria's] Joseph Fessio, S.J., and John McCloskey (spokesperson for Opus Dei), say that if the Church changes the teaching on contraception, it will cease to exist."

60. See, for example, Richard John Neuhaus, "Salvation Is from the Jews," *First Things,* November 2001. See also the statement of theological commonality between Christians and Jews, signed by more than 170 Jewish scholars, "Dabru Emet: A Jewish Statement on Christians and Christianity," *First Things,* November 2000, 39–41.

61. See Richard John Neuhaus, "Israel and Anti-Semitism," The Public Square, *First Things,* May 2002, 69–70; Neuhaus, "While We're At It," The Public Square, *First Things,* August/September 2002, 105; and Neuhaus, "While We're At It," The Public Square, *First Things,* December 2002, 82.

62. Daniel Jonah Goldhagen, "What Would Jesus Have Done?" *New Republic,* January 21, 2002, 21–45.

63. "Goldhagen v. Pius XII," *First Things,* June/July 2002, 37–54. See also Joseph Bottum's summary of the ongoing controversy surrounding Pius, from a decidedly theoconservative perspective, "The End of the Pius Wars," *First Things,* April 2004, 18–24.

64. Michael Novak was even more ecstatic about the film in a review published nearly six months before its release. See "Passion Play," *Weekly Standard,* August 25, 2003, 31–34.

65. Richard John Neuhaus, *"The Passion of Christ,"* The Public Square, *First Things,* February 2004, 62.

66. Leon Wieseltier, "The Worship of Blood," *New Republic,* March 8, 2004, 19–21.

67. David Denby, "Nailed," *The New Yorker,* March 1, 2004, 84–86.

68. Charles Krauthammer, "Gibson's Blood Libel," *Washington Post,* March 5, 2004; Gertrude Himmelfarb, "A 'Passion' Out of Proportion," *Washington Post,* March 7, 2004.

69. Richard John Neuhaus, "Whatever You Do, Don't Mention the Jews," The Public Square, *First Things,* May 2002, 59.

70. Ibid., 61.

71. Ibid.

72. Ibid.

73. Ibid., 62.

74. This was an old neoconservative argument—one that Irving Kristol had been making for years. See, for example, the 1991 essay "The Future of American Jewry," in *Neo-Conservatism: The Autobiography of an Idea* (New York: Free Press, 1995). Needless to say, the argument's force and implications were somewhat different coming from a Catholic priest instead of a secular Jew.

75. David Berger, "Jews, Christians, and 'The Passion,'" *Commentary,* May 2004, 23–31.

76. Quoted in Richard John Neuhaus, "Anti-Semitism and False Alarms," The Public Square, *First Things,* August/September 2004, 93.

77. See Correspondence, *First Things,* December 2004, 11–12, for Berger's letter to the editor in response to Neuhaus's criticism. Berger expresses dismay at Neuhaus's "in-

cendiary" comments—to which Neuhaus replies by asserting that "my observation about fear and loathing is not incendiary but is very sobering and is, I am afraid, supported by a fair reading of the evidence." See also "While We're At It," The Public Square, *First Things*, February 2001, 73, where Neuhaus writes that, in addition to the "long history of Christian anti-Judaism," there has also been "a long history of Jewish anti-Christian hostility." To which David L. Schaefer of Holy Cross College responded by writing to the editor (in Correspondence, *First Things*, May 2001, 7): "What can [this statement] possibly mean? Does the sheer refusal of Jews to regard the Christian religion as true merit comparison to the long history of Christian pogroms against the Jews? Nor is the 'long history of violence against Jews' that you go on to acknowledge balanced, as you imply, by the 'long history of Christian peoples providing refuge for Jews': against what was the refuge being provided except the persecution by other Christians? Should Jews therefore feel grateful to Christianity, as distinguished from individual Christians, for that occasional refuge?"

78. Neuhaus, "Anti-Semitism and False Alarms," 93.

79. Back in 1991, Neuhaus summarily pronounced atheists to be bad citizens. Now he was suggesting that Christian America might do something similar to secular Jews who refused to abide by standards of acceptable public discourse set by the country's conservative Christian majority. See Neuhaus, "Can Atheists Be Good Citizens?" *First Things*, August/September 1991, 21, and the discussion of the essay in chapter 2, this volume.

80. One need not assume that the church itself would have to advocate violence in order for it to become a factor in the country. Violence against Jews in Christian Europe, for example, was rarely, if ever, explicitly fomented by the Vatican. It was rather an expression of paranoia and fear on the part of lay Christians, sometimes spontaneous, often provoked or manipulated by local clerics and political leaders. But in nearly every case it drew on and grew out of orthodox Christian teachings and beliefs.

7: AGAINST THE THEOCONS

1. After Senator Frist's snub, and with Pennsylvania senator Rick Santorum facing a tough reelection fight in 2006, Kansas senator Sam Brownback has emerged as the theocons' main hope for 2008. Given that as of 2005 nearly 50 percent of registered Republicans declared that they cared more about social issues than reducing the size of government, it is possible that Brownback (a staunch opponent of abortion and gay marriage, and a former evangelical who converted to Catholicism in 2002) could secure the nomination—though it is hard to imagine him winning a general election contest against a mainstream Democrat. See David D. Kirkpatrick, "Kansas Senator, Looking at Presidential Bid, Makes Faith the Bedrock of Campaign," *New York Times*, October 14, 2005; and Ryan Lizza, "Beached Party," *New Republic*, October 31, 2005, 23.

2. The president's second choice for the job—Judge Samuel Alito of the Third Circuit

Court of Appeals—fared much better with the right. His nomination also inspired a round of self-congratulation in theocon circles about the fact that Alito would be the fifth Catholic on the Court, confirming Catholicism's ascendancy to dominance of the religious right's intellectual leadership. See, for example, Alan Cooperman, "Court Could Tip to Catholic Majority," *Washington Post*, November 7, 2005.

3. James Madison, *Memorial and Remonstrance Against Religious Assessments*, *The Founders' Constitution* (Chicago: University of Chicago Press, 2000), vol. 5, amendment 1 (Religion), document 43, paragraph 7.

4. Thomas Jefferson, letter to General Alexander Smyth, January 17, 1825, in *The Writings of Thomas Jefferson*, ed. Albert Ellery Bergh, vol. XVI, 100–01 (Thomas Jefferson Memorial Association, 1907); Thomas Jefferson, letter to John Adams, April 11, 1823, in *The Adams-Jefferson Letters: The Complete Correspondence*, ed. Lester J. Cappon (Chapel Hill: University of North Carolina Press, 1987), 591–94.

5. *The Autobiography of Benjamin Franklin*, in *Autobiography and Other Writings*, ed. Kenneth Silverman, (New York: Penguin Books, 1986), 63–64.

6. Brooke Allen, "Our Godless Constitution," *Nation*, February 21, 2005, 14–20. See also, more generally, Isaac Kramnick and R. Laurence Moore, *The Godless Constitution: The Case Against Religious Correctness* (New York: Norton, 1996).

7. For a largely persuasive defense of this interpretation, see Gertrude Himmelfarb, *The Roads to Modernity: The British, French, and American Enlightenments* (New York: Knopf, 2004), 204–17.

8. Voltaire quoted in Jerry Z. Muller, *The Mind and the Market: Capitalism in Western Thought* (New York: Anchor Books, 2002), 27.

9. The relevant essays are *Federalist Papers*, nos. 10 and 51, in Alexander Hamilton, John Jay, and James Madison, *The Federalist: The Gideon Edition*, ed. George W. Carey and James McClellan (Indianapolis: Liberty Fund, 2000), 42–49, 267–72. See especially 270–71, where Madison writes, "If a majority be united by a common interest, the right of the minority will be insecure. There are but two methods of providing against this evil: the one, by creating a will in the community independent of the majority; the other, by comprehending in the society so many separate descriptions of citizens, as will render an unjust combination of a majority of the whole very improbable, if not impracticable. . . . The second method will be exemplified in the federal republic of the United States. Whilst all authority in it will be derived from, and dependent on the society, the society itself will be broken into so many parts, interests, and classes of citizens, that the rights of individuals, or of the minority, will be in little danger from interested combinations of the majority. In a free government, the security for civil rights must be the same as that for religious rights. It consists in the one case in the multiplicity of interests, and in the other, in the *multiplicity of sects*" (emphasis added).

10. The Vatican's unambiguous support for Italian and Spanish fascism is rarely mentioned in theocon discussions of Pope Pius XII's equivocal opposition to Nazism in Germany.

11. This is already Neuhaus's view of Jefferson. See "The American Mind," The Public Square, *First Things*, December 2001, 67–85.

12. This comes close to Neuhaus's view back in the mid-1970s. At that time, he freely admitted that "in American public discourse, both political and legal, the secularist side . . . has been dominant during these two hundred years and has enjoyed an almost complete monopoly during the last forty." See Richard John Neuhaus, "A Carter Presidency and the Real Watershed," *Worldview,* September 1976, 29. See also Neuhaus, *Time Toward Home* (New York: Seabury Press, 1975), 66, where he conceded that his eschatological views about the intimate connection between salvation and American history and politics are "alien to the piety that dominates church life in America, and to the piety that has prevailed throughout a large part of Christian history." He conceded, in other words, that his views were radical not only in an American context, but even in the much broader context of Christianity as such.

13. See, for example, Richard John Neuhaus, *The Naked Public Square: Religion and Democracy in America* (Grand Rapids, MI: Eerdmans, 1984), 36: "A dilemma, both political and theological, facing the new religious right is simply this: *it wants to enter the political arena making public claims on the basis of private truths.*"

14. Garry Wills, "Fringe Government," *New York Review of Books,* October 6, 2005, 46–49.

15. The theocons deny this, of course, but their analysis of Europe's problems—including and especially its low birthrates—is marred by hysteria and exaggeration. See the discussion in chapter 4, this volume, as well as Neuhaus's comments (on the *First Things* weblog, www.firstthings.com, November 8, 2005) about the November 2005 riots in France, which he described as an "intifada": "The temptation to indulge in *Schadenfreude* should be resisted. What is happening in France and other parts of Europe is a tragedy of historic proportions. . . . We are witnessing the death of a continent."

16. See Tony Judt, "Europe vs. America," *New York Review of Books,* February 10, 2005, 37–41.

17. Latin America does have some of the world's most stringent abortion laws. Yet it also has the developing world's highest abortion rates, far surpassing Western Europe and coming in second only to formerly communist Eastern Europe. See Juan Forero, "Push to Loosen Abortion Laws in Latin America," *New York Times,* December 3, 2005.

18. The theocons are well aware of Poland's importance to their argument. Neuhaus, Novak, and Weigel have traveled to Krakow every summer since 1992 to lead the two-week "Tertio Millennio Seminar" for young Americans and Poles, in which the students are introduced to key elements of theoconservative ideology. For more on the importance of Poland to the theocons' highly idiosyncratic vision for Europe's future, see Richard John Neuhaus, "The New Europes," *First Things,* October 2005, 12–15.

19. On this point, see Gary Rosen's insightful review of *John Courtney Murray and the American Civil Conversation,* ed. Robert P. Hunt and Kenneth L. Grasso, in *The American Journal of Jurisprudence* 39 (1994): 471–87. Writing several years before the incendiary "End of Democracy?" symposium in *First Things,* Rosen concluded his discussion of Murray (and his influence on Neuhaus, Weigel, and other theocons) by writing, "In the end, the thought of John Courtney Murray reveals the

twin temptations to which natural law critics of [secular] liberalism are subject: he tends, by turns, to romanticize it and to demonize it, finding it on one occasion the rightful heir to the medieval order and on the next, a rationalist-individualist-nominalist heresy" (487).

20. In Neuhaus's dealings with the Catholic hierarchy, he often engages in both—affirmation and denunciation—at the same time. During the sex-abuse scandal, for example, he regularly attacked priests and bishops (and even the American bishops' conference as a whole) in the name of upholding the authority of the church. A similar dynamic took place during the debate about withholding Communion from prochoice Catholic Democrats in the run-up to the 2004 presidential election.

21. In *The Catholic Moment,* Neuhaus engaged in an extended discussion of the case of Emanuel Hirsch, a noted theologian in the interwar period of Germany who went on to embrace National Socialism. Neuhaus treated Hirsch's story as a "cautionary tale" about the danger of attempting to mix piety and politics—and yet he insisted that his own effort to sanctify American political life could avoid similar mistakes. See Richard John Neuhaus, *The Catholic Moment: The Paradox of the Church in the Postmodern World* (New York: Harper & Row, 1987), 214–31.

22. See Richard John Neuhaus, "Our American Babylon," *First Things,* December 2005, 28: "God is not indifferent to the American experiment. . . . It is time to think again—to think deeply, to think theologically—about the story of America and its place in the story of the world." See also a recent book, which Neuhaus has warmly endorsed, by a young theocon who similarly encourages providential thinking about America's role in the world: Stephen H. Webb, *American Providence: A Nation with a Mission* (New York: Continuum, 2004).

23. For a recent example, see Richard John Neuhaus, "While We're At It," The Public Square, *First Things,* November 2005, 79, where he claims to have "an Augustinian sensibility, marked by an abiding awareness of the fallenness of our human circumstance, the ambiguities that surround and the ironies that confound our prideful certitudes, and our radical dependence upon the grace of God." Yet in the very next issue of the magazine he endorses providential thinking about America and criticizes Reinhold Niebuhr (whom he describes as an "Augustinian") for failing to engage in such thinking himself. According to Neuhaus, Niebuhr was "perhaps too much impressed by what he called the irony of American history. So skeptical was he of the pridefulness that often accompanied the idea of a national mission . . . that he failed to engage constructively the irrepressible devotion to a national story" in the United States. See Neuhaus, "Our American Babylon," *First Things,* December 2005, 27.

24. See James Nuechterlein's largely sympathetic review of Neuhaus's 1978 book, *Christian Faith and Public Policy* ("Christians and Politics," *The Cresset* 41, no. 6 [April 1978], 7–15), in which Nuechterlein pointed out numerous ways in which Neuhaus's flirtation with eschatological radicalism belied his professed moderation. The same tension persists in Neuhaus's writing to this day.

25. Richard John Neuhaus, "A New Order of Religious Freedom," *First Things,* February 1992, 17.

INDEX

A

abortion, 1, 4, 52, 124, 146–56, 161,
    163, 190
  Bush-Kerry presidential campaign and,
    169–73
  First Things symposium and, 95–96,
    100–102, 105–7, 152
  and frustration and discontent of theo-
    cons, 88, 90–96, 100–102, 105–7
  Jews and, 95, 105, 205
  legislation on, 9, 13, 149–50, 152–55,
    170
  Neuhaus and, 27–28, 45, 77, 90, 92,
    114, 153, 156, 169–73
  and redemption of theocons, 113–14
  Supreme Court and, 27, 77, 89–94,
    100–101, 106, 150–52, 154–56,
    169–70, 178, 216
  theocon alliances and, 62, 77–79, 84
  theocon ideology and, 9, 12–13,
    209–10, 216
Abu Ghraib prison, 136
Adams, John Quincy, 121
Afghanistan, 13, 120, 177
  war in, 123, 129, 141

Allitt, Patrick, 70
Al Qaeda, 120, 137
American Enterprise Institute (AEI), 43,
    57–58
American Revolution, 25
Arkes, Hadley, 110
  abortion and, 95, 105, 149, 151–54
  First Things symposium and, 95,
    100–101, 105, 107
  ideological influence of, 9–10
atheists, atheism, 93, 143, 183,
    225
  theocon alliances and, 80–81
Augustine, Saint, 128, 222–24, 226
Ave Maria University, 195–96

B

Bailey, Michael, 198–99
Behe, Michael, 184–85
Belief and Unbelief (Novak), 22–23
Bell, Daniel, 32, 37, 55, 57
Benedict XVI, Pope, 11, 187, 213–14
  abortion and, 172–73
  Bush-Kerry presidential campaign and,
    149, 169, 172–74

and premodern notions of religious
 authority, 194–95
theocon alliances and, 63, 68
Bennett, William J., 60, 111, 181
Berger, David, 206–7
Berger, Peter, 20–22, 43, 188
 First Things symposium and, 105–6,
  115–16
Bernanos, George, 23, 37
Berns, Walter, 103, 105
"Bill Clinton and the American Character"
 (Neuhaus), 112–13
bin Laden, Osama, 120
bioethics, 13, 155–61, 208
 Kass and, 149, 156–60, 163
Blackburn, Elizabeth, 159–60
Bork, Robert H., 10, 83, 111
 First Things symposium and, 98–100
Born-Alive Infants Protection Act, 9,
 149, 152–54
Bottum, Joseph, 3
Bradford, M. E., 59–60
Bradley, Gerard V., 9, 149, 162
Buckley, William F., Jr., 60, 83, 127
Bush, George H. W., 93, 114, 168
 abortion and, 90–91, 148, 151–52
 just war reasoning and, 128–29
Bush, George W., xi–xiii, 15, 113–25,
 166–81
 abortion and, 1, 9, 113–14, 147–50,
  153–56, 161
 bioethics and, 149, 155–57, 159–
  61
 evolution-ID debate and, 183, 187
 gay marriage and, 149, 162, 166–68
 Iraq war and, 12–13, 119, 130–41
 and line between religion and politics,
  1–4
 Miers nomination and, 208–9
 militarism and, 120–21
 in presidential campaign vs. Kerry, 5,
  136, 149, 168–76
 and redemption of theocons, 88,
  113–17
 and Schiavo right-to-die case,
  178–81, 208
 September 11 terrorist attacks and, xii,
  120, 122–23, 125

theocon ideology and, 5, 7–9, 12–13,
 217, 220
and U.S. hostility toward Europe, 142,
 145
and war on terror, 118–20, 123–24,
 129, 141, 177
and White House access of theocons,
 117–19, 135–36, 140, 162
Bush v. Gore, 115, 150

C
capitalism, 6, 8, 11, 16, 57, 177
 Novak's ideological evolution and, 36–
  41, 55
 theocon alliances and, 73–76, 84
capital punishment, 79, 170, 172–73
Carson, Benjamin, 159
Carter, Jimmy, 41–45, 220
*Catholic Ethic and the Spirit of
 Capitalism, The* (Novak), 76
*Catholicism and the Renewal of American
 Democracy* (Weigel), 67
Catholic Moment, The (Neuhaus), 65,
 67–69, 73–74
Catholics, Catholicism, Catholic Church,
 xiii, 5–9, 11–14, 51–52, 116–17,
 126–32, 148–49
 abortion and, 28, 77–79, 95,
  100–102, 105, 107, 114, 169–73,
  178, 216
 alliance between evangelicals and,
  11–12, 54, 81–86, 109–10
 animosities between Protestants and,
  62–64, 83, 85
 Bush-Kerry presidential campaign and,
  149, 168–74
 capitalism and, 73–76
 evolution-ID debate and, 183, 186–87
 First Things symposium and, 95,
  100–102, 104–10
 foreign affairs and, 126–29
 gay marriage and, 162, 164–66
 Iraq war and, 130–32
 just war reasoning and, 127–29
 and line between politics and religion,
  3, 66, 69
 Novak's early radicalism and, 22–24,
  40

Novak's ideological evolution and,
    35–36, 40, 55
and path to power of theocons, 54,
    62–86
pedophilia scandal in, 196–202
and premodern notions of religious
    authority, 193–202, 207
and redemption of theocons, 110,
    113–14, 116
and relating to Jews, 202–3, 206
repoliticization of, 69–76
and Schiavo right-to-die case, 180,
    182
theocon alliances and, 11–12, 62–87,
    109–10, 213
theocon ideology and, 5, 7–9, 11–13,
    52, 210–19, 222–23, 226
theocon-neocon comparisons and, 6–7
and theoconservative U.S. in future,
    177–78, 196
and U.S. hostility toward Europe,
    143–45
"Catholics in Political Life," 171–72
Center on Religion and Society, 60–61
Centesimus Annus, 74–76
Central Intelligence Agency (CIA), 145,
    209
Challenge of Peace, The, 67, 126–27
China, U.S. standoff with, 121–22
Christians, Christianity, xiii, 7–10,
    12–14, 37, 59, 111, 117–19,
    124–26, 159, 175, 209–12
abortion and, 9, 78–79, 100, 102,
    105, 107, 161, 216
evolution-ID debate and, 183, 185
First Things symposium and, 95,
    99–102, 104–8
gay marriage and, 161, 167
Neuhaus's early political activism and,
    18, 21
Neuhaus's ideological evolution and,
    28–31, 36–37, 41
Neuhaus's theocon manifesto and,
    49–52
Novak's early radicalism and, 24–25
and premodern notions of religious au-
    thority, 193–94
and relating to Jews, 202–7

theocon ideology and, 4, 8–10, 12–13,
    210–12, 214–20, 222–26
and theoconservative U.S. in future,
    177–78
and U.S. hostility toward Europe, 142,
    144–45
and war on terror, 118–19, 124, 126
citizenship, 27, 80–81, 221
City of God, The (Augustine), 222–23
civil rights, xiii, 29–30, 59
Neuhaus's early political activism and,
    7, 10, 16, 18–20
Civil War, 59, 72, 90, 92, 96, 109
Clergy and Laity Concerned About
    Vietnam (CALCAV), 19, 24
Clinton, Bill, 118, 121, 161, 168, 221
abortion and, 90–91, 148, 150
and frustration and discontent of
    theocons, 87–88, 90–91, 110–13
cloning, 9, 78, 114
bioethics and, 155–56, 159–60, 163
Colson, Charles W., 81, 83, 85
First Things symposium and, 99–101,
    109
Commentary, 57, 88–89, 102, 203–4,
    206
Congress, U.S., 9–10, 22, 34, 57, 60, 81,
    98, 120, 142, 146, 210–11
abortion and, 9, 89, 106, 148, 150–
    54
and frustration and discontent of
    theocons, 100, 106, 111–12
gay marriage and, 161–62, 167, 208
and Schiavo right-to-die case, 178–82,
    208
conservatives, conservatism, xiii, 2–5, 7,
    15, 52–54, 58–62, 88–90, 114,
    127, 142, 148–50, 187, 209
abortion and, 52, 62, 89, 150
bioethics and, 155, 159
Bush-Kerry presidential campaign and,
    171, 176
First Things symposium and, 103,
    109
and frustration and discontent of
    theocons, 88, 90
gay marriage and, 162, 166–67
Iraq war and, 135–36, 138

and line between religion and politics,
2–3
militarism and, 121, 129–30
and neocon-paleocon relations, 59–61
Neuhaus's Catholic conversion and,
82–83
Neuhaus's ideological evolution and,
41, 43–44
Neuhaus's theocon manifesto and, 48,
52–53
Novak's ideological evolution and, 35,
37, 40
and premodern notions of religious authority, 194–95
and relating to Jews, 202, 206
and Schiavo right-to-die case, 180–82
theocon alliances and, 62, 64, 70,
81–83, 109–10
theocon ideology and, 4, 10–11,
214–16, 222–23, 226
and White House access of theocons,
117–19
Constitution, U.S., 96, 148
abortion and, 79, 92–93, 102, 151,
155, 216
Federal Marriage Amendment (FMA)
to, 9, 13, 161–62, 164–68, 178,
208–10
First Amendment to, 51, 212–13
Fourteenth Amendment to, 102,
106–7, 216
and frustration and discontent of
theocons, 92–94, 98–100, 102,
106–8
and Schiavo right-to-die case, 180–
82
theocon ideology and, 211–13, 216
contraception, 28, 79, 95, 114, 147–48,
166, 190, 194–96, 200–201
Cuban missile crisis, xi–xii
*Cultural Contradictions of Capitalism,
The* (Bell), 37
culture, 2–6, 15–16, 54–58, 118, 128,
149, 164, 167, 178–82
abortion and, 4, 52, 62, 77–79, 84,
100, 151, 153–55, 205
evolution-ID debate and, 185–86, 188
and frustration and discontent of

theocons, 90, 92, 103, 105, 108,
112–13
neocon infrastructure and, 57–58
Neuhaus's ideological evolution and,
27–28, 32, 34, 42, 44–46
Neuhaus's theocon manifesto and, 46,
48–49, 51–52
Novak's early radicalism and, 22, 24,
40
Novak's ideological evolution and, 35,
37, 39
and premodern notions of religious authority, 194–95, 200–201
and redemption of theocons, 113–14,
116
and relating to Jews, 205–6
rightly ordered family and, 188, 191
and Schiavo right-to-die case, 179–82
theocon alliances and, 62, 64–65, 77,
79, 82, 84–85
theocon ideology and, 4–5, 11, 210,
219
theocon-neocon synergy and, 55–57
and U.S. hostility toward Europe,
142–45

D
Davis, Joseph, 199
Dawson, Christopher, 143–44
Declaration of Independence, 9, 71, 97,
107, 153–54
Decter, Midge, 102–5
Defense of Marriage Act (DOMA),
161–62, 167
Dembski, William, 184–85
democracy, 2, 7, 10–13, 23, 58, 121,
140, 144
First Things symposium and, 12, 152,
179, 203, 221
and frustration and discontent of
theocons, 88, 94, 98–101, 105–8,
113
Neuhaus's early political activism and,
19, 21
Neuhaus's ideological evolution and,
31–32, 43–44
Neuhaus's theocon manifesto and,
47–48, 51–52

Novak's ideological evolution and,
    36–40, 55
and redemption of theocons, 88, 116
theocon alliances and, 62, 65, 70–72,
    76, 84
theocon ideology and, 8, 10–11,
    213–16, 218–21, 224–25, 227
Democrats, Democratic Party, 16, 20,
    115, 148–49, 180
  abortion and, 148, 152–53, 169–71,
    178, 205
  Bush-Kerry presidential campaign and,
    136, 168–71, 174, 176
  and frustration and discontent of
    theocons, 111–12
  Neuhaus's ideological evolution and,
    41, 45
  Novak's ideological evolution and,
    34–35
  theocon alliances and, 64–65
Denby, David, 204
Dignitatis Humanae (Declaration on
    Religious Freedom), 71
Di Noia, Augustine, 203
Discovery Institute, 183–87
Dobson, James C., 105, 109
Doing Well and Doing Good (Neuhaus),
    75–76
Dred Scott v. Sanford, 27, 92
Dula, Peter, 136–37, 139

E
Economic Justice for All, 67
education, 25, 43, 51–52, 84, 145–47,
    169, 172, 190, 204
  evolution-ID debate and, 13, 178,
    182–83, 185–88, 207
  and frustration and discontent of
    theocons, 91, 112–13
  gay marriage and, 163–64
  and premodern notions of religious au-
    thority, 194–96
  school prayer and, 51, 62, 93
  sex and, 1, 91, 146–47
  theocon ideology and, 4, 13, 219
Elders, Jocelyn, 91
embryonic stem-cell research, 1, 9,
    78–79, 114, 124, 146

bioethics and, 155–56, 159–60, 208
Ethics and Public Policy Center, 58, 89,
    130
ethnicity, 35, 55, 62
Europe, 134
  theocon ideology and, 13, 212–14,
    218–19, 223, 225
  U.S. hostility toward, 141–46
Eusebius of Caesarea, 222
euthanasia, 4, 78–79, 114, 155, 173
  and frustration and discontent of
    theocons, 88, 95–96, 100, 106
  and Schiavo right-to-die case, 1, 13,
    178–82, 208
  theocon alliances and, 62, 79, 84
  theocon ideology and, 9, 12, 216
evangelicals, 78, 148, 162, 180, 193, 202
  alliance between Catholics and, 11–12,
    54, 81–86, 109–10
  evolution-ID debate and, 183, 186–87
  First Things symposium and, 105,
    108–10
  Neuhaus's ideological evolution and,
    45–46
  Neuhaus's theocon manifesto and, 46,
    49, 51–53
  political rise of, 2–3
  and redemption of theocons, 110, 114–16
  in shifting to Republican Party, 44–47
  theocon alliances and, 11–12, 63–65,
    68, 80–87, 105, 108–10
  theocon ideology and, 5, 7, 11–12,
    215–16, 226
"Evangelicals and Catholics Together"
    (ECT), 11–12, 83–87, 109
Evangelium Vitae, 98
evolution, ID vs., 13, 178, 182–88, 207

F
Falwell, Jerry, 11, 44–45, 47, 50
family, families, 52, 172
  gay marriage and, 163–64
  Neuhaus's ideological evolution and,
    43–44
  and premodern notions of religious au-
    thority, 194–95
  rightly ordered, 13, 178, 188–92, 207,
    216

theocon alliances and, 62, 84
theocon ideology and, 13, 216
Federal Communications Commission, 1,
    148
Federalist Papers, 211–12
feminists, feminism, 78, 112, 163
    Neuhaus's ideological evolution and,
        28, 44
    rightly ordered family and, 189, 191
Fessio, Joseph, 195
First Things, 7–8, 12–13, 61–62, 79, 83,
        88–89, 128, 133–37, 142, 162
    bioethics and, 157–58
    evolution-ID debate and, 183–84, 186
    and frustration and discontent of
        theocons, 88, 94–110
    Iraq war and, 130, 134–37
    Jews and, 95, 101, 104–5, 203–7
    judiciary and, 95–102, 105–7, 115–16
    and premodern notions of religious au-
        thority, 196–200
    and redemption of theocons, 110, 113
    symposium of, 12, 88, 94–110,
        115–16, 152, 179, 203, 221
    theocon alliances and, 108–9
    and war on terror, 123–25
Fish, Stanley, 89
Fleming, Thomas, 61
Food and Drug Administration, 147–48
foreign affairs, 7–8, 58, 67, 124–32, 145,
        147
    Iraq war and, 131–32, 134, 139
    militarism and, 120–22, 129–30
    and war on terror, 118, 124
France, 70, 141–42, 223
Franklin, Benjamin, 211
Frist, Bill, 208

G
gay rights, gay marriage, 1, 4, 12–13, 79,
        146, 149, 161–68
    constitutional amendment on, 9, 13,
        161–62, 164–68, 178, 208–10
    and frustration and discontent of
        theocons, 88, 90, 93–94
    legislation on, 161–62, 167
    Neuhaus's ideological evolution and,
        28, 44–45

states in legalizing of, 162, 167
Sullivan vs. George on, 165–66
theocon ideology and, 9–10, 13,
    209–10, 216
George, Robert P., 195
    abortion and, 9, 95, 101–2, 152, 216
    bioethics and, 159–60
    First Things symposium and, 95,
        100–102, 106–7, 152
    gay marriage and, 149, 162, 165–66
Germany, 98, 104, 142, 223
Gerson, Michael, 114, 117
Gibson, Mel, 203–4, 206
Gingrich, Newt, 12, 91
Glazer, Nathan, 55, 57
Glendon, Mary Ann, 10, 159, 162, 195
Goeglein, Timothy, 117–18
Goldhagen, Daniel Jonah, 203
Gómez-Lobo, Alfonso, 159–60
Gore, Al, 115, 150, 168
Grammond, Maurice, 199–200
Gulf War, 8, 128

H
Hamilton, Alexander, 211
Hartford Appeal for Theological
    Affirmation, 48
Heilbrunn, Jacob, 104
Heschel, Abraham Joshua, 19, 202
Himmelfarb, Gertrude, 103–5, 204
Hittinger, Russell, 95, 99
Humanae Vitae, 200–201
Hunt, Dave, 85
Huntington, Samuel, 76, 123–24
Hussein, Saddam, 129–32
    Iraq war and, 12–13, 119, 130–32,
        137–39

I
immigration, 59, 61
"Inhuman Use of Human Beings, The," 156
Institute on Religion and Democracy,
    64
Institute on Religion and Public Life, 61,
    117, 166
intelligent design (ID), 13, 178, 182–88,
    207
Iran, 44, 129

Iraq, Iraq war, 8, 12–13, 119, 129–42, 170, 209
  Dula's accusations and, 136–37, 139
  just war reasoning and, 129–30, 135, 137–39
  U.S. military and, 129–31, 133–35, 139–40
  Weigel and, 130–34, 137, 139, 142
Ireland, John, 67, 79–80
Islam, 13, 144
  militarism and, 129, 141
  and war on terror, 119, 124, 126
Israel, 134, 202–3

J
Jefferson, Thomas, 71, 211
John Paul II, Pope, 8, 11, 39, 73–79, 89, 98, 154, 182, 194
  abortion and, 77–79, 100–101, 107
  evolution-ID debate and, 186–87
  and relating to Jews, 202–3
  theocon alliances and, 63, 68, 73–78, 83
Johnson, Lyndon, 19, 188
Johnson, Phillip E., 183–84
Judaism, Jews, 6, 80, 157
  abortion and, 95, 105, 205
  anti-Semitism and, 61, 202–7
  First Things and, 95, 101, 104–5, 203–7
  neocon-paleocon relations and, 59, 61
  Neuhaus's ideological evolution and, 30–31, 41
  Neuhaus's theocon manifesto and, 51–52
  problems in relating to, 178, 202–7
  theocon ideology and, 9–10, 215, 222, 225
judiciary, 1, 51, 148–52
  abortion and, 12, 27, 77, 89–96, 100–101, 146, 150–52, 154–56, 169–70, 209–10
  First Things and, 95–102, 105–7, 115–16
  and frustration and discontent of theocons, 88, 91–102, 105–7, 109
  gay rights and, 93–94, 161–62, 167
  and redemption of theocons, 115–16
  and Schiavo right-to-die case, 180–81
  theocon ideology and, 4, 10, 12
  see also Supreme Court, U.S.
Judt, Tony, 133

K
Kagan, Robert, 121
Kass, Amy, 190
Kass, Leon, 10, 149, 156–60, 163, 190
Kennedy, John F., 168–69
  Cuban missile crisis and, xi–xii
  and line between politics and religion, 66, 69
Kerry, John F.:
  abortion and, 170–73
  presidential campaign of, 5, 136, 149, 168–76
Kimball, Roger, 111
King, Martin Luther, Jr., 7, 16, 19–20, 41, 98
Kmiec, Douglas, 181–82
Kristol, Irving, 38, 55–60
Kristol, William, 89, 103, 121
Kyoto Protocol, 142–43

L
Lawler, Peter, 159–60
Lawrence v. Texas, 144, 161–62
"L'Chaim and Its Limits" (Kass), 157–58
Lee v. Weisman, 93
liberal bargain, 224–27
liberals, liberalism, xiv, 3–4, 6, 12–13, 15, 40–41, 55, 58, 60, 112, 121, 159, 179, 193, 205, 209
  abortion and, 4, 78, 89
  gay marriage and, 161–62
  Iraq war and, 133, 135
  Neuhaus's ideological evolution and, 30–31, 33, 41, 45
  Neuhaus's theocon manifesto and, 47, 49–50, 52
  and redemption of theocons, 115–16
  theocon alliances and, 62, 64, 68–71, 85
  theocon ideology and, 4, 9–10, 12, 211, 213–16, 221–27
Lincoln, Abraham, 39, 59, 71–72, 80, 92, 107
Luther, Martin, 17–18
Lutherans, Lutheranism, 105
  of Neuhaus, 7, 17–18, 23, 65, 67
  Neuhaus's Catholic conversion and, 82–83

M

McCarrick, Theodore Cardinal, 172–73

McGovern, George, 29, 35, 170

Madison, James, 211–12, 214, 226

Mahler, Jonathan, 177

Marx, Karl, 26, 31, 36–37

May, William, 159–60

megachurches, 192–94

Meilaender, Gilbert, 10, 159–60, 189

Miers, Harriet, 208–9

military, militarism, 7–8, 139–41
    foreign affairs and, 120–22, 129–30
    Iraq war and, 129–31, 133–35, 139–40
    and national myth of U.S., 122–23
    neocons and, 7, 57, 120–22, 125
    Neuhaus's early political activism and,
        21–22
    September 11 terrorist attacks and,
        120–23
    theocon ideology and, 8, 12–13
    and U.S. hostility toward Europe,
        144–45

Mills, C. Wright, 21, 56

Monaghan, Thomas, 195–96

"Moral Clarity in a Time of War"
    (Weigel), 130–31

"Moral Clarity in the Nuclear Age"
    (Novak), 126–28

Moral Majority, 11, 44, 65, 215
    Neuhaus's theocon manifesto and, 47,
        50, 52

morals, morality, 3–5, 15, 25, 44–46, 66,
        113, 121–24, 176
    abortion and, 4, 28, 77–79, 84, 89,
        91–93, 95–96, 100–101, 124,
        151–52, 155–56, 170, 172, 190, 216
    bioethics and, 155–60
    Bush-Kerry presidential campaign and,
        170, 172, 174
    and frustration and discontent of theo-
        cons, 88, 91–97, 100, 104–11
    gay marriage and, 163–66
    Iraq war and, 131–32, 136–37
    just war reasoning and, 128–29
    Neuhaus's early political activism and,
        19–22
    Neuhaus's ideological evolution and,
        28–29, 31, 41, 45–46

Neuhaus's theocon manifesto and,
        48–50, 52

Novak's ideological evolution and, 35,
        37

and premodern notions of religious
        authority, 193, 196–97, 199–200,
        207

and Schiavo right-to-die case, 179–82

theocon alliances and, 63, 68, 72–77,
        79–81, 84–86

theocon ideology and, 4–5, 9–10,
        12–13, 210–11, 215–16, 223, 227

and U.S. hostility toward Europe,
        142–44

and war on terror, 123–24

Movement and Revolution (Berger and
        Neuhaus), 20–22, 105

Murray, John Courtney, 39, 49, 128
    theocon alliances and, 70–73

N

Nadler, Jerrold, 153

Naked Public Square, The (Neuhaus), 16,
        59–60, 177, 215
    theocon alliances and, 64–65, 81
    as theocon manifesto, 11, 46–53

National Abortion Rights Action League
        (NARAL), 152–53, 170

National Council of Churches (NCC),
        48, 64, 67

National Review, 60, 127

Nazi Germany, 98, 104, 223

neocons, neoconservatives,
        neoconservatism, 11, 38, 204
    comparisons between theocons and,
        6–7, 126
    First Things symposium and, 102–5,
        108, 110
    infrastructure of, 54–55, 57–60
    militarism and, 7, 57, 120–22, 125
    relations between paleocons and,
        59–61
    synergy between theocons and, 54–62

Neuhaus, Clemens, 17

Neuhaus, Richard John, 7–12, 132–41,
        161–77, 179–80, 185–88
    abortion and, 27–28, 45, 77, 90, 92,
        114, 153, 156, 169–73

on atheism, 80–81
bioethics and, 155–56
Bush-Kerry presidential campaign and, 149, 168–76
on Carter, 41–45
Catholic conversion of, 82–83
Catholic sex-abuse scandal and, 196–202
comparisons between Novak and, 22–24, 26–27, 34, 36–37
early political activism of, 7, 10, 16, 18–22, 24, 26–30, 171, 202
evolution-ID debate and, 183, 185–87
First Things symposium and, 95–98, 101–5, 107–8, 110, 179
frustration and discontent of, 87–92, 94–98, 101–5, 107–8, 110–12
gay marriage and, 149, 161–67
ideological evolution of, 10–11, 16, 27–34, 36–37, 40–46, 55–56, 69
ideological influence of, 7–11
Iraq war and, 130, 132–40
just war reasoning of, 124–25, 128, 135, 138
and line between politics and religion, 42, 51, 108
neocon-paleocon relations and, 59–61
neocon-theocon synergy and, 55–56, 58–59, 62
and origins of theoconservatism, 15–24, 26–34, 36–37, 40–53
and premodern notions of religious authority, 193–202
problems with authority of, 17–20, 108
radicalism of, 7, 10, 16, 18–24, 26–29, 32, 41, 47, 54–55, 77, 108, 171
and redemption of theocons, 112–17
and relating to Jews, 202–7
revolution and, 20–22, 26–27, 29, 31–32, 41, 47, 49, 56, 88, 92, 94, 98
September 11 terrorist attacks and, 119–20, 123, 125
theocon alliances and, 62, 64–65, 67–70, 72–77, 79–83, 85–86, 88
theocon ideology and, 52, 210, 214–15, 217–18, 220, 222, 224–25
theocon infrastructure and, 58–62, 64
theocon manifesto of, 11, 46–53
and war on terror, 118, 123–26

Newman, John Henry, 193, 196–97, 201
New York Times, 61, 103, 133–34, 138, 187
Niebuhr, Reinhold, 18, 226
Novak, David, 10, 202
Novak, Michael, 43, 50–52, 89, 114, 117, 177, 188, 195, 210
comparisons between Neuhaus and, 22–24, 26–27, 34, 36–37
early political activism of, 10, 16, 23–26
foreign affairs and, 126–28
ideological evolution of, 10–11, 16, 27, 34–41, 55, 69
ideological influence of, 8–11
just war reasoning of, 127–28
neocon-theocon synergy and, 55, 58, 62
and origins of theoconservatism, 16–17, 22–27, 34–41
radicalism of, 16, 22–27, 34–35, 40, 54–55
revolution and, 22–27, 34–41
theocon alliances and, 62, 69, 73, 76, 83, 85
theocon infrastructure and, 58, 62
Nuechterlein, James, 96, 102–3

O
Oakes, Edward T., 184–85
Open Church, The (Novak), 22–23

P
paleoconservatives, paleocons:
First Things symposium and, 103
relations between neocons and, 59–61
Partial-Birth Abortion Ban Act, 154, 170
Passion of the Christ, The, 203–4, 206–7
Paul VI, Pope, 200
Pellegrino, Edmund, 160
Pfeffer, Leo, 205
Pius XII, Pope, 203
Planned Parenthood of Southeastern Pennsylvania v. Casey, 91–94
Podhoretz, Norman, 57, 102–3
Poland, 219
populism, 12, 91–92, 146, 165
and frustration and discontent of theocons, 92, 94, 100, 106, 111
neocon infrastructure and, 57–58

Neuhaus's ideological evolution and, 31–32, 41, 55–56
Neuhaus's theocon manifesto and, 49–50, 52
Novak's ideological evolution and, 34–36
and Schiavo right-to-die case, 181–82
and synergy between neocons and theocons, 55–56, 58
theocon ideology and, 210, 220, 226
and war on terror, 124–25
Protestants, Protestantism, 17, 53–54, 62–68, 78–80, 101, 109, 129
animosities between Catholics and, 62–64, 83, 85
Neuhaus's theocon manifesto and, 48–49, 53
and premodern notions of religious authority, 192–93
theocon alliances and, 11–12, 62–66, 68, 71–72, 76, 79–80, 83, 85
theocon ideology and, 7, 11–12, 215, 222–23, 226
see also evangelicals

R
Ramsey Colloquium, 156, 162–63
Reagan, Ronald, xii–xiii, 8, 11, 44–47, 53, 57–60, 114, 168
abortion and, 90–91, 148
evangelical support for, 44, 46–47
foreign affairs and, 126, 128
and frustration and discontent of theocons, 90–91, 93
neocon infrastructure and, 57–58
neocon-theocon relations and, 59–60
Novak's ideological evolution and, 38, 40
theocon alliances and, 64–65, 67, 72
religion, religiosity, xii, 6–8, 15–19, 21–55, 57–93, 123–32, 148–50, 176–80, 192–226
bioethics and, 156–57, 208
Bush-Kerry presidential campaign and, 168–74, 176
crisis of, 30–33, 36, 108, 210
evolution-ID debate and, 183, 185–87
and frustration and discontent of

theocons, 88, 90–93, 98–99, 104–6, 108
gay marriage and, 163–67
Iraq war and, 130–32, 137, 139
just war reasoning and, 127–29
line between politics and, 1–4, 13, 42, 51, 53, 66, 69, 84, 99, 108, 205, 226
neocon infrastructure and, 57–58
neocon-theocon synergy and, 55, 58
Neuhaus's early political activism and, 18–19, 21
Neuhaus's ideological evolution and, 28–34, 36–37, 41–46, 55
Neuhaus's theocon manifesto and, 46–52
Novak and, 22–27, 34–41
and path to power of theocons, 54, 62–86
politics without, 217–19
premodern notions of authority of, 13, 178, 192–202, 207
and redemption of theocons, 113–14
and relating to Jews, 178, 202–7
rightly ordered family and, 190, 192
and Schiavo right-to-die case, 179–80, 182
theocon alliances and, 62–87, 109–10
theocon ideology and, 4, 7–8, 10, 210–26
theocon infrastructure and, 58–61
and U.S. hostility toward Europe, 142–46
and war on terror, 123–26
Reno, Janet, 91
Republicans, Republican Party, 1, 3, 16, 35, 115, 117, 167–70, 191–93
abortion and, 79, 89, 146, 148, 152–54, 169–70, 210
Bush-Kerry presidential campaign and, 168–70, 174
evangelicals in shifting to, 44–47
and frustration and discontent of theocons, 88–89, 101, 111–12
just war reasoning and, 128–29
neocon infrastructure and, 57–58
Neuhaus's ideological evolution and, 27, 45

rightly ordered family and, 191–92
and Schiavo right-to-die case, 178–81, 208
theocon alliances and, 64–65
theocon ideology and, 5, 13, 210, 223
revolution, revolutions, 20–27, 221
and frustration and discontent of theocons, 88, 92, 94, 96–99, 101, 109
Neuhaus and, 20–22, 26–27, 29, 31–32, 41, 47, 49, 56, 88, 92, 94, 98
Novak and, 22–27, 34–41
Rise of the Unmeltable Ethnics, The (Novak), 35
Rockford Institute, 60–61, 103
Roe v. Wade, 27, 77, 89–91, 93, 100–101, 150–52, 154–56, 169–70, 178, 216
Romans, Letter to the, xii, 19
Romer v. Evans, 93–94
Rove, Karl, 2, 5, 114, 117, 137, 168

S
Santorum, Rick, 89, 153
Scalia, Antonin, 10, 89, 101, 161–62
Schaub, Diana, 159
Schiavo, Terri, 1, 13, 178–82, 208
Schoenborn, Christoph Cardinal, 187
school prayer, 51, 62, 93
Second Vatican Council (Vatican II), 22–23, 35–36, 186, 213
theocon alliances and, 63, 65–66, 70–71
secularism, xiii–xiv, 15–17, 23–24, 36, 59–60, 126, 134, 144–46, 157, 159, 174, 176–78, 186
and frustration and discontent of theocons, 88, 92, 101, 106, 111
gay marriage and, 161, 165
and line between religion and politics, 3, 13
neocon-theocon comparisons and, 6–7
Neuhaus's ideological evolution and, 30–34, 41–42, 44–45
Neuhaus's theocon manifesto and, 48–53
Novak's early radicalism and, 24, 40
and premodern notions of religious authority, 192–94, 196

and redemption of theocons, 88, 116
and relating to Jews, 205–7
theocon alliances and, 64, 69–70, 72, 85, 87, 109
theocon ideology and, 4–5, 9–12, 209–11, 214–15, 217–20, 225–27
and theoconservative U.S. in future, 177–78, 196
and U.S. hostility toward Europe, 144–45
Sensenbrenner, F. James, Jr., 181
September 11 terrorist attacks, xii, 12, 118–25, 130, 141, 147, 153
sex, sexuality, 4, 16, 25, 40, 89, 156, 194–202
contraception and, 28, 79, 95, 114, 147–48, 166, 190, 194–96, 200–201
education and, 1, 91, 146–47
Neuhaus's ideological evolution and, 28, 44–45
and premodern notions of religious authority, 196–202
theocon alliances and, 62, 84
see also gay rights, gay marriage; women
slavery, 90, 92, 98, 159
Smith, Adam, 39
socialism, 25, 36, 40, 67
Soviet Union, xi, 8, 104, 126–28
Spain, 142–43
Spirit of Democratic Capitalism, The (Novak), 8, 38–39, 73
Stenberg v. Carhart, 150, 152
Sullivan, Andrew, 122
gay marriage and, 165–66
and war on terror, 125–26
Supreme Court, U.S., 51, 98, 115, 144, 161, 181, 205, 209
abortion and, 27, 77, 89–94, 100–101, 106, 150–52, 154–56, 169–70, 178, 216
and frustration and discontent of theocons, 91–94, 101, 106, 109

T
terror, terrorism, 118–26, 129–30, 168
on September 11, xii, 12, 118–25, 130, 141, 147, 153

U.S. war on, 8, 12, 118–20, 123–26, 129, 141, 177
theocons, theoconservatism:
  alliances of, 11–12, 54, 58, 62–88, 102, 105, 108–10, 114–15, 146, 156, 207, 213, 217, 223
  finances of, 54, 61–62
  frustration and discontent of, 87–113
  in future, 177–78, 196, 207, 209
  goals of, xiii–xiv, 5, 8–9, 13–14, 52, 58, 191
  historical criticism of, 210–14, 224–26
  ideology of, 4–14, 27, 52–54, 73, 75, 77, 79, 85, 102, 148, 155, 159–60, 171, 177–78, 207, 209–27
  influence of, xiii, 6, 11, 53, 90, 117–19, 135–36, 140, 148–50, 162, 165, 174
  infrastructure of, 54, 58–62, 64
  manifesto of, 11, 46–53
  origins of, xii–xiii, 5, 7, 15–53
  path to power of, 5–6, 53–86
  political criticism of, 210, 217–19, 222–24, 226
  radicalism of, xiii, 12, 94–95, 103
  recent stumbles of, 208–9
  redemption of, 88, 110, 112–17
  sociological criticism of, 210, 214–17, 224, 226–27
Theology for Radical Politics, A (Novak), 23, 35
This World, 59–60
Thomas, Clarence, 10, 89, 161
"Thorough Revolutionary, The" (Neuhaus), 20–22
To Empower People (Berger and Neuhaus), 43
Tranquillitas Ordinis (The Peace of Order) (Weigel), 128
Trilling, Lionel, 56
Two Cheers for Capitalism (Kristol), 38
two kingdoms theory, 17–18, 23
"Tyrant State, The" (George), 100

U
Unborn Victims of Violence Act, 154–55, 170
United Nations, 130–31, 138, 142, 147

U.S. Conference of Catholic Bishops, 13, 149

V
Vietnam War, xiii, 126, 134
  Neuhaus's early political activism and, 7, 10, 16, 18–20, 24, 28–30, 202
Virtually Normal (Sullivan), 165–66
Voltaire, 208, 212

W
Wall Street Journal, The, 57, 74, 92
Washington, George, 211
Weekly Standard, 121–22
Wehner, Peter, 117, 137
"We Hold These Truths," 109–10
Weigel, George, 89, 114, 139–45, 162
  First Things symposium and, 95, 107
  and frustration and discontent of theocons, 93, 95
  ideological influence of, 8–9, 11
  Iraq war and, 130–34, 137, 139, 142
  just war reasoning and, 128, 130
  Neuhaus's Catholic conversion and, 82–83
  and premodern notions of religious authority, 200–202
  theocon alliances and, 67–70, 72–75, 83, 85
  theocon ideology and, 210, 222
  and U.S. hostility toward Europe, 142–45
Weyrich, Paul, 105, 111–12
White House Conference on the Family, 43–44
Wieseltier, Leon, 203–4, 207
Williams, Rowan, 138–39
Wills, Garry, 201, 217
Witness to Hope (Weigel), 8, 89
women, 52, 160, 177
  abortion and, 77–78, 84, 89, 151–52, 154, 209–10
  rightly ordered family and, 188–91, 216
  see also feminists, feminism
Wuthnow, Robert, 62